Building the Architect's Character

An understanding of architects' character traits can offer important insights into how they design buildings. These traits include leadership skills necessary to coordinate a team, honest and ethical behavior, being well educated and possessing a life-long love of learning, flexibility, resourcefulness, and visionary and strategic thinking. Characteristics such as these describe a successful person. Architects also possess these traits, but they have additional skills specifically valuable for the profession. These will include the ability to question the use of digital media, new materials, processes, and methods to convey meaning in architectural form. Although not exhaustive, a discussion of such subjects as defining, imaging, persuading, and fabricating will reveal representational meaning useful for the development of an understanding of architects' character. Through the analogies and metaphors found in Greek myth, the book describes the elusive, hard-to-define characteristics of architects to engage with the dilemmas of a changing architectural landscape. *Building the Architect's Character: Explorations in Traits* examines traditional and archetypal characteristics of the successful architect to ask if they remain relevant today.

Kendra Schank Smith is a Professor of Architectural Science at Ryerson University, Canada. With a Ph.D. in architecture from Georgia Tech, she has written on representation, urbanism, and education, and has published two books on architectural sketches. She is the co-author of *Developing Your Design Process: Six Key Concepts for Studio.*

Albert C. Smith is an Associate Professor of Architectural Science at Ryerson University, Canada. He holds a Ph.D., from Georgia Tech, in architecture with an interest in representation. Smith is the author of *Architectural Model as Machine* and co-author of *Developing Your Design Process: Six Key Concepts for Studio.*

Building the Architect's Character

Explorations in Traits

KENDRA SCHANK SMITH AND ALBERT C. SMITH

NEW YORK AND LONDON

First published 2018
by Routledge
711 Third Avenue, New York, NY 10017

and by Routledge
2 Park Square, Milton Park, Abingdon, Oxon OX14 4RN

Routledge is an imprint of the Taylor & Francis Group, an informa business

© 2018 Taylor & Francis

The right of Kendra Schank Smith and Albert C. Smith to be identified as authors of this work has been asserted by them in accordance with sections 77 and 78 of the Copyright, Designs and Patents Act 1988.

All rights reserved. No part of this book may be reprinted or reproduced or utilised in any form or by any electronic, mechanical, or other means, now known or hereafter invented, including photocopying and recording, or in any information storage or retrieval system, without permission in writing from the publishers.

Trademark notice: Product or corporate names may be trademarks or registered trademarks, and are used only for identification and explanation without intent to infringe.

Library of Congress Cataloging-in-Publication Data
Names: Smith, Kendra Schank, author. | Smith, Albert C., author.
Title: Building the architect's character : exploration in traits / Kendra Schank Smith and Albert C. Smith.
Description: New York : Routledge, 2018.
Identifiers: LCCN 2017033572 (print) | LCCN 2017034083 (ebook) | ISBN 9781315560748 (Master) | ISBN 9781317199175 (ePub) | ISBN 9781317199168 (Mobi) | ISBN 9781317199182 (Web PDF) | ISBN 9781138675360 (hardback) | ISBN 9781138675377 (pbk.)
Subjects: LCSH: Architects—Psychology. | Architecture—Miscellanea.
Classification: LCC NA2500 (ebook) | LCC NA2500.S553 2018 (print) | DDC 720.2—dc23
LC record available at https://lccn.loc.gov/2017033572

ISBN: 978-1-138-67536-0 (hbk)
ISBN: 978-1-138-67537-7 (pbk)
ISBN: 978-1-315-56074-8 (ebk)

Typeset in Univers LT Std
by Keystroke, Neville Lodge, Tettenhall, Wolverhampton

We would like to dedicate this book to our students.

Contents

List of Figures		ix
Acknowledgments		xiii
Introduction		**xv**
Character		xviii
Representation		xix
Challenges		xxiii
Assessing Good Character		xxvi
Structure of Topics		xxviii
The Chapters		xxix
1	**Defining**	**1**
	Architect as Definer	4
	Architect as Measurer	7
	Architect as Engaging Manner and Mode	11
	Architects and Play	16
	Architect as Setting Boundaries and Order	18
	Conclusion	22
2	**Imaging**	**27**
	Architect as Divinely Inspired	29
	Architect as Imitator	32
	Architect as Imaginer	37
	Architect as Mindful Mneme	39
	Architect as Prophesier	45
	Conclusion	47
3	**Transforming, Transitioning, Translating**	**54**
	Architect as Messenger	57
	Architect as Traveler	61
	Architect as Thief	64
	Architect as Magician	67
	Architect as Inventor	71
	Conclusion	74

Contents

4	**Persuading**	**80**
	Architect as Rhetorician	82
	Architect as Persuader	86
	Architect as Seeker of Beauty and Truth	89
	Architect as Seducer	94
	Architect as Developer of Trust	99
	Conclusion	102
5	**Fabricating**	**111**
	Architect as Craftsman	114
	Architect as Flawed	118
	Architect as Fabricator	120
	Architect as Inspired Inspirer	125
	Architect as Critical Thinker	130
	Conclusion	134
	Conclusion	**143**
	Critical Thinking	147
	Judgment and Decision Making	148
	Leadership and Influence	150
	Talent	152
	Design	154
	Index	160

List of Figures

I.1	Greek gods Hermes, Hephaestus, and Prometheus depicted in *Prometheus being chained by Vulcan*, Dirck van Babure (Amsterdam, the Netherlands), 1623	xvii
I.2	Interior of the Pantheon, Apollodorus of Damascus, The Pantheon (Rome, Italy)	xx
I.3	Scale model of Borobudur, Gunadharma, Borobudur (Java, Indonesia), 825 CE	xxi
I.4	Child playing	xxii
I.5	Child using a tablet	xxiv
I.6	Child in London's Chinatown	xxv
I.7	Chiasmus as symbolized by a reflection	xxix
I.8	Representation of the Tower of Babel	xxx
1.1	Bas relief of a labyrinth (Tuscany, Italy)	2
1.2	Depiction of the Minotaur on ancient Greek pottery (Madrid, Spain)	2
1.3	Model of Herod's Temple (Jerusalem, Israel)	6
1.4	Thales measuring the pyramid's shadow, adapted from a drawing in the archives of Pearson Scott Foresman, artist unknown	8
1.5	Stained glass windows, Champigny sur Veude Chapelle (Champigny sur Veude, France)	9
1.6	Notre-Dame de Paris from the Pont de l'Archêveché (Paris, France)	10
1.7	A full-scale architectural mock-up	14
1.8	*The Fall of Icarus*, Jacob Peter Gowy, 1615–1661 (Madrid, Spain)	15
1.9	Interior of the Solomon R. Guggenheim Museum, architect Frank Lloyd Wright (New York, NY, USA)	20
1.10	Similarities between mandala forms and the National Assembly of Bangladesh (completed 1982), adapted from image of the Mandala of Amitayus, Tibet	21
2.1	Detail on sarcophagus showing the Muses (Kansas City, Missouri)	27
2.2	Man the macrocosm within the Universal Macrocosm	34
2.3	Proportions of human form reflected in typical cathedral form, Francesco di Giorgio Martini, c. 1480 (Florence, Italy)	36
2.4	*The Architect's Dream*, Thomas Cole, 1840 (Toledo, Ohio)	39
2.5	*Mnemosyne and Memory*, Library of Congress, Olin Warner and Herbert Adams, 1896 (Washington, D.C.)	40

List of Figures

2.6	Dibutades depicted in *The Origin of Painting*, Jean-Baptiste Regnault, 1785 (Paris, France)	42
2.7	Washington Monument, Robert Mills, Washington Monument, 1884 (Washington D.C.)	43
2.8	Interior of Jewish Museum Berlin, Daniel Libeskind, 2001 (Berlin, Germany)	44
2.9	Man using divining rod	48
3.1	Hermes	55
3.2	Messenger	58
3.3	The Blur Building, Pavillion for Swiss EXPO, architects Diller, Renfro, and Scofidio, 2002 (Yverdon-les-Bains, Switzerland)	59
3.4	Travelers	61
3.5	Architecture must be experienced first-hand through travel	63
3.6	*Prometheus steals Fire from Apollo's Sun chariot*, Giuseppe Collignon, 1814, Collection of Palazzo Pitti (Florence, Italy)	64
3.7	The demolition of the Pruitt-Igoe housing project, 1972–1976 (St. Louis, Missouri)	65
3.8	Exterior Guggenheim Museum Bilbao, architect Frank Gehry, 1997 (Bilbao, Spain)	66
3.9	The Magician	68
3.10	Entrance Condition to the Caixa Forum Madrid, architects Herzog and De Meuron, 2007 (Madrid, Spain)	70
3.11	Futuristic drawings of power station, Antonio Sant'Elia, 1914	73
3.12	Statue of Janus' two faces upon one head	75
4.1	Pietho as depicted in a Roman fresco (Pompeii, Italy)	81
4.2	Demosthenes practicing oratory	83
4.3	Firmness, commodity, and delight compared to logos, ethos, and pathos, adapted from *The School of Athens* by Raphael, 1509–1511 (Apostolic Palace, Vatican City)	84
4.4	Replicas of Caryatids from the Erechtheion, northern side of the Acropolis, 406 BCE (Athens, Greece)	86
4.5	*The Drawbridge*, Le Carceri d'Invenzione series, Giovanni Battista Piranesi, 1750	89
4.6	Model of the monument for the Third International (*Maquette du Monument a la Troisiem internationale*), Centre Pompidou Metz, Vladimir Tatlin, 1919–1920 (Paris, France)	90
4.7	Plan of the Parthenon showing proportional relationships	91
4.8	Exterior of the Carpenter Center for the Visual Arts, architect Le Corbusier, 1963 (Cambridge, Massachusetts)	92
4.9	Exterior of Boston City Hall, architects Gerhard Kallmann and Michael McKinnell, 1968 (Boston, Massachusetts)	93
4.10	Statue of Imhotep, Louvre Museum (Paris, France)	96
4.11	The Cathedral of Light, architect Albert Speer, 1937 (Nuremburg, Germany)	98
4.12	Exterior of 8 House, Bjarke Ingels, 2010 (Ørestad, Denmark)	104
4.13	Hagia Sophia (Istanbul, Turkey)	105

4.14	Propaganda poster "Your Motherland will never forget"	106
5.1	Hephaestus as depicted in *Vulcano forjando los rayos de Jupiter*, Peter Paul Rubens, 1636 (Madrid, Spain)	112
5.2	Ancient Greek craftsman	114
5.3	Detailing in Brion Tomb, Carlo Scarpa, 1978 (Treviso, Italy)	117
5.4	Traditional Japanese house form	121
5.5	The destructiveness of technology as displayed by the "Baker" explosion at Bikini Atoll, 1946	123
5.6	Very humanlike doll, Centre International de la Mécanique d'Art, late nineteenth century (Sainte-Croix, Switzerland)	127
5.7	Earliest illustration of Frankenstein's Monster, frontispiece of first edition of Mary Shelley's *Frankenstein*, 1831	128
5.8	Convent Sainte-Marie de La Tourette, architect Le Corbusier, 1959 (L'arbresle, France)	130
5.9	Pandora and Pandora's Box	132
5.10	Hephaestus and automata	135
5.11	Intricacies of the roof structure of Terminal 3, Shenzhen Bao'an International Airport, made possible by parametric design, architects Massimiliano and Doriana Fuksas, 2013 (Shenzhen, China)	137
C.1	The Hal 9000 computer from *2001: A Space Odyssey*, directed by Stanley Kubrick, 1968	146
C.2	Interior vaulting conditions of the Basilica of St. Denis, eleventh century (St. Denis, France)	153

Acknowledgments

Our sincere appreciation goes to Meng (Lynda) Ye who assisted with initial research, drafted passages, and provided helpful insight throughout the project, and Jason Brijraj for his adapted drawings, the drafting of passages and especially for his critical editing.

We would like to thank Aubrey Deluca, Thais Alessandra Silva Mendes, and Alessia Commisso for their thoughts during early discussions concerning architects' character. Our appreciation goes to Hilary Neal and Jessica Stanford who thoughtfully commented on drafts, and Sharon Galvin for her editing.

We would also like to thank the Faculty of Engineering and Architectural Science and the Department of Architectural Science at Ryerson University for their assistance with research funding.

Introduction

The Renaissance architect Leon Battista Alberti's treatise *On the Art of Building in Ten Books* warns architects against "any frivolity, obstinacy, ostentation, or presumption, and anything that might lose him good will or provoke enmity among his fellow citizens."[1] This strongly worded statement reveals the importance historically accorded to the architect's character. Alberti specifically names traits necessary to being a successful architect; these include having "the greatest ability, the keenest enthusiasm, the highest learning, the widest experience, and above all, serious, of sound judgment and counsel, who would presume to call himself [or herself] an architect."[2] Interestingly, these traits are the same that contemporary society expects of architects.

An understanding of architects' character traits can offer important insights into how they design buildings. These traits include leadership skills necessary to coordinate a team, honest and ethical behavior, being well educated and possessing a life-long love of learning, flexibility, resourcefulness, and visionary and strategic thinking. Characteristics such as these describe a successful person. Architects also possess these traits, but they have additional skills specifically valuable for the profession.

Building the Architect's Character: Explorations in Traits examines traditional and archetypal characteristics of the successful architect to ask if they remain relevant today. It considers the qualities necessary for the transformation, transition, and translation involved in the architect's task of constructing environments, creating order, and setting boundaries for the understanding of the cosmos. The term "cosmos" can be defined as the universe regarded as an orderly, harmonious system, or how a society views the world.

After many years of educating future architects, we have identified certain characteristics necessary for designing and the successful realization of buildings. Discussing these traits can help understand those with special aptitude for the discipline of architecture. Furthermore, since architects reveal their character traits in their buildings, understanding these traits is conducive to a deeper understanding of their buildings.

Through a theoretical approach, illustrated by historical and contemporary architectural examples, this book will suggest ways to engage with the dilemmas of a changing architectural landscape. These will include the ability to question the use of digital media, new materials, processes, and methods to convey meaning in architectural form. Although not exhaustive, a discussion of such subjects as *defining*, *imaging*, *persuading*, and *fabricating* will reveal representational meaning useful for the development of an understanding of architects' character.

The ancient Greek word for theory was *theoria* which meant contemplation, speculation, seeing, or spectacle.[3] Indra Kagis McEwen, in her book *Socrates' Ancestor*, connects theory to the Greek gods. She writes that *théa* means seeing or spectacle, *theá* means goddess, and *theóros* is someone who performed services for, or had care of, a god (*theos*—god, *óra*—care). The term *theóros* was applied to a person who consulted an oracle.[4] *Building the Architect's Character: Explorations in Traits* may be viewed as a theoretical journey that will involve consulting the Greek gods for their insights into architects' character.

Greek myths have influenced many aspects of modern culture, such as medicine, literature, and language, and were the foundation of Western thought and philosophy. From an oral tradition, their many variations meant that they were open to a number of interpretations. However, their symbolic truths have remained constant and have manifested themselves in every society influenced by ancient Greece:

> [M]yths refer to relations inherent in the culture's value system and may be told with manifold emphases and variations within the confines of their basic plots. They constitute a discourse, a verbal medium, through which members of the community – those who share the same myths – use the past to talk about the present. They communicate with one another *through* but not *about* their past.[5]

The stories have been told and retold in various versions, and we have looked in these for common threads as analogies and metaphors for architects' character. The ancient Greek gods exhibited such human emotions as envy and anger, and often engaged in acts of retaliation. However, they were wiser than the human populace, superior to them, and therefore the gods believed that they were well qualified to instruct humans. In many cases, their attitude was parental as they taught and reprimanded. Unlike a Christian God, who is founded in goodness, the Greek gods were neither good nor evil but rather a manifestation of a force of power for the citizens. Often the myths depict people in competition with the gods, trying to rival them in skill and intelligence.

Contemporary societies, just like those of the past, use myths, and the allegories found in them, to help them understand circumstances that are difficult to explain. These myths often present moral lessons and analogies useful for finding order in a confusing world. The Greek gods were imperfect, and they had flaws: they were jealous, took revenge, and practiced infidelity, to mention just a few of their less attractive qualities. Their personalities reflected human character traits and revealed aspects of human nature. They demonstrated how people act and react in response to life challenges. The Greek gods and their stories, of course, chronicle the important beliefs of the culture.

We will use the analogies and metaphors found in Greek myth as a framework for the discussion of the elusive, hard-to-define characteristics of architects.

Introduction

Figure I.1 **Greek gods Hermes, Hephaestus, and Prometheus** depicted in *Prometheus being chained by Vulcan*, Dirck van Babure (Amsterdam, the Netherlands), 1623. Source: Rijksmuseum, 1623, CC-PD-MarkPD-Art (PD-old-100).

We have chosen Greek myths because of their recent popularity in architectural literature (including works by Marco Frascari and Alberto Pérez-Gómez), and because they are relevant to the points we would like to make about architects' character. Greek myths provide quintessential comparators for a consideration of architects' character and purpose. For instance, the human Daedalus and the god Hermes have qualities that relate directly to the role of architects both historically and in contemporary society. The privileging of Greek myths does not in any way imply any judgment that they are worthier than the myths of other cultures. Instead, we recognize the value of monomyths as described by Joseph Campbell. We also support the tradition that myths can illustrate many aspects of the profession of architecture.

Buildings have always been constructed by people whose specific job this was, but in ancient Greece the *profession* was limited. In Greece of the mid-fifth century BCE, the profession of architecture was beginning to take form, the same era during which myths were being recorded by Homer and others. Of course, Greek philosophy influenced Romans such as Vitruvius, and his work, in turn,

xvii

influenced architects of the Renaissance. It is not necessary to trace the history of the profession here, but the *professional* aspects of the profession of architecture adhere to tenets of being the primary work of that person, have a code of ethics (which may include a professional society or guild), and indicate a level of intention that a building is *planned* before construction and that construction standards are recognized.[6]

Architects have traditionally had to make decisions that take the environment into account and that influence how people live. It was necessary to establish a foundation for solid judgment in regard to making these important decisions. Recently, the role of architects has been changing. These changes include the use of new technologies in design processes, and a lack of contextual considerations or misaligned intent. These changes must be acknowledged, and it is important to question how architects have been responding and adapting to them. Has the traditional character of the architect been eroded and/or altered, or has it remained the same? To address these changes, architects must re-examine their abilities to define, image, transform, transition, translate, persuade, and fabricate. They must answer challenges with sound behavior and strong character. As a foundation, it is important to understand what we mean by character.

Character

The definition of character and an understanding of the historical use of the term can provide useful insight into its relationship to architecture. We often use *character* in the sense of ethical behavior, but the character of a person is his or her personality, identity, or individualism.[7] As one of the attributes or features that make up and distinguish an individual or a group, character encompasses their nature or persona.[8] Its etymology is similar to that of the word *design* since both are associated with the idea of a mark, a stamp, or a distinctive nature.[9] The origins of the word character adhere to a contemporary meaning of something that is strikingly displayed, distinct, or distinguished in its qualities as to imprint, inscribe, or represent, but it also touches on *ethos* as a habitual way of life.[10]

The term *ethos* suggests the habits of society that are reflected in how people inhabit buildings. Although the words *ethos* and *ethics* have similar roots, they do not mean the same thing. In classical philosophy, the term ethics was used to reflect aspirations of the good life, of vitality, exhilaration, and contemplation.[11] Ethos, by comparison, originated with Aristotle, who described human beings as political creatures designed by nature to live with others.[12] The "virtue of character (i.e. of ethos) results from habit [ethos]; hence its name 'ethical,' slightly varied from 'ethos.' Hence it is also evident that none of the virtues of character arises in us naturally."[13] For Aristotle, a state of character emerged from the repetition of familiar activities, mainly habits of the mind.[14] It was the philosopher Martin Heidegger who connected dwelling with ethos and being-in-the-world.[15] He was suggesting not that ethos can be demonstrated by buildings, but rather that it manifests itself through contemplation of the human experience, and through making and the truth of things. Ethos, in the context of rhetoric, was seen as the argument based on the reputation, the character, of the speaker.[16]

Using a word with a similar meaning to character, Joseph Rykwert, Neil Leach, and Robert Tavernor write about the translation of the word *virtus* in their 1988 edition of Leon Battista Alberti's *On the Art of Building in Ten Books*. They acknowledge that the word is hard to translate, but that *virtù* was used by Alberti to "convey gifted activism in matters pertaining to civic life and society in general."[17] For their interpretation, they cite Carroll William Westfall, in writing that *virtù* "is an extension of collocatio (see *concinnitas*), because 'it brings together the intentions and abilities of the architect and the intentions and achievement of God in creation and of man in society. Through his concern with *concinnitas* the architect enters society'."[18] Through his use of the term *virtù,* Alberti may have been connecting the traits of architects to virtue, good behavior, and character.

For eighteenth-century French architectural theorists, determining architectural character involved considering the use of a building in relationship to its form, since to articulate the character of a structure would be to identify its genre or style.[19] The depiction of character emerged in the related term *taste*, as it pertained to aesthetic choice, but also choice in the context of moral and political engagement. As taste in beauty or style changes, so do morals and customs.

Writing on aesthetics, Charles Batteux made a connection between art and judgment stating that "taste is the facility to sense the good, bad, and mediocre, as opposed to intelligence which distinguishes true and false."[20] Often considered a definition of art, the twentieth-century aesthetic philosopher George Santayana implied that beauty is an abstract ideal, but also wrote that character represents the truth.[21] The contemporary architectural theorist Dalibor Vesely references eighteenth-century architectural thinking and writes that character finds its meaning in historical precedent, as it relates to architecture's order and an emerging meaning of style.[22] He likens style to the Italian words *maniera*, *ordine*, and genre that evoke the words *manner* or *orderly*.[23] As a concept related to order in its Greek origin, *symmetry* meant measuring together, or measured together.[24] For Vitruvius, symmetry meant rules for good design, good proportions, or even simply style.[25] Eugéne-Emmanuel Viollet-Le-Duc wrote about style as a part that can represent the character of the whole. But he also described style in terms of the architectural process when he wrote that style is "the perfect harmony between the result and the means employed to obtain it."[26] More importantly for the study of character, he wrote about art in relation to intention, particularly as a mediator. "Style can also be understood as mode; that is, to make the form of an art appropriate to its objective."[27] The word character can be tied to mode and manner as it implies a customary method of acting or behavior.[28] The word *manner*, stemming from belonging to the hand, touches on morals and modes of life.[29] Character, then, involves both personality and identity but also pertains to style and order. With an underlying connection to taste and good judgment, the character represented in a building and human character affects the habits of the inhabitants.

Representation

Traditionally, architects have had a desire to represent meaning in their buildings. Representation, as an issue in the visual arts, is at least as old as Plato and

Aristotle, and initially referred to the imitation of what is seen as well as to the imitation of other artists' styles. Historically, imitation questioned the replication of reality and also made a distinction between what was viewed and a period's style.[30] Issues regarding representation have always involved the amount of likeness between the imitation and the original, and how these are represented either symbolically or abstractly. Thus, representation was seen as imitation with a change of dimension or an abstraction of the original.[31] For example, it is well known that the *Pantheon* in Rome replicates a model of the universe, whereas a Gothic cathedral presents more abstract ideas of narrative and light.

In another example, the *Great Stupa* shrine in Borobudur, Java (800–850 AD) is a quintessential symbol of Buddhism and, like the *Pantheon*, replicates its society's view of the universe. Its three levels symbolize the micro-cosmos.

Figure I.2
Interior of the Pantheon, Apollodorus of Damascus, The Pantheon (Rome, Italy).
Source: National Gallery of Art, CC-PD-MarkPD-Art (PD-old-100).

Figure I.3
Scale model of Borobudur, Gunadharma, Borobudur (Java, Indonesia), 825 CE. Source: Albert Smith, CC-BY-SA-2.5 Self-published work.

The first level represents the human world of desire and the negative influences evoked by desire. The middle level represents the world in which humans can control their negative impulses and utilize their positive impulses. This is put into contrast by the highest level, in which the world of humans is no longer bounded by physical and worldly ancient desire.

A building's form can evoke emotional responses by association; this is one way in which architecture expresses meaning. The study of meaning-making and meaningful communication is called semiotics. In the late nineteenth century, the pragmatist philosopher and logician Charles Sanders Peirce wrote that a *sign* is an indication in communication. He identified signs as standing for other objects in some respect of capacity.[32] The study of semiotics (in all its many branches) explored symbolism, analogies, communication, and signification, to name a few.

To present a more contemporary view, Dalibor Vesely, when describing representation beyond mere imagery, writes, "We may...apprehend that representation is not limited to the physiognomy of buildings and spaces but relates more closely to the situational structure and meaning of architecture."[33] Critical to the theme of this book on architects' character, Vesely references the philosopher Hans-Georg Gadamer, who compared *making* to "creative imitation."

The problem of representation is closely linked with the process of making (*poiēsis*) and with creative imitation (*mimēsis*). Thus, as Hans-Georg Gadamer points out, in contrast to the conventional understanding,

> ...representation does not imply that something merely stands in for something else as if it were a replacement or substitute that enjoys a less authentic, more indirect kind of existence. On the contrary what is represented is itself present in the only way available to it.[34]

Vesely also discusses the mediating role of representation, its relationship to phenomenological experience, and how that experience, can be made more easily accessible through representation.[35] He writes that

> A line of poetry or a single painting very often can tell us much of the hidden meaning and beauty of a landscape, just as light in a sacred space tells us of the intelligibility of the sky and the divine.[36]

Not just limited to media in the design process, representation constitutes the less definable, the allusions that give a building a depth beyond mere substitution.[37] This dimension of representation is often considered in terms of ontology, as in theorist Marco Frascari's discussion of the essential characteristics of architecture.

The design process used by architects to develop their buildings may be compared to concepts of *play* and, thus, it is in the character of architects to be playful. Although we will be discussing play more thoroughly in Chapter 1, play as a philosophical concept involves the actions of "give and take" and can contribute to a design dialogue. Play is important as regards both the intelligence involved in it and the learning that results from it; the fact that it is repeated allows opportunities to alter and manipulate to discover something new.[38] The repeatability and intelligibility of play are particularly important for architects since most design by manipulating forms or materials. The celebrated architect Frank Gehry's cut and assembled models illustrate the iterative process so critical to design exploration. Other aspects of play include the boundaries that surround the activity of play, since architects' decisions are always guided by external conditions or internal restrictions. Architects often use concepts from play, for instance in avant-garde

Figure I.4
Child playing.
Source:
Joymaster,
CC-BY-SA-3.0.

architect Zaha Hadid's paintings, or the fantasy drawings called *ideagrams* that Michael Rotundi uses to begin his design process.

Looking at two words with their roots in play may further clarify the architect's design process. An *allusion* can be defined as a reference; the word takes on connotations of a brief or indirect mention. It originates from the Latin word *ludere*, to play, to joke, jest, or touch lightly upon a subject.[39] The term *allusive*, when used in the context of architects' design process, may refer to the ideas tied to a building's conceptual framework. In a world influenced by postmodern philosophy where everything is a reference and little can be defined, allusions may help us understand the world better, but they may also keep us forever suspended in a time, or place, of unknowns.[40]

The act of playing with a design can be cyclical in nature. Such cyclical play can be advantageous since it allows a design to remain fluid and for new solutions to appear. In our examination of play as related to the design process, we can consider the etymology of the word *illusion*. Also from the Latin *ludere*, it means to mock or ridicule, a meaning that suggests "against play."[41] An illusion is a false or unreal appearance, being deceived or eluded by appearances. It also can be defined as a false conception of ideas or the sensuous perception of an external object. In contrast to its negative connotations, however, an illusion may be understood as something that enables us to *envision* what has never before been seen.

Challenges

As mentioned earlier, the education of architects and architectural practice has changed substantially over the last few decades, particularly in response to differing concepts of what buildings represent. It is important to question whether these changes have affected architects' character. It is the responsibility of architects to engage these changes, to understand their importance, and to set trends with innovative ways of thinking. The computer has been a major contributor to these changes, along with new technologies, materials, and processes, trends toward globalization and specialization, and the welcome integration of sustainable practices. As architects embrace these new paradigms, they may be losing their characteristic ability to draw upon their critical judgment and understand their primary goals.

Digital media is increasingly becoming everything and everywhere, and it is important to ask what this means for architects' character. Our connection with computers begins early in our lives, and the fact that we constantly use them means that we may feel our minds are actually in coordination with them. For architects, the computer encourages rapid alterations to needed documentation and facilitates viewing a range of options that assist decision making. The quality of architects' designs improves when they can visualize and communicate a broad range of possibilities. It allows architects to see things in new and unusual ways and helps them to comprehend more complexity in their design. In professional practice, new digital programs connect architects to the allied professions with whom they need to collaborate. The ability to quickly duplicate components with advanced digital applications also allows for more efficient design processes.

Figure I.5
Child using a tablet. Source: CC-BY-SA-2.0.

Traditionally, architects have persuaded others not only verbally but through convincing images. They have always utilized their abilities to produce seductive images for visualization in their design process and also presentation. Today, new digital tools available for both design and construction are changing how architects convey information, persuade their intentions, and most importantly convey how they think. It is important for architects to engage these changes to effectively understand and use new technology. It remains essential that, though change occurs, architects remember the importance that the meaning and position of buildings traditionally play in meeting human needs.

Introduction

Figure I.6
Child in London's Chinatown.
Source:
CC-BY-SA-3.0
Self-published work.

Globalization may be distancing the current practice of building from human need to create a form of commonality where function, societies' ideals, and traditions have been diluted. In her book *Architecture, Ethics, and Globalization*, Janice A. Newson expresses what globalization means for architecture:

> I use the term globalization to reference a complex interplay of economic, political, social and cultural changes which are neither inevitable nor uniform.

> While this interplay of changes has gradually and increasingly influenced world development over at least the past century, its effects are contingent and indeterminate, leading not to a conventional homogeneous ending but rather to a range of alternative responses. Such a view allows that it is possible for human agents to intervene in these processes of change in ways that significantly affect the direction of local as well as global transformation.[42]

This new understanding of the world is essential to the trans-national circulation of ideas, languages, and popular culture, and of course architecture. For example, the many North American architectural practices with offices in China accept globalization and recognize that it provides a fruitful exchange of ideas. However, at the same time, it should be questioned if the richness and distinctive nature of a locality have been sacrificed to globalization. Comparatively, the design disciplines must deal with trends, including the mobility of the profession (architects do not need to be in-country to design), economic growth (money moves quickly from region to region), and world regionalization (crossing boundaries can be done easily). With competition, and economic pressures to build quickly, architects may be forced to disregard issues such as the context of the communities in which they build and thus cannot rely on previous definitions of character. The question arises whether architects can continue to rely on traditional approaches.

As the profession of architecture has become globalized, it has also become more specialized. It is important for students and practicing architects to question this apparent dichotomy and to engage in a discussion of their character in the context of the modernization of architectural tools and processes.

As specialization alters architects' responsibilities, the individual expression that once represented the profession may be lost. With these paradigm shifts, specialization has become a more important focus in education and practice, so much so that students and professionals now strive to be first and foremost experts in one area, with taking a broader view a secondary consideration. This allows for groups of experts, or specialists, to essentially dominate the design process. This event presupposes the building as the final product rather than the collaborative development at each stage led by expert individuals. Architects may ask if specialization and stratification have enabled the emergence of an industry that will be able to alter the current trajectory and restructure itself. The future will require architects to engage their character to effectively deal with these issues.

Assessing Good Character

How do architects and architectural students engage the question of their character in the design process? The only apparent answer is by learning *good judgment.* This sounds easy, but how do architects develop and exercise good judgment? It depends on being a connoisseur, a gourmet, critical, discerning, self-reflective, constantly questioning and, most of all, being well educated with an extensive repertoire of knowledge and experience that will allow them to understand when choices are right and when they are wrong—and whether their decisions are sound and correct. Deciding involves knowledge and character to utilize good judgment.

When discussing character and good judgment, it may be necessary to introduce the concept of *ethics*. Ethics as an area of study has a long history in philosophical and psychological works, and it is not necessary to fully explore it here. We are interested primarily in the study of ethics as it pertains to character, and as to how it affects judgment. Briefly, ethics are described as the "the moral principles by which a person is guided."[43] Morality involves living within social norms, while ethics involves questioning whether actions are right or wrong. If architects influence and make decisions on how people should live, then they should not blindly accept social norms but should, rather, question basic assumptions.

The origins of the word *ethic* come from the Greek (*hē) ēthikē (tekhnē)* meaning the science of morals; it is based on *ethos*, the Greek word for character, guiding beliefs, nature, or disposition. But ethics involve more than just making the right or best decision based on moral or technical judgment or a person's creative talent. The philosopher Immanuel Kant theorized that it was not the actions of an individual that were right or wrong, but instead the motives behind these actions.[44] Therefore, it is reasonable to consider that ethics are a synthesis of all three, in addition to good intentions. Ethics can provide guidelines for the creation of an architecture that is not false or corrupt, but rather honest and good-willed.

Part of good judgment and the ability to be critical may rely on the character of architects to interpret. This is especially true given that the rules of the profession are constantly changing, and architects are being called upon to make decisions about environmental sustainability, for example. The area of philosophy called hermeneutics studies the theory and methodology of interpretation. It examines the ways in which we interpret and attempt to understand the phenomena such as texts, works of art, actions, and gestures. Chapter 3 of this book will return to the subject of interpretation, but it is important to introduce the concept.[45]

The philosopher Martin Heidegger, who connected hermeneutics to the Greek god Hermes, clarified this traditional definition, emphasizing the study of texts: "hermeneutics is a science that deals with the goals, ways, and rules of the interpretation of literary works."[46] To apply hermeneutic methodology to architecture, we can look to Martin Heidegger who wrote in his seminal work on language that "Accordingly, the word 'hermeneutics,' used in a broader sense, can mean the theory and methodology for every kind of interpretation, including, for example, that of works of the visual arts."[47] Contemporary theorists, such as Robert Mugerauer, expand that definition to encompass human understanding as well.[48] Interpretation plays a large part in architectural design. Many architects, educators, and theorists of architecture view hermeneutics as a stepping-stone to interpretation.[49]

The philosophers Damian Cox, Marguerite La Caze, and Michael P. Levine believe that design is related to integrity and tied to desires, needs, commitments, and values.[50] Although Alberto Pérez-Gómez acknowledges that clients will ultimately decide the final significance of what we build, he also insists

> . . .that there is an inherent phenomenological continuity between thinking and making, between our words in our particular language and our deeds. Thus what we control and must be accountable for are our intentions. . . intentions imply a whole style of thinking and action that takes into account a past life and a thick network of connections within a culture.[51]

While it may be evident that natural forces, and specific socio-political and economic climates, influence architects' ideas, it is also important to consider the impact of their education and training, as well as their professional and personal experiences.

Structure of Topics

Building the Architect's Character: Explorations in Traits is organized into two broad parts, both investigating the character traits of architects. The first part is Chapters 1 and 2, the second is Chapters 4 and 5, and Chapter 3 serves as a crossing between the two parts. The first part discusses the way architects traditionally design and what has changed. These first chapters entitled "Defining" and "Imaging" question the processes of conceiving where architects must "play with" conceptual thinking. Chapter 3, entitled "Transforming, Transitioning, Translating," is a center point; it discusses how the character of architects allows them to develop a point or position that can assist with transition or transformation. This chapter explores strategies for actively engaging design process. The second part represents the contemporary dilemmas architects face when designing. These final two chapters specifically concern how contemporary architects must call upon their character when "Persuading" and "Fabricating."

The book is structured similarly to the rhetorical notion of a *chiasmus*. The etymological root of the word chiasmus comes to us from the ancient Greek, "to shape like the letter X." It is a figure of speech in which two or more clauses are related to each other through a reversal of structures to make a larger point. A chiasmus may be the place of inversion where the positive and negative reflect each other to demonstrate new meaning.[52] In other words, things can be clearer when discussed from two perspectives. For example, the phrase *the architecture of drawing and the drawing of architecture* allows us to view how drawings can be constructed and also how drawing can illustrate architectural artifacts. Through such a crisscross arrangement, the reflective impact of an architectural issue can be countered with an equally valid opposing position. This crisscross can point out that when considering context, era, situation, or economy, each case can be justified. Although each side of the chiasmus may be reflective, revealing opposites or opposing positions, each version may not always be of equal value or importance. Of course, there are always two sides to every story, and it is architects' responsibility to determine the best course of action.

Introduction

The Chapters

Defining

Chapter 1 addresses traits associated with defining. This chapter will investigate the analogy of the prototypical architect from Greek mythology, Daedalus. Architecture's ability to impose order and define boundaries can be understood through his labyrinth. Part of defining involves activities that architects are familiar with, such as measure, modes and manners of dwelling, and the cultural rituals that inform architectural design. The topic of defining is further analyzed through the subtopics of definer, measurer, engaging with manner and mode, the ability to play, and acceptance of boundaries and order. Each subtopic engages with the way architects use their ability to define spaces and orders, and to ultimately define the world we live in. The chapter looks at numerous theoretical works to understand the architect's role as definer, including Le Corbusier, Louis Kahn, Spiro Kostof, James S. Hans, and Hermann Kern. The chapter also uses many notable architectural works as a means to express the ideas of the chapter in physically built forms. This includes the ideas of measuring the unknown, as expressed through built examples of stained glass windows in a cathedral and ancient temple forms.

Imaging

Chapter 2 addresses the topic of imaging. The roots and definitions of the topic are established with analogies to the Greek myth of the Muses. The Muses imbue

Figure I.7
Chiasmus
as symbolized
by a reflection.
Source: Putnik
CC-BY-SA-3.0.

xxix

Introduction

Figure I.8 Representation of the Tower of Babel. Source: CC-PD-MarkPD-Art (PD-old-100).

architects with the inspiration used to produce various mediums of work, from drawings and models to completed buildings. The topic of imaging is further analyzed through the subtopics of architects as divinely inspired, imitators, imaginers, mindful mnemes, and prophesiers. Each subtopic engages the methods architects use to produce the images in the discipline. They may employ their imaginations, memories, and inspirations to predict how their future buildings, and subsequently how the future world, will be perceived. The chapter looks at numerous theoretical works to understand architects' role as imagers, including Edward S. Casey and David Hume. The chapter also uses many notable architectural works as a means to explain the ideas of imaging in physically built forms. This includes buildings that represent the idea of memory such as Daniel Libeskind's *Holocaust Museum*.

Transforming, Transitioning, Translating

Chapter 3 addresses the topics of transforming, transitioning, and translating. As this chapter is a turning point for the book, where Chapters 1 and 2 address traditional areas of architecture involving architects' thinking, Chapters 4 and 5 discuss issues that arise in contemporary practice. Chapter 3, the middle chapter, engages with this middle ground, discussing architects' changing education and practice. It uses the analogous Greek myth of Hermes to explore numerous traits that allow architects to engage with the changing face of architecture incorporating the idea of interpretation. The chapter is divided into the subtopics of the architect as messenger, traveler, thief, magician, and inventor. Each section examines how the possession of each trait influences the decision-making abilities of architects in both historical and contemporary contexts. This chapter looks at numerous theoretical works to understand these pivotal topics, such as the work of Oliver Brown, Plato, and Robert Venturi and Denise Scott Brown. The chapter uses architectural examples where relevant, including Antonio Sant'Elia's *Citta Nuova*, Peter Zumthor's *Therme Vals*, and Frank Gehry's *Concert Hall* in Los Angeles.

Persuading

Chapter 4 addresses the topic of persuading. The chapter references the myth of Peitho, the Greek goddess of persuasion and seduction, who has close ties to Aphrodite, the goddess of love and beauty. Peitho's character is one that captures the traits architects must exhibit to create persuasive representation, arguments, and ultimately built works. The subtopics of architect as rhetorician, persuader, seeker of beauty and truth, seducer, and developer of trust analyze the various aspects of persuasion in respect to architecture. The chapter addresses the duality behind persuasion and its negative connotations, as architects' relationship with persuasion can lead to works with varying success. The chapter explores numerous theoretical works to understand the architect's relationship with persuasion, including the authors Lee Morrissey, John Ruskin, and Aristotle. The chapter also uses various architectural examples to explain the subtopics presented in the chapter. Considering how architects' use persuasion, Le Corbusier's *Carpenter Center* and *Boston City Hall* are used to explain how material characteristics can capture or deter its users.

Fabricating

Chapter 5 addresses the topic of fabrication. The chapter explores the Greek god Hephaestus, the god of smithing, as an analogy to analyze architects' role in construction and fabrication systems that provide accuracy for production. Hephaestus, the deformed craftsman, is the skilled yet flawed figure presenting a duality of character that can be used to understand the multifaceted relationship that architects have with their craft, technology, and fabrication. The subtopics discuss the characteristics of architect as craftsman, flawed, engaging the technologies of fabrication, inspired inspirer, and critical thinker to further analyze the issue of fabrication. The chapter discusses Hephaestus, compared to a traditional architect, as one who is fully immersed in their craft and the process of making, contrasted to modern-day mechanization that has created a disconnect between craft and design. The chapter looks at numerous theoretical works to understand the changing relationship between architects and fabrication, such as the work of Joseph Rykwert, Richard Sennett, and Marco Frascari. The chapter also uses numerous architectural examples to explain the changing relationship with fabrication, including works by Carlo Scarpa and Ludwig Mies Van der Rohe.

The conclusion presents various topics in which architects must understand to fully realize and address the topics covered by each of the chapters. This includes the topics of archetypes, critical thinking, leadership and influence, and design. With the foundations of the topics laid out using theories of notable philosophers, architects, and the Greek myths, a critical perspective addresses the use of proper judgment in the architectural profession. This chapter utilizes theoretical work presented by James George Frazer, Carl Jung, and Vitruvius to reinforce the arguments put forth.

Notes

1 Leon Battista Alberti, *On the Art of Building in Ten Books*, trans. Joseph Rykwert, Neil Leach, and Robert Tavernor (Cambridge, MA: MIT Press, 1988), 315.

2 Ibid.

3 Indra Kagis McEwen, *Socrates' Ancestor* (Cambridge, MA: MIT Press, 1993), 20–22.

4 Ibid, 21.

5 William Blake Tyrell and Frieda S. Brown, *Athenian Myths and Institutions: Words in Action* (New York: Oxford University Press, 1991), 8; original emphasis.

6 See Spiro Kostof, ed., *The Architect: Chapters in the History of the Profession* (New York and Oxford, UK: Oxford University Press, 1977).

7 *Oxford English Dictionary*, s.v. "character."

8 Ibid.

9 Ibid.

10 *Oxford English Dictionary*, s.v. "character"; Lily H. Chi, "An Arbitrary Authority: Claude Perrault and the Idea of Character in Germain Boffrand and Jacques- Francois Blondel" (Ph.D. dissertation, McGill University, 1998), 173.

11 Aristotle, *Nicomachean Ethics*, trans. David Ross (Oxford, UK: Oxford University Press, 2005), Book 1, Section 5.

12 Aristotle, *Aristotle's Politics*, trans. Benjamin Jowett (New York: Modern Library, 1943), Book 1, Part 2.

13 Aristotle, *Nicomachean Ethics*, trans. Terence Irwin (Cambridge, MA: Hackett Publishing Co., 1985), 1103a14–19.

14 Ibid., 1103b21.

15 See Martin Heidegger, "Building, Dwelling, Thinking," in *Poetry, Language, Thought* (New York: Harper Periennial Classics, 1975), 141–160. Also see Karsten Harries, "Thoughts on Non-Arbitrary Architecture," *Perspecta* 20 (1983): 9–20.

16 Aristotle, *The Art of Rhetoric*, trans. John H. Freese (Cambridge, MA: Harvard University Press, 1926), 17.

17 Alberti, *On the Art of Building in Ten Books*, 426.

18 Ibid.

19 Chi, "An Arbitrary Authority," 219.

20 Ibid., 170.

21 George Santayana, *The Sense of Beauty; Being the Outline of Aesthetic Theory* (New York: Collier Books, 1961), 43–45, 124–126.

22 Ibid., 259–261.

23 Ibid., 261.

24 *Oxford English Dictionary*, s.v. "symmetry"; also see George Hersey, *Architecture and Geometry in the Age of the Baroque* (Chicago, IL: University of Chicago Press, 2002).

25 See Hersey, *Architecture and Geometry in the Age of the Baroque*.

26 Eugéne-Emmanuel Viollet-Le-Duc, *The Foundations of Architecture: Selections from the Dictionnaire raisonné*, trans. Kenneth D. Whitehead (New York: George Braziller, 1990), 23.

27 Ibid., 232.

28 *Oxford English Dictionary*, s.v. "manner."

29 Viollet-Le-Duc, *The Foundations of Architecture*, 232.

30 Monroe C. Beardsley, *Aesthetics from Classical Greece to the Present* (Tuscaloosa: University of Alabama Press, 1975), 33–39.

31 Richard Wollheim, *Art and Its Objects* (New York and Evanston, IL: Torchbook Library Edition, 1971), 14–20.

32 See Charles Sanders Peirce and Justus Buchler, *Philosophical Writings of Peirce* (New York: Dover Publications, 2011).

33 Dalibor Vesely, *Architecture in the Age of Divided Representation* (Cambridge, MA: MIT Press, 2006), 13.

34 Ibid., 13–14.

35 Ibid., 18–19.

36 Ibid., 19.

37 See Marco Frascari, *Monsters of Architecture; Anthropomorphism in Architectural Theory* (Savage, MD: Rowman & Littlefield, 1991).

38 See Johan Huizinga, *Homo Ludens: A Study of the Play-element in Culture* (London: Routledge, 2002); Gregory Bateson, *Steps to an Ecology of Mind* (Northvale, NJ and London: Jason Aronson, Inc., 1972); James S. Hans, *The Play of the World* (Boston and Amherst: University of Massachusetts Press, 1981); and Hans-Georg Gadamer, *Truth and Method* (New York: Seabury Press, 1975).

39 *Oxford English Dictionary*, s.v. "allusion."

40 See Richard Kearney, *The Wake of Imagination* (New York: Routledge, 1994).

41 *Oxford English Dictionary*, s.v. "illusion."

42 Janice A. Newson, "Re-making the Space for Professional Response-Ability: Lessons from the Corporate-Linked University," in *Architecture, Ethics, and Globalization*, ed. Graham Owen (New York: Routledge, 2009), 51.

43 *Oxford English Dictionary*, s.v. "ethics."

44 Immanuel Kant, "Section I: Transition from the Common Rational to Philosophical Moral Cognition," in *Groundwork of the Metaphysic of Morals,* ed. Mary Gregor (Cambridge, UK: Cambridge University Press, 1997), 8.

45 A.R. Lacey, *A Dictionary of Philosophy* (London: Routledge & Kegan Paul, 1976), 91–92.

46 Martin Heidegger, *On the Way to Language*, trans. Peter D. Hertz (New York: Harper & Row, 1970), 10.

47 Ibid., 11.

48 Robert Mugerauer, *Interpreting Environment: Tradition, Deconstruction, Hermeneutics* (Austin: University of Texas Press, 1995), xxvi. "Hermeneutics aims not so much to develop a new procedure as to clarify how understanding takes place" (Mugerauer, xxvi) and ". . .all understanding is interpretation, that is, contextual" (Mugerauer, xxvii).

49 See Alberto Pérez-Gómez, "Hermeneutics as Architectural Discourse in Design," *Design Research* 15, no. 2 (Summer, 1999): 71–79; and Adrian Snodgrass and Richard Coyne, "Models, Metaphors and the Hermeneutics of Designing," *Design Issues* 9(1) (1992): 56–74.

50 See Damian Cox, Marguerite La Caze, and Michael Levine, *Integrity and the Fragile Self* (London: Ashgate, 2003).

51 Alberto Pérez-Gómez, "Ethics and Poetics in Education," in *Architecture, Ethics, and the Personhood of Place*, ed. George Caicco (Hanover, NH: University Press of New England, 2007), 128.

52 *Oxford English Dictionary*, s.v. "chiasmus."

Chapter 1

Defining

It has been traditionally part of architects' character to clearly define their future buildings the process of design. But architects have greater responsibilities than just defining buildings: they also influence the definitions of a culture's cosmos through their creations. *Definition* is described as comprising the essential characteristics of the thing being defined. It presents meaning for things that are not clearly understood, in a context of things that are understood. The act of defining can be similar to the act of designing in many ways. Architects define through measuring, creating boundaries, establishing manners of dwelling, play, and the cultural rituals that inform architectural design.

This exploration will be illustrated with examples of how architects have traditionally measured in an effort to determine if their character has undergone changes. This chapter will investigate five characteristics of architects in an effort to clearly define, understand, and create an architectural measure that inhabitants can engage with; recognize manner and select appropriate modes within which to design; play with ideas and media; and set boundaries to establish order. Specifically, it will investigate the chiasmus formed between *defining the design and designing the definition,* and will attempt to clarify the relationship between definition and design. As a means to engage architectural definition, the discussion will employ the story of the prototypical architect from Greek mythology, Daedalus. It will consider the design of his labyrinth that has been traditionally invoked as analogous to the creation of order.[1]

There are solid reasons for choosing Daedalus, although some might believe that Prometheus would be a more appropriate Greek god to explain definition in the context of architecture. After all, it was he who stole fire from the gods and presented it to humans, an act that has been interpreted as an analogy for technology. Prometheus has been credited with creating humankind, a powerful act of defining. However, we find that myths concerning Daedalus, although he was human and not a god, are more suitable in the context of definition. He designed and built the labyrinth to contain the Minotaur, a metaphor for humanity's search for order. The labyrinth represents a ritual that helps architects in their search for knowledge, and presents an analogy for the things that they do not know. The story of Daedalus and his labyrinth built to hold the monster offers an archetypal explanation of the architect's position within early society. This myth presents a recurring theme that reflects the common ideals of Greek culture, especially in regard to how they viewed architects. It not only delineated, but also reinforced the social position, customs, and cultural importance of architects within Greek society, and demonstrated their relationship to humans, technology, construction, and the gods.

Figure 1.1
Bas relief of a labyrinth (Tuscany, Italy).
Source: Beatrice, CC-BY-SA-2.5-IT.

Figure 1.2
Depiction of the Minotaur on ancient Greek pottery (Madrid, Spain).
Source: Museo Arqueológico Nacional de España, CC-BY-2.5.

Though it is not necessary to regard the tale of Daedalus as a true story, it remains important because it was commonly believed to be an analogy that offers poetic insight into current conditions.[2] Analogies are forms of inference, since the assertion of some similarities between two things is extrapolated to encompass their likely similarities in other respects.[3] With this description, the myth is told through the following story:

Having killed his nephew Talos out of professional jealousy, Daedalus was forced to leave Athens. He went to Crete, where he served in the court of King Minos at Knossos. Among his amazing achievements, there was the construction of a "daidalon", a life-like wooden cow covered with leather in which Queen Pasiphae hid to seduce a magnificent bull (a gift from Poseidon to the Minoan King) with which she had fallen in love. Daedalus' success with this task confirmed, once again, his skill as a demiurge. When, after seducing the bull, the queen gave birth to the Minotaur, Daedalus was asked to design a structure to contain this monster.[4]

While the myth itself serves as an analogy, the creation of the labyrinth by Daedalus may be considered a metaphor for the creation of architecture. The labyrinth represents human existence and Daedalus as its creator presents a paradigm of order, the "primordial ideal of architecture."[5] He addresses humans' basic need to find order in a chaotic environment and formulates this order with the Knossos labyrinth. Daedalus' ability to create order is likely the reason why he held an important position within ancient Greek society. To further elaborate on this position, Françoise Frontisi-Ducroux writes:

All sources agree that he (Daedalus) was an Athenian, son or grandson of Metion, a man who had been endowed with "metis," a kind of practical intelligence and ingenuity which could be deployed in many ways but was mostly associated with the wisdom of craftsmanship in the Athenian tradition. . .While in Athens, Daedalus worked as a sculptor. He was the reputed inventor of agalmata, statues of the gods which had open eyes and moveable limbs, a compelling manifestation of the mystery of divinity (the verb "to see" was reciprocal in Greek: whoever saw was also seen, and the blind were invisible). These statues were so lifelike that Plato remarked upon their amazing and disconcerting mobility, which was accomplished with techniques that are clearly those of the *daidala*. Daedalus was also an inventor. Pliny enumerates the instruments that he invented while in Athens, including the saw, the axe, glue and, more significant for architecture, the plumb-line (*cathetos* or *perpendiculum*).[6]

The architectural historian and theorist Alberto Pérez-Gómez suggests that the name Daedalus is a play on the Greek word *daidala* which appears in archaic literature as a complement of the verb to make, manufacture, to forge, to weave, to place on, or to see.[7] *Daidala* were the implements of early society and included defensive works, arms, and furniture. Pérez-Gómez writes of the importance of the *daidala*:

> The "daidala" in Homer seem to possess mysterious powers. They are luminous—they reveal the reality they represent. It is a metaphysical "light" of diverse and often bizarre qualities, evoking fear and admiration. "Daidala," particularly jewels, are endowed with "charis" (charisma) and thus with "kalo" (beauty) and "amalga" (festive religious exaltation). "Charis" is a product of "techne" (art, skill, craft) but it is also a god-given grace. This mysterious emanation, whether artificially created or given by the gods, has the power of seduction. "Daidala" are therefore capable of creating dangerous illusions.
>
> "Daidala," or art objects, can appear to be what they are not, and the metal plates give a value to the objects that they would not otherwise have. The principal value of "daidala" is that of enabling the inanimate matter to become magically alive, of "reproducing" life rather than "representing" it. Hence the word also designates "thaumata," marvelous animated machines with brilliant suits of armor and scintillating eyes. The more primitive Homeric texts emphasize the ability of the "daidalos" to seem alive. . .[8]

Certainly, Daedalus can be linked to the *daidala* through his creation of automata such as lifelike statues, a machine-like cow (which he built for Queen Pasiphae), his wax-and-feather flying machine, and finally the labyrinth at Knossos. Daedalus' ability to create the machine-like *daidala* placed him in an extremely powerful position in his society. Again, the labyrinth at Knossos serves as a model of society's attempt to find order. Pérez-Gómez writes, "The labyrinth is a metaphor for human existence: ever-changing, full of surprise, uncertain, conveying the impression of disorder."[9] In this way, the *daidala* (mechanism) of the labyrinth symbolizes the ancient Greek cosmos.

The monster symbolized a seemingly chaotic message sent from the mythical Greek gods. A key concept behind the understanding of the Minotaur as a monster arises from its origin in the Latin words *monstrum*, which means portent (an omen or prodigy), something marvelous, and *monere*, to warn.[10] In a way, monsters are similar in meaning to soothsayers in that they foretell the future.[11] The labyrinth demonstrates an understandable definition of an ideal (more perfect) message. Here is the connection between Daedalus, the labyrinth, and definition. To understand aspects of architects' character, it is important to begin with defining.

Architect as Definer

The myth of Daedalus relates that he designed the labyrinth to contain the Minotaur. Through the marking out and subsequent building of the wall, Daedalus defined how its inhabitant, the Minotaur, would be confined. The myth, the labyrinth, and the monstrous Minotaur were attempts to define to humans the unexplainable; similarly, architecture can be used to help explain by creating definition. It is for this reason that it is part of the character of architects to be able to define clearly.

Concerning definition, the philosopher John W. Miller writes, "by what method, therefore, can the study of philosophy proceed?. . .Only through the definition of a term."[12] The etymology of the word *definition* comes from the Latin word *definire* that means the setting of bounds or limits.[13] To define something is to put boundaries around it in order to designate its exact meaning. It is interesting to note that the word "designate" is closely related to the word "design," which means to mark out.[14]

There are many rules used for establishing a good definition. A primary one stipulates that a definition must indicate the essential characteristics of the thing being defined. A thing can be a material or an inanimate object, such as a matter of concern, deed, act, or accomplishment that exists as a separate entity. "Things," as described by Miller, can be distinguished from pure objects of thought since they can be artistic compositions or pieces of architecture: they are used for creating definition. It is not necessary for things to be precisely designated and this is why certain buildings fluctuate in meaning. There are several important properties of definition. Again, the most important function of a definition is to present meaning for things that are not clearly understood, in a context of things that are clearly understood. Definitions increase knowledge and impart information; they prevent ambiguity, imprecision, and complexity. They are resolutions, declared intentions that indicate both how to use a thing in a specific manner and for what the thing is used.[15] When discussing the transitory qualities of definition, Miller points out that "A static definition is neither experimentally nor logically possible. . .we are compelled therefore to search for a relative permanence, and we find that definition as a whole changes in respect to other definitions."[16]

Buildings throughout history have presented various solutions to how people should live—some have done this better than others. For example, *The Temple of Jerusalem* served to demonstrate and define a prevailing concept of the divine—an idea of God. A temple is considered a measured sacred space and is an edifice perceived as the residing place of, or dedicated to the worship of, a deity.[17] The definition of a temple is the measured space of a divine ideal. There are several basic architectural elements that typically define (mark out the measure of) a temple. These elements include the enclosure, the gate, the altar, the tower, a column standing within the enclosure, and, finally, the *cella*, which is the most sacred space contained within the sanctuary, or temple proper, where the image of the deity (ideal) or his/her symbol is kept. These are the significant elements that have been clearly discussed in accounts of *The Temple of Jerusalem*.[18]

The Temple of Jerusalem was the center of ancient Israeli worship and national identity. The First Temple was constructed during the reign of King David's son, Solomon, and was completed in 957 BCE as an abode for the ark and as a place of assembly for the people.[19] Over the centuries, *Solomon's Temple* was rebuilt by Zerubbabel and later by Herod. The exact location of *Herod's Temple* on the mount is unknown, although it is recorded that it was destroyed by the Romans in 70 AD.[20] The First Temple served to reflect the supposed order of the ideal. This holy building was derived architecturally from a divine pattern revealing the shape of the tabernacle and the temple: "God's guidance is implied in David's rejection (II Samuel 7:5, 13; I, Chronicles 17:12) and the choice of his son Solomon as a

Figure 1.3
Model of Herod's Temple (Jerusalem, Israel). Source: CC-PD.

builder."[21] As Rudolf Wittkower writes in *Architectural Principles in the Age of Humanism*, "This order was believed to have been originally inspired directly by God when he charged Solomon to build the Temple. Architects, therefore, attempted to re-create this perfect archetype from which all other orders were thought to be derived."[22] God was the original or ideal considered for, or deserving of, imitation, and the Second Temple was considered to be based on the first.

The Temple of Jerusalem also served to represent the ideal in the Christian mind. For example, Jesus is said to have described the destruction and rebuilding of the temple in reference to his death and resurrection. Medieval Christians described the temple as setting the ideal standard for their soaring sanctuaries.[23] On entering the restored Santa Sophia, the Byzantine Emperor Justinian I (c. 482–565), is reported to have cried, "Solomon, I have outdone you."[24] Charlemagne supposedly built his churches and palaces following Solomon's example, and the *Sistine Chapel* is, in a medieval way, modeled explicitly on *The Temple of Jerusalem* by repeating its dimensions.[25] His vision of the temple represented a paradox, a building located on a particular site but also one that was increasingly coming to be regarded as universal and transcendent.

Universal and transcendent buildings can be considered archetypes.[26] Here it is important to consider the psychology of Carl Jung, who believed that archetypes were the patterns of thought, or imagery that emerged from the collective unconscious of humankind. For example, Jung described the deep emotional appeal of the mandala, the square surrounded by, or including, a circle. Numerous buildings, such as churches in the form of a Greek cross, have been based on such a form.[27] The concept of the temple, although originally connected with a sacred site, was transformed into a universal archetypal building. Christians interpreted the temple as an archetypal predecessor of the church, while Jewish religious doctrine saw it as a realization of their concept of invisible things: "It is, therefore, not an ill-founded notion but a sign of spiritual continuity that the reformers of Christianity and of Judaism set out to build 'temples' to God in search for a wider spiritual concept."[28] The creators of temples attempted to define their concept of the divine through their designs. Part of definition involves *measuring* and, as we have seen, it is used as a comparison or to measure against something else, a known or an ideal.

Architect as Measurer

As we have stated, people have a basic need to find order in a chaotic environment. Daedalus' structure served as a paradigm for attempts to form order. The word *paradigm* comes from the Greek *paradeigma*, "pattern, model; precedent, example," and from *paradeiknynai*, "exhibit, represent," literally "show side by side."[29] The labyrinth demonstrates how order can be found through myth, symbol, and allegory, and explains a conceptual notion of architecture through an understandable measure and scale.

Traditionally, it has been part of architects' character to clearly define their future buildings through the design process. The ability of architects to understand and effectively use measurement is critical to this process. Having clear measurement is, of course, important for all involved with building the project, so things do not become confused during construction. It is also important for those living in these buildings to be able to understand the logic of their dwelling. Thus, it is characteristic for architects to use measure in a search for an ideal way for people to live in the world. To understand measure, it can be stated that "Measurement is the process used to answer the questions: how many? How much? Measurement, broadly defined, can be made by the unaided human senses and brain—for example, in estimating distances dimensions, temperatures, and weights."[30] On a basic level, measure and scale are represented through systems of ordered marks arranged at fixed intervals and used as standards of reference—such as the architectural drafting tools, ruler, and scale.[31] Being able to measure and scale allows architects to metaphorically *climb towards* a definition, and also to develop a balance, or medium, between things that we know and things we do not know.[32]

Stories recount how the ancient Greek philosopher, mathematician and astronomer Thales measured the height of the pyramids by the length of the shadows they cast. He measured these shadows at the hour when the length of his own shadow equaled his height. The shadow offered Thales an understandable scale so that he could measure the unknown—something he did not know.[33] Similar to Thales, when architects develop a measure (in architecture often called a "concept"), they are establishing a standard, an acceptable unit of quantitative or qualitative value by which something intangible is determined or regulated. For example, when architects place walls here instead of there, they are making choices about the way the inhabitants will live and understand the world around them. However, if the measurement is not fully defined, then the development of the measurement process becomes itself an essential part of the process of understanding.

The concept of measurement reflects both tools and processes. Measuring devices such as rulers, scales, and various kinds of meters are manufactured in accordance with an understood, and socially accepted, standard. Each measurement of something unknown involves comparing it with an accepted known; however, the development of measurement involves several (not always apparent) steps. An unknown is measured by comparing it directly with a known device or with a measuring device or instrument that has been previously developed to agree with established measurement standards.[34] These reference standards are calibrated from time to time by comparing them with higher-level reference

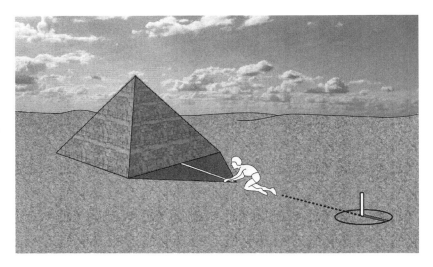

Figure 1.4
Thales measuring the pyramid's shadow, adapted from a drawing in the archives of Pearson Scott Foresman, artist unknown. Source: Jason Brijraj, CC-BY-SA-2.5 Self-published work.

standards that have been agreed upon. These high-level reference standards can be as simple as the length of an inch, or may involve complex systems such as cultural norms (or paradigms).

It is through society's attempts to measure invisible things that people produce not only units of measure such as inches, liters, and pounds, but also the philosophies and belief systems needed to measure and define the forms of any architectural period. What individuals see reflected in measurements is affected by current concepts (*reference standards*) of what is invisible. In other words, architects may simply accept a prevalent way of measuring by using typical building methods and incorporating the beliefs of a community. In this way, the community would set the standards for how its members should live. However, often architects have new ideas and devise new ideal ways for people to live. This may happen when architects influence local zoning laws, introduce a new building material, or devise a new construction technique that changes a community's thinking about how buildings should be built. Thus, architects often guide the redefinition of the community's standards.

It is through the attempt to measure invisible things that a society produces analogies—types of reference standards—that serve to interpret the things they do not know about. For this task, measurers', in our case architects', relationship with the invisible is important as they try to define such through a building. For example, the Catholic religion is measured through the cathedral. The churches of the fifth to fifteenth centuries demonstrated the message of medieval Catholicism to an illiterate population through sculpture and stained glass windows. Each door and window told a story from the religion, and presented it in a direct way to the observer; these buildings also served as media that considered and determined the measurements of the organization and doctrine of the Catholic Church.

A Catholic cathedral illustrates concepts of its religion as well as of its community. It offers a good example of how a building presents an understandable surface (framework) from which to project and define invisible things. It is a form

Defining

Figure 1.5
Stained glass windows, Champigny sur Veude Chapelle (Champigny sur Veude, France).
Source: Albert Smith, CC-BY-SA-2.5 Self-published work.

of measurement that mediates between the order of the known and the chaos of the unknown. This ability to use measurement provides people some control over confusing things. But, like a crystal ball, tea leaves left in a cup, or smoke in an alchemist's tort, users can never be sure how the message of the building will be interpreted on any given day.

9

Defining

There are, of course, many parts of a building that can be exactly measured, for instance the width of doors and the number of windows. However, the overall *meaning* of a building as perceived by its inhabitants may be more difficult to measure, since many things in people's lives cannot be measured precisely or numerically. For example, many people have spiritual or mystical beliefs that are difficult to explain scientifically but that nevertheless remain an important part of their lives. Similarly, there are many conceptual ideas that architects consider when designing a building that are ambiguous and never perceived consciously by visitors. The manifestations of these ideas will require interpretation.

Again using the example of early Christianity, the Catholic Church desired that controlled measures be defined in specific ways that were compatible with Church doctrine. Architectural designs that supported their tightly controlled definitions were the acceptable ones. The cathedral, through its design, maintained solid control over its users' interpretations. The Church did not necessarily wish the parishioners to assume wrong conclusions. The cathedrals presented their *readers* with a relatively tightly controlled narration or measurement that provided the specific interpretation of the canons of the Catholic religion desired by its leaders. It is not surprising that competing measurements such as myths, legends, witchcraft, and modern science were frowned upon in such a controlled environment. The Church did not allow the *reader* of the cathedral many opportunities for misinterpretation of the measure.

The Catholic Church's control over the cathedral's message reflected the paradigm of medieval society. In a similar way, the measure of Daedalus' labyrinth metaphorically demonstrated the ancient Greek concept of order. Most often, contemporary architects also build within the accepted norms of a community.

Figure 1.6
**Notre-Dame de Paris from the Pont de l'Archêveché (Paris, France).
Source: Atoma, CC-BY-SA-2.5.**

This consideration of manner and mode results in what is often referred to as *regionalism* or style.

Architect as Engaging Manner and Mode

An important character trait of architects is the ability to understand the manner and mode of their society and of those who will live in their buildings. Manner and mode are two related words; *manner* is a habit or custom reflective of society, whereas *mode* involves the atmosphere or emotions embedded in the perception of architectural space. To explain these concepts, we will return to the myth of Daedalus and the labyrinth. As described at the beginning of the chapter, the Minotaur/monster's movements were intentionally restricted to the path of the labyrinth. Alberto Pérez-Gómez has compared the significance of Daedalus' construction to the idea of dance: "In archaic times, the dance was the architecture. The space of architecture was the space of ritual and not an objective, geometrical entity."[35] This quote suggests that the ritual of dance was not the prescribed form of a labyrinth (or the shape of a maze) but instead indicates that movement through space was architectural because it reflected the patterns of how people lived their lives.

In the book *Through the Labyrinth*, Hermann Kern discusses the origins and ritual structure of the relationship between the labyrinth and dance:

> One approach is to examine early descriptions of the graphic figure or, alternatively, the dances that were described in antiquity as labyrinthine. Should the literary, visual and dance traditions ever be traced to a common source, this source could indeed be called the archetypal labyrinth. Much is to be said for the hypothesis that the concept of the labyrinth first manifested itself as a group dance and that a chain of dancers followed a path much like the one depicted on the tablet from Pylos and the corresponding Bronze Age petroglyphs in the Mediterranean basin.[36]

Pérez-Gómez also finds that, after slaying the Minotaur, Theseus (who represented the mythical Greek hero) engaged in a dance, which imitated the meandering of a labyrinth:

> The connection between this image and the Trojan games described by Virgil in the "Aeneid" has often been observed, as have the possible relationships between these ritual dances and the rituals of the foundation of cities in Roman times, which made the city secure; the ritual was so important, in fact, that it had to be re-enacted periodically.[37]

Ritual can be connected with the patterns of dance since ritual is defined as pertaining to or connected with rites, a prescribed order of performing a religious or other devotional service.[38] Two predominant circles of thought concerning ritual give different dimensions to the repetitive action involved in it.[39] The anthropologist Roy Rappaport's cultural studies stressed how rituals reflect fundamental notions about the world, and that they are inherently connected with religious beliefs. Religious rituals are developed through a set of beliefs (that may be considered boundaries), which attempt to explain, through a form of worship, the true meaning of the universe or of an ideal. Anthropologist Victor Turner, whose interests involved social change, proposed that rituals are based on the repetition of a procedure: they are performances according to defined habits or conventions. As ceremonial acts, rituals are ways to understand things that are not known. It can be seen that both ritual and religion offer a way to understand shared assumptions that attempt to explain the truth inherent in phenomena and in the invisible. When architects engage the manners of a time period, ritual influences the future building and its inhabitants. Various cultures employ ritual ceremonies related to the creation of architecture. For example, some Western societies believe that certain actions must be performed to successfully celebrate the completion of a building; it is common for contractors to conduct a topping-off ceremony for a modern high-rise building. In a ritual called "stealing the golden beam," the Dong tribes of Southwest China choose an auspicious day to cere-moniously cut and prepare the first tree that will be used in constructing a sacred building.[40] These rituals serve to retain the traditional visual traits of vernacular buildings, and also to ensure the structural integrity of constructions. Still practiced today, these rituals are important to the community as they guide the process at every stage, "expressing the awareness of the time and space that defines the Dong sensibility of creating a building."[41]

Manner

It is in the character of architects to understand and effectively engage the human manner. The etymology of the word *manner* is related to that of *modus*. One of the primary definitions of the word manner is connected to a characteristic that makes an architect's work uniquely his or her own—that is, a style. But this does not mean architects can create without limits, since they have a responsibility to the people living in their buildings, and to the society that contains the buildings. Interestingly enough given its relation to building, the word manner has its origin in a Latin term meaning "of the hand."[42] Specifically, the word means a characteri-stic or customary mode of acting, as in habit, usage, or custom. In this case, we are using this term to refer to the society within which an architect builds. This relationship relates manner to the word *habit* which means an acquired behavio-ral pattern regularly followed until it becomes almost involuntary, or a customary practice or use. Manner as linked to the word *custom*, meaning a habitual prac-tice, is the usual way of acting in given circumstances.[43] The manner, habits, and customs of a society are a reflection of how they define their cosmos, the term cosmos being understood as the world or universe regarded as an orderly, harmonious system. Thus, it is important to understand the concept of manner in architecture because it reflects the normal behavior of a society and, in turn, influences the people who live in the buildings which architects construct.

In many large cities, the floor area of condominiums has been greatly reduced as people tend to live in small bachelor or studio apartments. Architects may ask if this trend is a function of a culturally changing paradigm of the family, or if it has been imposed by the buildings' developers. The movement towards smaller families and staying single longer may be part of the reason, along with the cost of real estate in cities. Studies of vernacular architecture have revealed how various housing types reflect a culture's customs—from the indigenous people of North America's longhouses to contemporary communal living in the Netherlands.

Ritual has been studied as a social and cultural phenomenon; in its relationship to architecture, it represents the habits of a person's life. When architects design, they should consider a society's customs and ceremonies—these include attending school, getting married, interactions for work and recreation—and the way spaces are sequenced. To give an example, Pérez-Gómez in his references to dance speaks of placing walls around the ceremonial actions that mark events in peoples' lives. This brings our conversation back to Daedalus' labyrinth. The labyrinth was said to have been constructed to confine the Minotaur. This can be seen as similar to the way architects construct walls that influence the rituals of inhabitants:

> As a graphic linear figure, a labyrinth is best defined first in terms of form. Its round or rectangular shape makes sense only when viewed from above, like the ground plan of a building. Seen as such, the lines appear delineating walls and the space between them as a path, the legendary "thread of Ariadne"; the walls themselves are unimportant. Their sole function is to mark a path, to define choreographically, as it were the fixed pattern and led to the center by winding its way in circuitous fashion across the entire labyrinth.[44]

Architecture, as it involves the construction of walls to define space, becomes a form of definition. It is through an understanding of the manner of architecture that it becomes possible to comprehend what is being measured and thereby to establish a definition. Buildings reflect architects' relationship with an accepted concept of the tangible, but also with the invisible: the divine, or in other words, the non-physical things that guide our beliefs.[45]

Mode
It is part of architects' character to understand and determine the *mode* within which to design. The word mode is related directly to *model* and measure, and is also linked etymologically to the word manner. Although mode refers to a prevailing fashion or style of dress or behavior, it can also mean a musical arrangement or rhythmical scheme. Mode relates to architecture by setting a mood, a temporary state of mind or feeling.[46] When speaking of mode, the philosopher Immanuel Kant used the word *modalität*, usually translated as modality, which meant the manner—as actual, as possible, or as necessary—in which something existed.[47] The philosopher John Locke defined mode as the manner in which an idea is known, and mode to the philosopher Baruch Spinoza was "that which exists in and through, something other than itself."[48]

In architectural terms, mode can be the atmosphere of interior spaces that reveals an underlying intention. Architects have long recognized the value of imbuing their buildings with mode. Steven Holl reinforces these concepts in his

Defining

preface to Juhani Pallasmaa's book *Eyes of the Skin: Architecture and the Senses*.[49] Holl explores the element of light in his buildings, utilizing spectacular light wells and skylights in buildings such as the *Herning Museum of Contemporary Art*. In this design, folded and stepped ceilings create gaps that reflect light and emit glowing light from above.

For architectural thinking, the use of scale, in various forms, serves as a mode or a mechanism for measuring or defining manners. Architects understand scale primarily as proportional comparison, in other words, through its relationship to our bodies. The meaning of the Minotaur also assists architects in understanding human scale. Architects consider scale when drawing or modeling to avoid designing on a one-to-one basis—that is, full scale. Thus, scale can help architects perceive a future building without the costs of full-size construction. It is important to consider scaled drawings and models in contrast to sketches, drawings, or computer graphics that are presented without scale—or designed in CAD. While it is true that all of these forms of graphic representation are useful in the design process, scaled media can produce results that are less ambiguous. For example, according to Stanford Hohauser, architectural scale models are the most easily understandable of all presentational techniques.[50] They are useful in allowing architects to perceive their developing concepts more clearly. Even though architects are typically experienced in spatial thinking, their clients are generally not. Such scaled media (sketches, renderings, and models) help clients to more quickly understand a potential design. Thus, through the use of scale, architects can directly communicate ideas such as mood or feelings to clients, as well as to the public. Scale can indicate the measure and mode of a building.

The word mode is also related to the word *modest* through the Latin *modus*. Modest means having a limited and not exaggerated estimate of one's ability or

Figure 1.7
A full-scale architectural mock-up.
Source:
Mr Martini, CC BY-SA 4.0.

14

worth, or lacking in vanity or conceit, or not bold or self-assertive.[51] Its definition includes being free from exaggeration or overstatement. To be modest is to be reasonable, moderate, conventional in dress and behavior, or limited in size or amount—in other words, not excessive. In its archaic form, to be modest means to exercise control over, to act as a mediator, or to be in the middle.[52] This is quite similar to the word *moderate*, which is characterized by an avoidance of extremes of behavior.[53] Thus, the modest measure reflects the mode.

Using another episode from the story of Daedalus, once he created the labyrinth, he attempted to escape his island prison. He crafted a pair of wings made of wax and feathers for himself and his son, Icarus. Daedalus warned Icarus to travel a moderate path as they escaped Crete on their fabricated wings. Flying too low would cause the moisture from the sea spray to soak the feathers, and flying too high would take him too close to the sun, melting the wax that held the wings together. Icarus, however, was so excited with his ability to fly that he ignored his father's warning and flew too high. Thus, his wings melted and he fell into the Icarian Sea and died. Just as in the case of Daedalus' labyrinth, Icarus' wings are a story of technology; they present evidence of Icarus' rejection of limits and are a recommendation for the moderate use of technology.

Figure 1.8
The Fall of Icarus, Jacob Peter Gowy, 1615–1661 (Madrid, Spain). Source: Museo Del Prado, CC-PD-MarkPD-Art (PD-old-100).

An architectural construction is a reflection of current thoughts and a measure of modernity. Since the word *modern* also originates from *modus*, meaning something that reflects the manner of today, the measure of architecture has always been related to its manner. Without manner, it becomes impossible to understand what is being measured. This is why, as society changes, so does the definition of manner. As mode is the predominant style or behavior, it reflects the feelings inhabitants experience in their buildings. Buildings extend architects' modest ability to measure the perceived chaos of the unknown. Architecture is our modest mode in which the manner is measured.

Architects and Play

Architects need character to help them define their design decisions and thus their buildings. This section explores architects' relationships to the design process, and how architects should be able to engage play as part of definition. The philosophical theories of play developed by Hans-Georg Gadamer, Johan Huizinga, Gregory Bateson, and, more recently, James S. Hans can provide insight into how architects can effectively engage their design process.[54] Play is an activity in which all humans engage, even when "working."[55] It is a function of learning that involves acts of manipulation, and its implementation enhances interpretation to find truth. A philosophical definition of play includes a consideration of boundaries, creates a dialogue of interaction (action and response) that explores possibilities, considers its role as simulation, and highlights the ability to concede one's conscious efforts to play. It incorporates the understanding that to play is to provide intelligibility to any given process. Daedalus' abilities as an *architect*, as the designer of the labyrinth, and as a sculptor exhibit the concept of play in architecture.

To construct buildings in most cases, architects need to work within the established limits of site, program, the nature of materials, and especially gravity. They must also establish limits that may involve imbuing the building with conceptual meaning or deciding the *feel* of spaces. It is through the action of designing (or playing) that they try various alternatives or combinations, explore different aspects of materials, analyze by disassembling components to inspect the parts, test different ideas against a pre-determined proposal, and/or stretch against established boundaries by experimenting with new techniques. When designing the wings for his escape from prison, Daedalus was attempting something completely new—challenging the boundary of the accepted notion that people cannot fly. Using play, he was building and testing his invention, although, unfortunately, he did not test sufficient iterations of his design before flight. Architects can develop their projects using the actions of playing, and it is therefore instructive to look to how we play games.

It is well known that games require an adversary, an opponent, rules, a chance (luck), or a boundary of space, time, or physical being.[56] Physical boundaries, such as a tennis court or a chessboard, define games. Similarly, rules, such as limiting the sequence of play or the number of participants, are another form of boundary. These limits create the challenge. By comparison, architects' design processes are enhanced by physical restrictions or self-imposed limitations, and they react to physical boundaries to help them make decisions. For example, an irregularly shaped site may present architects with an opportunity to use their imaginations and arrive at an unusual solution. A steeply sloped site presented challenges that proved to be opportunities for the architect Richard Meier when he designed his well-known *Douglas House*. In an effort to maximize the view, the design for this house on Lake Michigan required extending the building above the trees. The limits of the difficult site encouraged a creative solution.

A limited budget for building materials led the Swiss architect Mario Botta to construct his early buildings using dyed concrete blocks. The *Giuseppina Bianchi Danilo House* in Ligornetto, Ticino, uses common, relatively inexpensive blocks to form a pattern of horizontal stripes on the façade. These lines pay homage to the landscape at the same time as the building itself presents a physical boundary with heavy exterior walls that enclose the living spaces inside. This innovative and beautiful design was partially the result of budgetary constraints.

Play is only productive during the act of playing. When the play stops, so does the immersion in the play mode. For instance, in a game of soccer, when the ball goes out of bounds, players physically relax and abandon the playing stance. They know play has ceased, and they take on a different mind-set. The anthropologist Gregory Bateson uses the terms "frame" and "context" to clarify the meaning of boundaries in play. He compares his use of the term "frame" to the frame of a picture, which is used "to order or organize the perception of the viewer."[57] Similarly, play helps to define what tools, methods, or ideas are appropriate for a session of play. As Joel Weinsheimer writes, "It is also true that the limits imposed are themselves restricted by the need for play."[58] The rules are chosen specifically to support the play and what is hoped to be achieved through it. As Daedalus defined a society's search for knowledge with the labyrinth, he was also defining the movement (play) of the Minotaur with boundary walls.

Part of the definition of play includes the fact that it can be, and needs to be, repetitive. At the same time, there remains the importance of infusing the familiar with the different. The philosopher James S. Hans suggests that play requires both novelty and repetition and that the course of play involves a relationship between these two.[59] A game's rules may be constant, but the strategies and level of skill of the players make the game different each time it is played. In this way, "play shares one thing with games: a familiar structure that allows one to play with the unfamiliar."[60] Architects may play within the rules, freely accepted, of the media they are manipulating, but they often work outside these rules to explore alternatives. They repeatedly play with a basic palette of common building materials but can employ them very differently. They, as others who are engaged in play, find that through play, the players adapt to a changing world, and it is this change that enriches play.[61] It is also important to note that play cannot be repeated exactly, for then it is no longer play. Play's function is primarily to learn, and once something is learned, repetition is unnecessary. Examples of the iterative qualities of architectural sketches demonstrate that many variations on a theme reveal architectural play.

James S. Hans writes about why humans engage in play: "The why of play is quite obvious: one seeks to play because one believes that the understanding achieved through play is more valuable than the kinds of understanding achieved in other ways."[62] Architects may alter forms, move spaces around, or apply various materials on a façade to see which works better—judging from their pre-determined boundaries. Play presents a dialogue or discourse to help architects determine decisions, and each decision is met with a new opportunity for interpretation: "Play fulfills its purpose only if the player loses himself in the play."[63] This means that the work of art (architecture) "becomes an experience changing the person experiencing it."[64] It does not mean that someone is *not present*, or distracted, but rather it means that they are present through the attention to something, not themselves—thus not only a self-forgetting but a self-finding.[65] Part of this includes a willingness to give up pre-judgments—to believe the play is true—and become self-absorbed: "the player begins with his own fore-conceptions, but he must be led by the work itself, must accept the rules the work itself offers."[66] This dialogue of architectural design may help architects to avoid pre-conceived ideas and to open up possibilities for them to explore. The many possibilities of meaning bring play to life, and also assist learning. Hans writes:

> Man may have a purpose in his play, but this purpose is always no more than an orientation if his play is really to be play. Man may play with certain ideas in the hope of resolving a particular problem, but if he is really playing with the ideas, the play of ideas directs him rather than the other way around.[67]

Another primary feature of play is its dependence upon representation. The actions of play often replicate an action of not-play. As children play house or war, they are simulating within a safe environment. This is also true of architecture. To simulate by using design media avoids the costly ramifications of changes on a large scale. Architects can manipulate media to learn about a project and make decisions before a building is constructed. Specific models, drawings, and computer renderings may be understood only by the architect who made them and, in this way, architects are able to think through design decisions by using design media.[68] Thus, play is a very serious activity that utilizes not-serious methods.

Play revels in ambiguity. In the early stages of design, ideas, drawings, and models are vague and unformed. The manipulation of design materials helps to interpret this ambiguity. A common analogy equates a labyrinth to the idea of the thesaurus: both are structured like a meander. Such meanders work like a web where every point is connected to every other point. Marco Frascari pointed out that meanders are full of Minotaur-like monsters. He stated, "These Minotaurs, monsters conceived by inconceivable unions, demonstrate the possibilities of union between different kinds of realities. They are not abnormalities but rather they are extraordinary phenomena that indicate the way to how—to design for architecture."[69] It is understood that Daedalus' labyrinth represents a search for truth, and that the building of the labyrinth's walls limits play.

Architect as Setting Boundaries and Order
In the previous parts of this chapter, we have discussed how the act of play assists the evolution of architectural definition, as it provides architects with numerous

new possibilities to engage during the design process. But to play with a purpose, there must be a set of boundaries within which the play takes place. *Defining* is the act of demarcating what is within or outside what constitutes something, and boundaries frame a definition within specific parameters. By establishing boundaries, architects are essentially delineating order that initiates and subsequently governs the act of play. In this section, we will examine the character of architects as those who employ order and boundaries to assist in defining their buildings.

As discussed in the introduction to this chapter, Daedalus' invention of the labyrinth serves as an analogy for architectural definition. By containing the monster inside the labyrinth walls, Daedalus was essentially defining the chaos of the unknown through a set of understandable boundaries. Defined by its walls, the labyrinth is able to demarcate the spaces of its path, and its concentric circles collectively produce its iconic pattern and form.[70] Clearly, Daedalus was able to interpret an order, built upon this logic, that he displayed in his design. In other words, the search for order through the labyrinth is analogous to the search for the order fundamental for building.

Dictionaries define *order* as the "formal, regular, methodical, or harmonious arrangement in the position of the things contained in a particular space or area, or composing any group or body."[71] Order can also mean "a regular mode of procedure. . .or a method of action."[72] For architecture, the importance of order can be understood in terms of the order imposed on the physical and metaphysical landscape. Humanity's search for order, since the beginning of architecture, was encapsulated by the architectural historian Spiro Kostof:

> Boundary and monument both imply a determined marking of nature. Humans impose through them their own order on nature, and in doing so introduce that tug of balance between the way things are and the way we want them to be.[73]

Definitions of order, as understood today, allude to a relationship of parts to the whole that results in a work's formal and experiential harmony. Vitruvius wrote that architecture consists of proportion (among other things) so that buildings are in balance between the details in relationship to the whole to provide a good arrangement.[74] As will be fully discussed in the section on beauty in Chapter 4, Leon Battista Alberti also discussed the harmony of a building's parts in relationship to the whole.[75] Consistent with these descriptions, the twentieth-century Modernist architect Le Corbusier described order as a "necessity" which "brings satisfaction to the understanding," and thus "a sense of beauty."[76] In Le Corbusier's words, we find parallels to Kostof's statement that order gives rise to a set of rules, principles, or limits that govern the design of buildings, mediating the unknown with understandable boundaries.

For these architects, order ensured a systematic approach to design that fostered harmony, unity, and beauty, since it served to guide and transform invisible ideas precisely into definitive forms. With a slightly different approach, the twentieth-century architect Louis Kahn wrote that "design is form-making in order." For Kahn, there existed in order a "creative force" that was executed through design. His manifesto on order described a "system of construction," which intuitively guides form-making to realize the "unfamiliar."[77] He closed his manifesto by stating that order is intangible, as it is a level of creative consciousness that is forever elevating: the higher the order, the more diversity in design.[78]

Throughout history, there are many examples of where architects defined their buildings in accordance with a particular order or set of boundaries that reflected certain ideals of the time. To illustrate, the architect Frank Lloyd Wright was known for his use of geometry as an order governing the entirety of a design. In his *Guggenheim Museum*, the geometry of the double circles, as a labyrinth, governed the plan, form, and details of the building. The geometry can thus be said to have set boundaries for the design. Wright possessed the transcendentalist belief that "the universe is represented in every one of its particles. Everything in nature contains all the powers of nature. . .Each one is an entire emblem of human life."[79] In other words, the universe infinitely repeats itself in the smallest details, while each detail encapsulates the universe. Wright's use of the double circle motif, basically a labyrinth, at every scale of the building, aims to imitate a relationship that can be seen as a way of defining the invisible and boundless, that is, the universe, through comprehensible means.[80]

To give another example, analyzing Kahn's work demonstrates his success in achieving an expression of order. The *National Parliament Building* in Bangladesh takes the form of an imposing fortress lying in an artificial lake in the country's capital: its grandness expresses the authority of the government. The plan of the building features eight halls concentrically arranged around the circular central parliamentary grand chamber. The equality of the supporting chambers that revolve around the central chamber emphasizes the importance of the central government. The design exemplifies a formal expression of order. The poured-in-place concrete and inlaid marble, as well as geometric *punched-out* openings, offer unique lighting scenarios. The building speaks to the vernacular architecture

Figure 1.9
Interior of the Solomon R. Guggenheim Museum, architect Frank Lloyd Wright (New York, NY, USA).
Source: Alex ProimosMedia, CC-BY-2.0.

of Bangladesh and to its climate, as well as to Modernist principles. These are demonstrated distinctly in the centralized plan that resembles a Hindu mandala pattern, a circle imposed inside a square.[81] A mandala is a spiritual and ritual symbol representing the universe. Its geometric pattern is usually organized as a square of four main gates containing a central circle with a center point. As a symbol of the cosmos, the mandala is an ordering device: it makes something unknown understandable as it expresses a microcosm of the universe.[82]

We have seen how it is within architects' character to use boundaries and order to define their buildings. The limiting aspects of play also result in "a structure, a framework or order that has been confirmed by the play itself."[83] The postmodern philosopher Jacques Derrida questions the order of play and describes the constant reflection or interpretation of experience as "freeplay."[84] In contrast to this position, the philosopher Hans-Georg Gadamer conceded that all experience involves interpretation and believed that all interpretation hinges on pre-judgments that are traditional and occur in culture—something that is found to be true throughout the centuries.[85] This idea is crucial to the nature of boundaries within a discussion of defining. When building, architects cannot ignore their buildings' place in the world as being reflective of society and culture. A way to synthesize and unite these issues for architects may be seen in Gadamer's quote, "To stand within a tradition does not limit the freedom of knowledge but makes it possible."[86]

Figure 1.10 **Similarities between mandala forms and the National Assembly of Bangladesh (completed 1982), adapted from image of the Mandala of Amitayus, Tibet. Source: Jason Brijraj, CC-BY-SA-2.5 Self-published work.**

Just as Daedalus imposed order through constructing walls as boundaries to demarcate paths and thus differentiated the understandable from a chaotic world, so architects have re-interpreted order through their work. In a context of shifting circumstances, having the character to establish and reinforce order is essential, as it guides judgment and decision making throughout the design process. Therefore, architects should possess the ability to formulate thoughtful boundaries to define their future buildings' meanings. This should be considered using their own belief systems within a contextual paradigm.

Conclusion

We began our study of architects' character with the concept of defining for several reasons. The first reason is that it is fundamental human nature to search for meaning. Second, connecting definition with the design process helps us to see architecture's greater role in society, one that transcends simply protecting us from the physical forces of nature. Beginning with definition allowed a discussion of how architects design, which is central to being an architect.

Through exploring the meaning of definition, this chapter discussed the connection between definition and design. Subsequently, it explained that to define something is to create boundaries that designate exact meanings. Again, we would like to reiterate that the word *designate* is closely related to the word *design*, which means "to mark out." It is the marking out of a thing that led us to the concept of measuring, and it is through humanity's attempts at measuring invisible things that humans produce not only units of measure such as inches, liters, and pounds, but also the philosophies and belief systems needed to measure and define.

Architects measure many things, but one of the most important of these is the human manner. They have a responsibility to a building's inhabitants and to the society within which the building will be constructed. It has been argued that it is important for architects to understand the appropriate mode within which to design. In pointing out that a static definition or design is neither experimentally nor logically possible, architects continue their search for meaning. But in this search, they persistently seek relative permanence in their definitions. Using design as part of this search, architects work within the established limits of construction, even as they create their own limits to respond to the criteria of each project.

In this—and subsequent chapters—it is important to ask if the illustrative Greek myths are still relevant. To return to the myth of Daedalus, he was reported to have constructed the wooden cow for the queen Pasiphae, the labyrinth at Knossos, and artificial wings for himself and his son Icarus, and even to have sculpted animated figures. Daedalus served as a reflection of other ancient Greek architects. Today, as we consider his role, we can recognize Daedalus as the prototypical example of how architects have always attempted to create order in a diverse, and yet to be structured, environment. We must also be mindful of the fact that, while he may be prototypical, there are differences between architects then and now, especially in regard to social standing but that, nevertheless, many of the characteristics we have discussed remain relevant.

It has been noted that the architectural design process not only is used as a means of designing our life-sustaining buildings, but also plays an important role in defining a culture's belief systems. It is possible to argue that the end product of this process, architecture, is typically used as a way to define. Although examples of architecture from different historical periods may look similar, there can be substantial differences as to what these buildings define. Through the use of analogy and metaphor, architecture can serve as a measuring mechanism that projects meaning onto a complex and confusing whole. However, while certain aspects of architectural designs are constant, the representational meanings of designs may be in transition. This transition occurs when a society changes, or when our relationship with the unknown shifts.

By posing questions about the characteristics contemporary architects need, it is important to ask if the labyrinth still serves as a metaphor of human existence and whether Daedalus' creation of it can be seen as a paradigm of order, the primordial ideal of architecture. Every time we create architecture that responds to our environment and reflects meaning, we engage in the search for order. For example, if architects design a courthouse that reflects and helps define the idea of justice and presents the seriousness and gravity of a judicial system, then they are participating in this search. Every time we build a road, create a philosophy, or vote, for example, we are reflecting our basic and continuing need to establish order where there was previously chaos. While today some buildings may seem to participate in this search more than others, all buildings define their culture in some way.

If we accept that it should be in architects' character to be able to define clearly, what characteristics do they use to define? The topic of Chapter 2, "Imaging," presents an overview of the traditional characteristics architects need to envision, conceive, and imagine. It will explore representational media, how images inform architectural thinking and how architects engage the images they make—drawings (either analog or digital) and models. Thus, the aspect of architects' character that pertains to dexterity, conveying messages through the built work, creativity, and intention will be made clear.

Notes

1   Hermann Kern, *Through the Labyrinth: Designs and Meanings over 5,000 Years* (Munich: Prestel Publishing, 2000), 12.

2   Françoise Frontisi-Ducroux, *Dédale: Mythologie De L'artisan En Grèce Ancienne* (Paris: F. Maspero, 1975), 90.

3   *Oxford English Dictionary*, s.v. "analogy."

4   Frontisi-Ducroux, *Dédale*, 90.

5   Alberto Pérez-Gómez, "The Myth of Daedalus," *AA Files* 10 (1985): 51.

6   Frontisi-Ducroux, *Dédale*, 90.

7   Pérez-Gómez, "The Myth of Daedalus," 50.

8   Ibid.

9   Ibid., 51.

10   *Oxford English Dictionary*, s.v. "monster."

11   For additional information on this subject, see Marco Frascari, *Monsters of Architecture* (Savage, MD: Rowman and Littlefield, Publishers, Inc., 1991).

12 John W. Miller, *The Definition of a Thing* (New York: W.W. Norton and Co., 1980), 38.

13 *Oxford English Dictionary*, s.v. "definition."

14 *Oxford English Dictionary*, s.v. "design."

15 Peter A. Angeles, *Dictionary of Philosophy* (New York: Barnes and Noble Books, 1981), 55–59.

16 Miller, *The Definition of a Thing*, 42, 50.

17 *Webster's New Third International Dictionary*, s.v. "temple." The word "temple" comes from the word *templum* which, in its original Latin meaning, defines a measured sacred space on earth or in heaven.

18 Alan H. Smith, *Encyclopaedia Americana* (Danbury, CT: Encyclopedia Americana, 1982), 459.

19 Ibid., 460.

20 Helen Rosenau, *Vision of the Temple: The Image of the Temple of Jerusalem in Judaism and Christianity* (London: Oresko Books, 1979), 7.

21 Ibid., 4.

22 Ibid., 14.

23 Ibid.

24 Joseph Rykwert, *On Adam's House in Paradise* (Cambridge, MA: MIT Press, 1981), 122.

25 Ibid.

26 According to the *Oxford English Dictionary*, the word "archetype" comes from the Latin *archetypum* which means first impression, stamp, or type.

27 Rosenau, *Vision of the Temple*, 163.

28 Ibid.

29 *Oxford English Dictionary*, s.v. "paradigm."

30 "Measurement, principles and instruments of", *Encyclopedia Britannica* (Chicago, IL: Encyclopedia Britannica, 1974), XI, 728.

31 Other definitions of the word scale can offer interesting and unusual insight into a deeper meaning of scale. The word scale derives from the Latin *scalae,* which means a ladder and, currently, scale can mean to climb. A scale can be a mechanism that provides an understandable balance between a known and an unknown. When a fisherman scales a fish he or she, through the act of peeling away, reveals something which was previously unseen underneath.

   A standard of reference or reference standard is a term borrowed from the field of measuring and simply means to direct to the established fixed rules. In measuring, an unknown is measured by comparing it with a known thing that has been previously developed. Such reference standards are calibrated from time to time by comparing them with a higher-level, generally agreed upon, reference standard.

32 *Oxford English Dictionary*, s.v. "scale."

33 Aristotle describes Thales of Miletus as the founder of European philosophy. For this reason, Thales is important to bridging the worlds of myth and reason.

34 "Measure," *Encyclopedia Americana* (Danbury, CT: Encyclopedia Americana, 1982), XVIII, 585.

35 Pérez-Gómez, "The Myth of Daedalus," 52.

36 Kern, *Through the Labyrinth*, 12.

37 Pérez-Gómez, "The Myth of Daedalus," 52.

38 *Oxford English Dictionary*, s.v. "ritual."

39 See Richard Bradley, *Ritual and Domestic Life in Prehistoric Europe* (London: Routledge, 2005); Victor W. Turner, *The Ritual Process: Structure and Anti-Structure* (Piscataway, NJ: Transaction Publishers, 2011); and Roy A. Rappaport, *Ritual and Religion in the Making of Humanity* (Cambridge, UK: Cambridge University Press, 1999).

40 Xuemei Li and Kendra Schank Smith, "Space, Time and Construction: Starting with Auspicious Carpentry in the Vernacular Dong Dwelling," *Journal of the Society of Architectural Historians*, 70(1) (2011): 7–17.
41 Ibid., 7.
42 *Oxford English Dictionary*, s.v. "manner."
43 *Oxford English Dictionary*, s.v. "custom."
44 Kern, *Through the Labyrinth*, 23.
45 For further information, please refer to Albert C. Smith, *Architectural Model as Machine* (Oxford, UK: Architectural Press, 2004).
46 *Webster's II New Riverside University Dictionary*, s.v. "mode."
47 See Immanuel Kant, *Metaphysical Foundations of Natural Science*, trans. Michael Friedman, Cambridge Texts in the History of Philosophy (Cambridge, UK: Cambridge University Press, 2004).
48 Angeles, *Dictionary of Philosphy*, 177.
49 Juhani Pallasmaa, *Eyes of the Skin: Architecture and the Senses* (Hoboken, NJ: John Wiley and Sons, 2005). See also Steven Holl and Juhani Pallasmaa, *Questions of Perception: Phenomenology of Architecture* (San Francisco, CA: William K. Stout Publishing, 2007).
50 Stanford Hohauser, *Architectural and Interior Models* (New York: Van Nostrand Reinhold, 1970), 6.
51 *Oxford English Dictionary*, s.v. "mode."
52 *Oxford English Dictionary*, s.v. "modest."
53 *Oxford English Dictionary*, s.v. "moderate."
54 See Hans-Georg Gadamer, *Truth and Method* (New York: Crossroads, 1989); Johan Huizinga, *Homo Ludens: A Study of the Play Element in Culture* (Boston, MA: Beacon Press, 1955); Gregory Bateson, *Steps to an Ecology of Mind: A Theory of Play and Fantasy* (Northvale, NJ and London: Jason Aronson, Inc., 1972); and James S. Hans, *The Play of the World* (Boston and Amherst: University of Massachusetts Press, 1981).
55 Hans, *The Play of the World*, 26–32.
56 Joel C. Weinsheimer, *Gadamer's Hermeneutics: A Reading of 'Truth and Method'* (New Haven, CT: Yale University Press, 1985), 104.
57 Bateson, *Steps to an Ecology of Mind*, 187.
58 Weinsheimer, *Gadamer's Hermeneutics*, 104.
59 Hans, *The Play of the World*, 28.
60 Ibid.
61 Psychologists refer to this as "feedback."
62 Hans, *The Play of the World*, 11–12.
63 Hans-Georg Gadamer, *Truth and Method*, 102.
64 Ibid., 92.
65 James S. Hans, "Hermeneutics, Play, Deconstruction," *Philosophy Today* 24(4) (1980): 305.
66 Ibid.
67 Hans, *The Play of the World*, 32.
68 Huizinga, *Homo Ludens*, 166. Huizinga has doubts about the plastic arts in a definition of play because a two- or three-dimensional object is a finished product and the key to play is in the practice of making. He writes, "for where there is no visible action there can be no play."
69 Frascari, *Monsters of Architecture*, 108.
70 Kern, *Through the Labyrinth*, 32.
71 *Oxford English Dictionary*, s.v. "order."

72 Ibid.

73 Spiro Kostof, *A History of Architecture* (New York: Oxford University Press, 1985), 21.

74 Vitruvius, *On Architecture*, trans. Frank Granger (Cambridge, MA: Harvard University Press, 1931), 25. His use of the word *proportion* is more appropriate in this context. His use of the word *symmetry* is understood to mean *proportion* rather than our definition of symmetry as two equal balanced parts.

75 Leon Battista Alberti, *On the Art of Building in Ten Books*, trans. Joseph Rykwert, Neil Leach, and Robert Tavernor (Cambridge, MA: MIT Press, 1988), 156.

76 Le Corbusier, *Towards a New Architecture*, trans. Frederick Etchells (New York: Dover Publications, 1986), 1–3.

77 Ulrich Conrads, *Programs and Manifestoes on 20th-Century Architecture*, trans. Michale Bullock (Cambridge, MA: MIT Press, 1971), 169–170.

78 Ibid.

79 Edward Ford, *The Architectural Detail* (New York: Princeton Architectural Press, 2011), 93–96.

80 Ibid.

81 William J.R. Curtis, "Louis Kahn: The Space of Ideas," *The Architectural Review* 1389 (November 2012): 78–87.

82 Kern, *Through the Labyrinth*, 34.

83 Ibid.

84 Jacques Derrida, "Structure, Sign, and Play in the Discourse of the Human Sciences," in *The Structuralist Controversy*, eds. Richard Macksey and Eugenio Donato (Baltimore, MD: Johns Hopkins University Press, 1972), 65, 264.

85 Weinsheimer, *Gadamer's Hermeneutics*, 105.

86 Gadamer, *Truth and Method*, 324.

Chapter 2

Imaging

Architects' character, as discussed in the Introduction, encompasses their nature, personality, or attributes, and may also indicate their talents. As talent is an aptitude, gift, inclination, or capacity for achievement or success, it can be proposed that architects have talent and the skills necessary to conceive, design, and construct architecture.[1] A person may choose to enter the discipline of architecture because they exhibit a propensity for image-making, possess a desire to alter the built environment, or have a gift for envisioning the future. Thus, it is in architects' nature, or character, to demonstrate advanced skills in the use of imagination and creativity. It is also architects' responsibility to hone these skills and to critically assess their use of images. To explain the imaging characteristics (*divinely inspired*, *imitator*, *imaginer*, *mindful mneme,* and *prophesier*) that architects require to successfully perform their tasks, it is important to begin with the Greek goddesses known as the Muses.

The Muses, or *Mousai*, were the goddesses of the arts, music, and philosophy who inspired mortals and gods alike. They were respected in Greek society, especially by artists, poets, and musicians, and cults and festivals were established

Figure 2.1
Detail on sarcophagus showing the Muses (Kansas City, Missouri).
Source: Nelson-Atkins Museum of Art, CC-PD-MarkPD Old.

in their honor. Born to Mnemosyne, the goddess of memory, and Zeus, the Muses resided with Apollo, the god of music, truth, and prophecy.[2] Each of them embodied a particular realm of knowledge that Greek civilization held important—collectively they formed "the world's memory."[3] Greek poets emphasized the wisdom and knowledge of the Muses, portraying them as goddesses who "know what is worth telling and can give the poet the ability to tell it, and also to remember it."[4] The number of Muses varies depending on the historical or literary source or period. Ephialtes and Otus introduced three, whose names were Melete (meditation), Mneme (memory), and Aoede (song); by contrast, nine Muses were established by the Thraco-Boeotian cults.[5] Although the Muses were named individually, they can be collectively referred to by the name *Mneiae*, meaning Remembrances. It should be noted that the Muses sang in chorus and that their intents were the same.[6] They were said to have lived beside the Graces, and Himeros (Desire), and they often appeared in literature with the Graces.[7]

The Muses lived with Apollo on Mount Helicon and visited various gods (the immortals) and mortals at their will, granting inspiration and insight according to their field of expertise. Many prominent Greek mathematicians, poets, and artists cite the Muses as inspiration and as having had a large role in their success.[8] Today, many words associated with the arts, knowledge, and inspiration have been derived from the term "Muses," including museums and music.[9] The goddesses were said to have received "unusually excellent education," which gave them the ability to confer delight.[10] Hesiod writes in *Theogony* that the Muses came to him in the mountains, "granted him his gift of song, breathing a divine voice into him to enable him to celebrate things that will be and things that have been in times gone by."[11] Homer asked the Muses to help him tell the stories of *The Iliad* and *The Odyssey* and described them as deities who "are present at all things, and know all things, while we hear no more than a rumour and have no knowledge." The Muses are a presence that was difficult to see and were perceived to have subtly influenced artists' creativity.[12]

The Muses had prophetic power and were connected to the god of Delphi. They gave the Sphinx riddles, educated Echo in playing music, and taught healing and fortune-telling to Aristaeus. According to Plato, at the birth of the Muses, men were compelled to sing with them until they starved to death. The Muses, then, turned these men into locusts, giving them the gift of song for the remainder of their lives. The Muses were also the companions of Dionysus, a patron of pleasure, and later a patron of the arts.[13]

The literature on the use of visual media in ancient Greece is limited and what survives today is primarily texts from philosophers and literary voices. Thus, very little writing exists that concerns art theory and nothing from the artists themselves. Plato wrote about artists but did not refer to the creativity of visual artists (labeling them imitators) even though he discussed the inventive abilities of poets. Although there are limited texts from this period on the subject of creativity, it does not mean that visual artists were not concerned with such concepts. It is through the myths describing the Muses that we understand ancient Greece's interest in inspiration and creativity. Although the Muses were not major goddesses, their support of artists, poets, and musicians reveals the importance of artistic endeavors in ancient Greek society. Architecture and the media used in the design process can also be considered arts.

Artists employ the images of imagination and media in many ways, but the primary objective for using paintings, drawings, and sculptures is to present an idea. The images they create convey an intended meaning. By contrast, architects typically use images to spark their imaginations, as a medium to explore design intent, present to clients, and represent a future building so that it will be constructed as they envision. For architects, the ultimate medium of meaning is the building: this is an inherent difference between artists and architects. More specifically, architects use images in the design process to record what they see, discover conceptual ideas and manipulate media, test what they make against what is in their minds' eye for appropriateness, visualize complex concepts, and persuade others, and for conventional documentation that anticipates construction.

Architects employ media to visualize future buildings. These media include various types of images for design exploration and presentation such as drawings, models, and digital renderings. But beyond the images that architects construct, there are also the images, or mental impressions, that are formed when they imagine, remember, envision the future, or invent something completely new. The Italian architect Carlo Scarpa expressed the importance of images for architects when he said that he used drawing to *see*. By using the term *see*, he meant the ability to understand both what he was observing and also the images formed in his imagination.[14] By employing the word imaging, this chapter will explore the character of architects' abilities to make images and also to comprehend the images that appear in their mind's eye.

Chapter 2, "Imaging," will investigate the historical and theoretical aspects of imaging as manifested in imitating, imagining, and visualizing for constructing, and will relate these to architects' character traits. It will also clarify the qualities of intention and interpretation critical to how architects utilize imaging. The chapter will discuss how architects envision the future through the use of imaging, and how the traits of the *divino artista* (God-given talents) assist in this ability to act as a soothsayer. The chapter will conclude with examples of how architects employ these traits in their design processes. Just as the Muses sang in chorus, there will be no equation of a specific Muse with a particular character trait; rather, the inspiration and creative qualities of the Muses collectively will be considered. The history of the Muses as goddesses in ancient Greece makes it appropriate to begin with a discussion of the perception of the character of architects as divinely inspired.

Architect as Divinely Inspired

Architects often are not able to credit their good ideas to any one factor in their skills or education, and may surmise that inspiration is a gift from an unknown source. Thus, it is possible to understand how the Muses were credited with inspiring writers, scientists, artists, and also architects. In some stories, Zeus slept for nine nights with Mnemosyne and fathered all nine Muses. From this union, the Muses were brought to life and tasked with praising the Greek gods. They were not interested in the everyday life of humans; instead, their primary role was to dedicate their lives to the arts. They supported and encouraged creation, thus enhancing artists' imagination. In this section, we will discuss the Muses' connection to the divinity of the gods, inspiration, and creativity. It will explore the concept of fantasy to understand the character of architects as *divinely inspired*.

While the concepts of imagination and fantasy are virtually synonymous, fantasy contains connotations of illusion and creative invention. People interested in aesthetics have long speculated about the mind's ability to create. Before there were scientific studies into the workings of the human mind, the occurrence of unexplained images or ideas led to speculation as to their origins. It may have been human nature to assign responsibility to the Muses or other divine intervention. Or creative inspiration may have been credited to the expanded associative capacity of certain individuals (their talents) or attributed to magic. To *inspire* is to breathe or blow into or upon. It also means to stimulate creative activity in an act, to bring about or produce.[15] *Inspiration* thus denotes the ability to make something entirely new or to bring to life. The word has ecclesiastic overtones, as inspiration and the force that creates life are similar notions.

Traditionally, to make inventive images has been the talent, and part of the character, of artists and architects. Although currently the word *fantasia* means creative imagination, this was not originally the case.[16] Literature from ancient Greece did not extensively discuss concepts of the creative imagination, but when the word *phantasia* first appeared in Western literature, it meant the appearance or the reflection of a thing. This interpretation was a metaphor of the mind as a mirror.[17] Although beginning in reflection, *fantasia* evolved to mean a *likeness* that did not need to be a replica. The visions of inspiration, "*phantasmata* of sense," needed to be accompanied by interpretation or higher judgment.[18] The art and architectural theorist David Summers wrote that *phantasia* and higher reality are linked by divination and are best described as the two sides of fantasy. He wrote of "one that reflects the world of sense, and another, allied with memory, that presents the reflected image to the higher faculties of the soul."[19] The historian Murray Wright Bundy, when discussing the Stoic philosophers of the Hellenistic and Roman periods, wrote of the creative imagination concerning fantasy and stated that "'*phantasm*' and '*phantastic*' [were] thus for the Stoics terms denoting the unreality of the vision."[20] Referencing ancient Greek culture, Summers compared Platonic thought to the creative mind: "In the ultimately Platonic tradition of *phantasia* as the meeting place of the higher and lower, is realized by an image in the fantasy."[21] He stated that this image has been in "combinatory fantasy to make 'what had never been seen.'"[22] Fantasy then leads the imagination into the "higher faculties of the soul," and its intelligence and inventiveness may be compared to illusion.

Definitions of inspiration and creativity were more completely developed by Renaissance writers, and discussion of the word *fantasia* established an understanding of what it means to be divinely inspired. In fifteenth-century Europe, the word *Renaissance* meant a return to the Classical; thus, it is possible to consider some ideas of inspiration as a continuation of Classical thought into this period. Renaissance artists' fanciful illusions established their reputations as thaumaturgists: "The active fantasy became one of the characteristics of genius. . .the word *fantasia* was used for the natural gifts of the painter."[23] This character trait was perpetrated by the artists themselves and by those who wrote about them. Giorgio Vasari, for example, in his book on the lives of

Renaissance artists, played on the quirks and chance beginnings which gave these artists mythical proportions.[24] Other publications elaborated by discussing artists' eccentric behavior, genius, madness, and melancholy.[25]

Rudolf and Margot Wittkower wrote that the beliefs of the Renaissance returned to the idea that artists, similar to the ancients, were placed in "the circle of inspired creators" along with poets.[26] The Renaissance concept of the *divino artista* or divine artist had two meanings, both of which divided artists from laypersons. The Wittkowers stated that "It was not only derived from Plato's theory of poetical enthusiasm but also from the medieval idea of God the Father as artist: as architect of the universe."[27] Artists, able to recognize divine beauty, were driven to divine madness and, consequently, they were forgiven eccentric behavior as it was seen as a personality trait necessary to, or at least distinctive of, their creative imagination.[28]

Summers added to this relationship when he described the Renaissance literary figure Dante Alighieri as a writer with incredible visual qualities: "Dante affirms more powerfully than anyone before him—both in theory and creative accomplishment—that fantasy was much greater than the sum of its parts."[29] Continuing this thought, "he [Dante] speaks of fantasy (or imagination) as a force initiated by divine grace which, like the intellect it serves, is able to approach the threshold of the vision of light itself."[30] This statement reveals Dante's unwillingness to define imagination solely as images worked on by our minds. He alluded to an intuitive God-given talent that enters a realm beyond, one of magic or divination.

David Summers, when defining *fantasia* as used by the Renaissance artist and architect Michelangelo, wrote that "*fantasia* is closest in meaning to *invenzione*."[31] Emerging from one of the five parts of rhetoric in ancient Greece, *invenzione* meant finding a theme of an argument. It was a term used extensively in the Renaissance and may be similar to the modern meaning of *invent*: to originate as a product of one's own device, or to make up or fabricate. This explanation is interesting for architects since it resembles a generating idea, an architectural *concept*. Specifically, "from this comes the invention—or the form (the words seem to be almost equivalent for Scamozzi), which is the explication of the Idea."[32] This "Idea" emanates from knowledge and helps make the images that appear in architects' minds. Invention recalls the Renaissance term *disegno*, "in Vasari's sense: the lines which express the mental conception."[33] "Design, then, could mean the Idea, or conception, or invention, itself; and could even be regarded, as Zuccari regarded it, as the sign, the stamp of God in man."[34] This connection between design and the gift of the Muses may help us understand the creative imagination's influence on architects' character.

The Renaissance spurred beliefs that creativity is not solely determined by hard work, education, or practice, but by a unique gift.[35] The belief was that the artist's talent was born in him or her.[36] Leon Battista Alberti in the fifteenth century added a specifically God-like flair to the artist, stating that this talent was divine; he saw "the artist's activity as that of a 'second God.'"[37] For instance, it was reported by Vasari that the early Renaissance artist Fra Angelico did not retouch his paintings after they were finished because God's will had been exhibited through his hand.[38] Artists and architects were seen as having special abilities sanctioned by a supreme being.

Architects today, along with artists, may wonder where their conceptual ideas come from, suggesting these inspirations may represent God-given or god-given talents. The Muses were tasked with praising the gods, but they also enhanced artists' abilities through divine inspiration. Architects, when designing the buildings so critical to society, need to do so diligently and with hard work, but talent also figures in the skills needed for success in the discipline. It is in architects' character to recognize the role of the creative imagination in inspiring their work, but they also desire to imitate the attributes of the divine.

Architect as Imitator

It is in the character of architects to desire perfection and many attempt to emulate through imitation. A myth from Ovid's *Metamorphoses* relates that the King of Macedon had nine daughters named after the Muses. The king believed that his daughters' skills could be matched against the Muses', and made the mistake of challenging them to a competition. The result of this was that his daughters were turned into chattering magpies for their presumption.[39] On the one hand, this story reveals that the Muses were protective of their powers and jealous of those attempting to reach the perfection of the gods. On the other hand, it explains how people can be inspired by the Muses to praise the divine gods through imitation of their perfection.

This section will discuss how it is in the character of architects to imitate nature and also emulate others. Imitation involves the ability to observe and reproduce. The etymology of the word *imitation* emerges from the Latin *imitāt-*, participial stem of *imitārī* meaning to copy.[40] The word is defined as to do or try to do after the manner of, to follow the example of, to copy in action. The Roman statesman Lucius Annaeus Seneca offered an example of the Classical position when he wrote, "All art is but imitation of nature."[41] We are also reminded of Pliny who asserted that trees were the first temples, and more specifically that they imitate columns.[42] This theme runs throughout history: Egyptian hypostyle halls have been interpreted as representations of forests of trees. The French writer and activist François-Marie d'Arouet, known as Voltaire, wrote that "originality is nothing but judicious imitation. The most original writers borrowed one from another."[43] Thus, currently, we may consider a broader understanding of imitation and its link to invention. As the American writer Mason Cooly states, "Art begins in imitation and ends in innovation."[44] Today, architecture's imitation of nature may not be so literal. For this reason, critically assessing imitation is important to the character of architects.

Historically, the ancient Greeks connected the notion of imitation to the arts. The word *mimesis*, from the ancient Greek, means *imitation* and is also related to the arts.[45] The French author John D. Lyons wrote that while mimesis, or imitation, has played a fundamental role in most theories of fine arts and literature since antiquity, it is usual to study two polar concepts of its meaning.[46] Mimesis enables the work of art or architecture to represent reality objectively and also calls attention to the presence of the artist in the work, something that may be labeled *style*. For the Greeks, mimesis was an idea that governed the creation of works of art, specifically with correspondence to the physical world, though it was understood as imperfect.[47] The words mimesis and counterfeit are synonymous. Mimesis is the name for art that represents (imitates) objects in the sensible world yet does not provide insight into the real and eternal world of forms since they are, as Plato wrote, merely imperfect copies.[48] In *Ion*, Plato believed that poetry is the art of inspiration or divine madness. Since poets are influenced by such divine madness and do not possess "art" or "knowledge" of the subject (532c), they cannot be truthful. Plato believed that truth is the territory of the philosopher.[49]

To clarify, in *The Republic*, Plato gave the example of three couches. He explained that one couch exists as an idea made by God viewed as an ideal. The next was crafted by the carpenter and was seen as an imitation of God's idea of the couch in physical form. The final couch was one created by the artist as an imitation of the carpenter's. In this way, the artist's couch replicated from observation was twice removed from the truth and would not attain the truth (of God's creation).[50] Recalling Plato's writings about mimesis, Aristotle defined mimesis as the perfection and imitation of nature. He believed art is not only imitation but also the use of mathematical ideas and symmetry in the search for the perfect and the timeless.[51] However, he did not agree with Plato's *Idea* (God's ideal) and *Appearance* (the painter's observation of objects). Instead, he saw the importance of the process in which the object takes shape, and thus becomes real.[52] This notion of production can be found in nature and in human activity such as in the crafting of things. Art and artistic objects are constructed from matter and are consequently formed into meaningful cultural artifacts.[53] This concept is particularly relevant for architects since the tools of the craftsman make objects— in the architect's case, buildings where people live.

Aristotle questions who moves the craftsman's hands and answers "it is his [the carpenter's] knowledge of his art, and his soul, in which is the form that moves his hands."[54] This relationship between the "tools and the hands" is based in knowledge, and these together influence the craftsman's creativity—the form producing the final object.[55] These notions have influenced the way architects think about their design processes, and they are intrinsic to their character.

Architects should be able to understand the reasons behind the work they are copying in order to know if they are making thoughtful choices. A good example of the use of imitation without understanding was found after World War II. Anthropologists discovered that a unique religion had developed among islanders of the South Pacific. Known as the *Cargo Cult*, this religion believed that if certain rituals were performed, shipments of riches would be sent from the heavens. This appeared logical to the islanders because they saw Europeans and Americans ordering shipments of wondrous things from unknown places. Cargo Cult members were motivated to create replicas of airfields and airplanes out of twigs and branches, and to make the sounds of airplanes to recreate the shipment of cargo. The islanders believed that by performing a magical ritual and imitating the image of the thing they desired, it would be delivered. A comparison can be made to *image magic* displayed in the prehistoric cave paintings of Lascaux that depict animal herds. Many scholars believe that early people thought the drawings retold stories of heroic events. Another interpretation suggests that the herds were replicated so that the images might act as a talisman to ensure successful future hunts. To avoid the potential falsehoods of imitation, contemporary architects should be conscious of what they are imitating. They should beware of trends that lack substance or ones where they do not understand the theoretical premise. In the 1990s, many architects were copying the *look* of Deconstructivist architecture, its sharp angles and fragmented forms, and did not necessarily consider the philosophical foundations of this movement. Imitation has always been part of the architect's palette and character, but needs to be applied thoughtfully.

Just as architects looked to the past for models, they have also looked to the human body as a subject for imitation. One of the primary ways people understand the world is through their bodies. Historically, concepts of space, time, and numbers were generated from the human body. For example, the square, the four cardinal directions, and the four seasons derive from the four directions of our bodies.[56] Since Greek antiquity, the human body has been regarded as a microcosm of universal harmony.

The body has long been used as an analogy for buildings. Babylonian and Egyptian architects employed units of measurement extracted from the length of arms, hands, and fingers. They passed these traditions on to the Greeks and

Figure 2.2
Man the macrocosm within the Universal Macrocosm.
Source: CC-PD-MarkPD-Art (PD-old-100).

Romans, who in turn created units of measure such as the cubit. Vitruvius in his treatise *On Architecture* wrote that the proportions initially adopted for temples and columns were based on the human body, an accepted model of strength and beauty. In his view, proportion is a correspondence between the measures of the members of an entire work and the whole, to a certain part selected as standard.[57] Renaissance architects such as Francesco di Giorgio Martini designed cathedrals whose floor plans represent the analogous proportions of the human body.[58] Most measurement systems around the world reference the human body: "Architecture is our primary instrument in relating us with space and time, and giving these dimensions a human measure."[59]

The understanding of architectural scale involves the constant awareness of buildings in relationship to our bodies. When looking at walls and ceilings, for example, people may be subconsciously measuring the space between their bodies and the limits of architectural space. Even today, people use the body as a way to explain the world through icons and symbols, such as measuring in feet. This image-making is closely tied to our perceptions of our bodies, as the human body presents one way to understand the unknown world around us. It is in the character of architects to project our image onto our buildings and thus to define the undefined. But architects should consider the amount of likeness, or imitation, in relationship to abstraction, that they use in designing the form of their buildings.

If analogies provide comparison, a metaphor involves the use of a name or descriptive term that is different from that usually employed. With this definition, it is possible to view how language terms can be transferred to physical objects. Metaphors can stem from sensory stimulation, so for humans to engage their imaginations they must have many experiences to draw upon.[60] Metaphors evoke ambiguous images or sensations that connect the pictorial with words, like poetic allusion.[61] Often word-play can spark interesting beginning points, such as literal or figurative expression—descriptions, tropes, or sensory terms.[62] These literary examples exhibit the importance of abstraction as a form of imitation in the design process. In many cases, architects reuse imitated forms by distorting them to give them new meaning.

Contemporary architects often employ the abstraction of metaphor to initiate conceptual ideas or convey subtle intention in a design process. The Spanish engineer/architect Santiago Calatrava is known to begin his design process by sketching references to human bodies, animal forms, or bird skeletons when designing his anthropomorphic structural systems. Often the bone-like forms appear as structural members on his bridges or building designs. The form on top of the completed *Milwaukee Art Museum* evokes a rib cage, or a bird preparing for flight. Slender white members link to a central spine that hovers over the museum. The finished building's exoskeleton-looking structure emerges from the roof and opens and closes several times during the day. The broad arms (a span of 217 feet) appear to fold and unfold in a manner reminiscent of the wide sweeping wings of a bird. The building's final form carries this strong analogy, but the shape of the structure most likely began, as many of Calatrava's projects do, with moment diagram sketches. Sketches in the design process can be an ambiguous medium conducive to exploring analogy or metaphor.

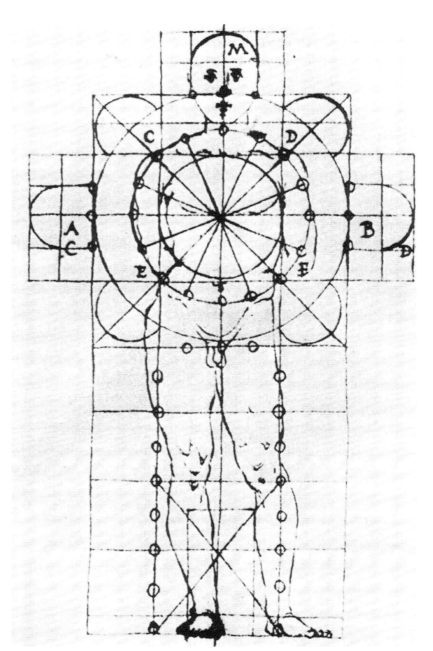

Figure 2.3
Proportions of human form reflected in typical cathedral form, Francesco di Giorgio Martini, c. 1480 (Florence, Italy).
Source: National Library in Florence, CC-PD-MarkPD-Art (PD-old-100).

Although imitation provides a fundamental beginning for architecture, architects should use it with caution, and not copy without understanding the ramifications of their actions. They should remember that imitation is a foundation that needs the transforming qualities of imagination.

Architect as Imaginer

All people, and particularly architects, constantly use imagination. Greek mythology conveyed how the Muses influenced the writings of poets, the drawings, paintings, and sculpture made by artists, and the compositions and performances of musicians. Architects, involved as they are in creative endeavors, are highly visual and typically design with, and ultimately represent through, images. Author Julia Forster links inspiration from the Muses to the transformation achieved by artists as they use their creative imaginations. She writes, "When the inspiration of the muses was invoked by Greek artists, poets or philosophers they would, in effect, be calling upon both the world's memory and their capacity to use their imagination to inform their work or composition."[63] Imagination is the faculty of the mind that assists architects to initiate, reuse, and transform mental impressions. It is, therefore, a character trait of architects to be imaginers.

The mental impressions of imagination are difficult to define. Humans all experience imagination, but our ability to describe what we experience is elusive. An explanation of imagination involves the study of perception, as the mental impressions of perception are often worked on by imagination.[64] The term imagination is primarily used in three ways: to envisage objects that are absent from view, to change or interpret that which can be observed, or to recognize and reuse items which are known.[65] In a comprehensive study of imagination, the philosopher Edward S. Casey wrote, "Imagining is remarkably easy to enter into. . .we can also imagine *whatever* and *however* we wish to. . .it is more difficult to fail than to succeed in imagining."[66] He defined the qualities of imagination by describing three pairs of words. The first pair he called spontaneity and controlledness.[67] By using these opposing terms, he pointed out that humans can control their imaginings by simply deciding to. Casey explained that the capability of being able to conjure up a mental impression is contrasted, or completed, by the chance of something spontaneous entering the mind: "[Spontaneity is] where imaginative acts and presentations appear in an irrepressible and sudden upsurge."[68] The second faculty he named involved self-containedness and self-evidence.[69] Here the imaginer's desire determines the range of possible imaginings, and the product of this will have features that the imaginative activity imposes on it.[70] The imagination is self-evident in that all information appears at once, and issues of inconsistency are unimportant. That is, when one is inspired by imagination, mental impressions often do not appear as fully rendered or completed scenes. Finally, Casey introduced indeterminacy and pure possibility: "Imagined objects are indeterminate as a whole. Their vagueness however, does not necessarily pertain equally to all of their parts."[71] It is difficult to determine exactly where imagined objects begin or end as imagination does not follow rules of perspective, for example.[72] In pure possibility, "the 'purity' of imaginative possibilities lies precisely in their independence of the mutually exclusive alternatives of reality and unreality."[73] This aspect of imagination makes anything hypothetical and all things possible. Identifying these aspects of imagination may help architects understand how they are touched by the Muses and how their creativity works.

Philosophers and physiologists view imagination as a complex faculty of the mind since memory, perception, and a creative capability are required to facilitate it. For example, the philosopher David Hume felt that the role of imagination was to mediate between impressions and aspects of memory or judgment.[74] He described imagination as having the liberty "to transpose and change its ideas."[75] The late eighteenth-century philosopher Immanuel Kant's "reproductive imagination" was "entirely subject to empirical laws, the laws, namely of 'association.'"[76] In this instance, Kant was describing how imagination can emerge from analogies or comparisons. Like Hume, Kant found an interdependence between intellect and perception, since the imagination acts to synthesize what is observed with new thoughts.[77] According to this line of thinking, any new mental impression cannot be radically new, because the imagination is a synthesis of memory and perception, and all that can be originated is dependent on them.[78] Since imagination is dependent upon memory and perception, architects in the present can both remember the past and anticipate the future at the same time. How architects perceive their surrounding environments can be translated into the images used in the design process since the dialogue of perception, reaction, and then action can form and re-form. The physical images of drawings, models, or digital renderings provide the tangible media with which to evaluate and manipulate ideas that may first present themselves as vague impressions, impressions that in turn translate into architectural environments. Architects often manipulate images to form what they know in an attempt to, through association, discover completely new constructs.

If architects' imaginations help them reconfigure images through use of association, then they should understand how conventional or non-conventional media affects their decision making. For example, design presentations may use conventional means of architectural representation such as plans, sections, or elevations. They may also employ unusual methods to convey emotion to create the experience (or atmosphere) of an intended space. These images, similar to a poem, may not necessarily be clear in their intent, since in some cases abstraction is an appropriate means of communication. Architects should question conventional representational media, asking if typical drawings sufficiently demonstrate what they envision, and if they evoke appropriate impressions.

Architects should understand the difference between imitation and imagination. One is a means of replication, and the other can be an abstraction requiring interpretation. The etymology of the word *abstraction* comes from the Latin *ab(s)* and *trahere* and means "to draw away from." One definition of abstraction is something distanced from reference to any particular object or event that represents symbolically or conceptually.[79] Buildings are inherently abstract since they cannot be *read* for specific meaning or intention.

The Architect's Dream, a nineteenth-century painting by Thomas Cole, demonstrates several characteristic aspects of architects' imagination. The painting depicts an architect reclining in contemplation (possibly being visited by the Muses) on a pedestal made of a classical column. The architect is surrounded by the tools of his trade, drawings, and books. Placing him on a pedestal gives him an elevated (or exalted) position, overlooking or overseeing various constructions from history. This position may echo the status he aspires to and allows him to imagine what he desires. In the background can be seen numerous monumental buildings from history (Greek, Roman, Egyptian, and English). Thus the architect is imagining and recalling (using memory to create mental impressions) simultaneously. Possibly he is reflecting on his visits to these buildings, using the power of his imagination to visualize things absent from view. Through his knowledge and memory, the buildings are rendered to replicate known building types. However, these structures also appear to be vague abstractions or generalizations, not of specific buildings but various styles in new combinations. Although from different parts of the world, the buildings have been placed in proximity to each other, and this juxtaposition suggests indeterminacy or pure possibility. This assemblage represents the limitlessness of the imagination: the mind allows anything to be imagined. Naming the painting *The Architect's Dream* suggests that the architect is projecting into the future, dreaming that he will be able to achieve greatness on the level demonstrated in these historic monuments.

This painting also demonstrates the ability to make use of imitation, memory, and fantasy as gifted by the Muses. Memories, worked on by the imagination, along with a vision of the future, display some of the uses of the characteristic imaging abilities of architects' imagination.

Architect as Mindful Mneme

Imagination, as it has been discussed, involves the image-making faculties of the mind. Memory is also connected to mental impressions, but of things previously seen and experienced. Most sources indicate that the Muses were born at the

Figure 2.4
The Architect's Dream, Thomas Cole, 1840 (Toledo, Ohio).
Source: The Toledo Museum of Art, CC-PD-MarkPD-old-100-1923PD-Art (PD-old-100-1923).

Figure 2.5 *Mnemosyne and Memory*, Library of Congress, Olin Warner and Herbert Adams, 1896 (Washington, D.C.). Source: PD US.

foot of Mount Olympus as the daughters of Zeus and Mnemosyne.[80] They are "tied to memory through their mother Mnemosyne, whose name shares a root with the word memory, and also through the Muse, Clio, whose special skills included knowledge of history."[81] Mnemosyne and memory are connected to the etymological root for *mnemonic*, which refers to an aid that helps to stimulate human memory.[82] According to Pausanias, the Muse Mneme was described as representing memory.

Memory is an accumulation of all our experiences: it encompasses who we are, our whole being, and can be elusive in that humans cannot retain every memory. Our minds do, however, tend to reinforce memories that are constantly being retrieved. Recognizing this may prompt architects to engage Clio to represent their history while acknowledging that the mother of all the Muses (creative arts) is Mnemosyne (memory). Architects' relationship with memory is demonstrated by their repertoire of visual communication techniques. Mental impressions from memory influence their designs, specifically the images in their minds' eye and those they bring to life.[83] Beyond their own memories, architects should recognize that the images they present are interpreted by audiences or viewers, based on their own experiences, associations, and emotional memories. Thus, it is in the architect's character to be a *mindful mneme*.

Pliny the Elder wrote an allegory to explain the beginning of drawing that illustrates a relationship between architects and memory. The story described a young woman, Diboutades, who etched (in charcoal) the profile of her departing lover on a rock.[84] This story was meant to express the primacy of sight in comparison to all of the human senses. But it also demonstrates pictorial imagery as something that retains a memory. Diboutades could have kept a vial of her lover's blood or a shirt permeated with his scent, things that would provide his true essence.[85] Instead, she recorded his image. This story describes a historical understanding of art (and especially imitation) and also suggests ways in which architects utilize images.

In general, all people, including architects, utilize memory since it is important to all of our activities. With memory, humans can retain knowledge and understand our past experiences; in the form of reminiscing, memory usually emerges without much effort. Memory was once viewed as a perceptual imprint on the mind. This mnemonic imprint was compared to a stamp or carving on a wax tablet.[86] Since both memory and imagination have image-making abilities, the connection between memory and intellect was common. Aristotle believed that "the thinking faculty thinks of its forms in mental pictures," and Plato noted that when humans are not perceiving, dependent entirely on knowing, they use the faculty of memory.[87] He believed that knowing is not only recollection but that the soul was elsewhere before it became part of the human body.[88] Thinking contains mental impressions from memory and, conversely, memory in learning affects intellectual activity.[89] In other words, memories are the conduit of knowledge, and these memories are the foundation all knowledge is based upon.[90] This may relate to a more contemporary belief concerning *body memory* that holds that "every fiber of our bodies, every cell of our brains, holds memories."[91]

Figure 2.6
Dibutades depicted in *The Origin of Painting*, Jean-Baptiste Regnault, 1785 (Paris, France). Source: Musée national du Château de Versailles, CC-PD-MarkPD-Art (PD-old-100).

There may be a difference between memory and reminiscence (or recollection).[92] Anamnesis, recollection or often reminiscence, is similar to the definition of memory as an imprint. However, a person with complete recall may not necessarily have skills in abstract thought. Recall itself is not the whole of memory since recollection is the recovery of facts.[93] Conversely, the concept of "recollective knowing" can be the highest level of knowledge since it is knowledge regained "from within," from already acquired cognitions.[94] Frances Yates wrote in *The Art of Memory* that memory does not necessarily involve just relearning or bringing the past to mind, but constitutes a return to knowledge, "Or more exactly, memory itself becomes a function of knowledge: 'Mnemosyne, supernatural power, has been interiorized so as to become in [humans] the very faculty of knowing'."[95] This discussion may represent the difference between active and passive memory.[96] One is basically storing incoming impressions; the other, active memory, "involves the creative transformation of experience rather than its internalized reduplication in images or traces construed as copies."[97] For architects, an active memory may be evident in the *working through* of mental impressions to transform them into useful designs through drawings and models. Employing active memory might be the *mindful* (*memor*) use of memory that is heightened in the character of architects.[98]

Important to architecture is the long-held belief that location is associated with memory, and that emotion accompanies locational memories.[99] Yates observed that because location is spatial, the movement of our bodies through spaces creates new stimuli to our memories as our position changes. As we reside in spaces, they become firmly imprinted in our memories. This idea has important ramifications for architects since they are influenced by the spaces they visit, and in turn use spatial memories to design new emotional spaces.

Imaging

Just as spatial recall is tied to places, memory is often spurred by metaphors and associations. Metaphors may represent "a thing less accurately than the description of the actual thing itself"; however, metaphors (*metaphoria*) "move the soul more and therefore better help the memory."[100] The mode of resemblance may be of issue here. Returning to Diboutades, the image of her lover was emotional because the visual image initiated associations. Resemblance in memory is an "indication," a sign that spurs an action by signaling an actual or possible

Figure 2.7 **Washington Monument, Robert Mills, Washington Monument, 1884 (Washington, D.C.). Source: Room237, CC-BY-SA-3.0.**

43

presence.[101] "[A] thing is only properly an indication if and where it in fact serves to indicate something to *some thinking being*."[102] Here it is possible to return to the historical belief that a *place* has an identity because it calls up associative memory. Spatial memory, then, is a distinctive constituent of the character of architects.

Buildings may act as memory devices. Most obviously, monuments and memorials are constructions meant to provide recollection and mindful memory. These architectural memory devices can be powerful in their ability to connect the consciousness of cultures. Almost every town contains a monument dedicated to fallen soldiers, and every tombstone or Japanese family shrine carries memories of ancestors. Museums—again, a word tied to the Muses—are places to find inspiration, but they can also be receptacles for memory. Not only do they hold objects from history, but their very forms transmit recollective memories. The *Jewish Museum Berlin* designed by Daniel Libeskind offers an example of a building that demonstrates a powerful sense of memory. Not only do victims' shoes become objects that induce memory, but the form of the building itself presents the horrors of the Holocaust. A line of void spaces (66 feet tall) slices through the length of the building to represent the erasure of Jewish life in Berlin. Even more emotionally evocative are the long, thin, shard-shaped windows that reference violence. Canted walls, while they may not make direct reference to any event, create an overall feeling of disorder and impending collapse. This museum is a moving example of a memory device.

Observers of architects' visual presentations also participate in active recollection. The fantasy paintings completed by the Italian architect Massimo Scolari reference emotional memory on a different level than a museum. Rather than referencing realism, Scolari renders associative images that speak of dream

Figure 2.8
Interior of Jewish Museum Berlin, Daniel Libeskind, 2001 (Berlin, Germany).
Source: CC-By-SA 3.0.

places. These rendered constructions question architectural space as they provide gates in the water or brown geometrical landscapes. The images play with perspective and perception, sometimes drawing the viewer into the frame and at other times providing a bird's-eye view. Often defying gravity, his images allude to places that have yet to be experienced, but that convey mindful remembrance.

Buildings' forms and spaces provoke remembrance as memory devices. The Muses, tasked with giving people artistic inspiration, also represent world memory, which is knowledge. In like manner, architects' images, whether built or intended for design or presentation, can evoke memories in clients or in architects themselves. Drawings and models can also portray a vision of the future that architects will reference as they design.

Architect as Prophesier

As builders of the future, architects should have as part of their character the ability to foresee what the constructed environment will look like. Again, the Chorus of the Muses was led by Apollo, the Greek god of the arts and prophecy, who was said to have educated the Muses in these areas. Mythology also reveals that the Muses were visionary, and were linked to the prophetic god of Delphi. It was reported that the Muses taught prophecy to others, and taught fortune telling to Aristaeus.

The word *prophecy* comes from the Greek verb *prophemi*, which means "to say beforehand, foretell."[103] Prophecy involves a process in which one or more messages allegedly communicated to a prophet are then communicated to other people.[104] Such messages typically involve inspiration, interpretation, or revelation of future events which can be compared to divine knowledge. Comparably, the character of architects must comprise the capacity to find inspiration, interpret the *signs* observed on a site, translate the needs of a client, or decipher the civic environment, to develop and define their intentions for the future. To achieve their visions, they must possess the character trait of a prophesier.

It is the primary job of architects to prophesize by creating the future. To have a premonition of the future, architects define, develop, and then build environments that others have not imagined. This ability to see what is to come is dependent upon intent, defined as the direction of an action toward a goal.[105] Intention can be viewed as a mental state that represents a commitment to carry out an action in the future. It involves mental activity such as planning and forethought.[106] Psychologists such as Bertram Malle note that intention helps explain our attempts to achieve goals that are directed by beliefs. He states, "Thus, an intentional action is a function to accomplish a desired goal and is based on the belief that the course of action will satisfy a desire."[107] In a similar vein, the aesthetic philosopher Richard Wollheim wrote how intention assists in the comprehension of what information the final work of art conveys. "Now, the notion of intention has most obviously an important part to play in any complete analysis of representation."[108] He continued, further explaining how something is perceived by others: "The intention, we might say, looks forward to the representational seeing."[109] After recognizing how intention can give meaning to the final work, Wollheim makes a very interesting proposition that pertains to abstraction, and states that "the correspondence between intention and action need not be exact."[110]

When architects design, they are expressing their own desires regarding what the future will look like. Intention and desire are not always perfectly aligned with the final product. A misalignment can arise because ideas cannot be literally manifested in a building, and also because the design process itself requires substantial iteration. Architects through the use of drawings and models design what might be a finished building, and consequently help clients visualize the future. Demonstrating this idea is the Renaissance painting *Michelangelo Presenting the Model of the Completion of St. Peters to Pope Pius IV*, by Domenico Cresti da Passignano, in the *Casa Buonarroti*, in Florence, Italy.[111] Michelangelo is seen expressively gesturing at the model, a form of presentation media easy for clients to comprehend. The rich interior setting and the seated position of the Pope reveal the power of the Catholic Church. The architect, Michelangelo, stands in a position that suggests he is persuading both verbally and visually. The model represents an early vision of what the building is intended to look like. Most likely, all involved realize that its design will progress through many iterations.

Before presenting a proposal, architects analyze their desires and intentions through design. Part of this process helps locate initial ideas. Sometimes they can find a conceptual beginning through rational means (such as logical reasoning) while other times a concept may be surmised through less rational thought. Architects can exercise their imaginations by intuitively or unintentionally helping their brains to construct images; they can learn to stimulate the parts of their brain that deal with visual imagery. They often use metaphors to search for the unusual connections between dissimilar notions. Because our minds are constantly trying to make sense of what we perceive, things that are clear, combined with things that are ambiguous, often expand the imagination.[112] Architects can make empathetic imagination metaphoric. Placing themselves in the mind of others, in different scenarios, or in the place of inanimate objects, helps them to discover conceptual beginnings. It is well known that ideas often appear when you first awake, or in the bath. This happens because your mind is at rest and not distracted, so that concepts can solidify and you can make sense of an idea. This may explain how association works in the imagination, and how subconscious intention surfaces in our conscious minds. This intentional thinking plays a major role in architects' design process.

When considering the attributes of a potential construction site during the design process, architects should assume the role of soothsayer. A good example of the skills of the architect as prophesier was recorded by Vitruvius:

I cannot too strongly insist upon the need of a return to the method of old times. Our ancestors, when about to build a town or an army post, sacrificed some of the cattle that were wont to feed on the site proposed and examined their livers. If the livers of the first victims were dark-coloured or abnormal, they sacrificed others, to see whether the fault was due to disease or their food. They never began to build defensive works in a place until after they had made many such trials and satisfied themselves that good water and food had made the liver sound and firm. If they continued to find it abnormal, they argued from this that the food and water supply found in such a place would be just as unhealthy for man, and so they moved away and changed to another neighbourhood, healthfulness being their chief object.[113]

Here Vitruvius was suggesting that architects should be able to read the signs that the site presents. He understood what the health of the natural environment meant for the future inhabitants. This reading of the signs is not unlike the soil testing and wind or sun analysis that architects currently complete before beginning to build. Vitruvius understood that a critical characteristic of architects must be the ability to comprehend what they intend to design and to interpret the information needed to create the work. For example, architects might program a future building by identifying intention. They would ask themselves how to interpret information gathered from the site, the interests of the patrons, and the general idea of what this building should be. Recognizing intent and interpreting its ramifications is part of the process of decision making.

Once architects read and interpret the messages of the signs, they can then define their intentions and can like a prophet communicate their concepts to others. Again, architects typically communicate these messages by way of a demonstration using media. Demonstrations gauge the general appearance or composition of the thing planned: "The word *demonstrate* comes from the Latin *monstrum*, and means to divine, portend or warn. A demonstration offers a foreshadowing of coming events and allows a certain prophetic indication of meaning through marvel, prodigy, and wonder."[114]

The idea of demonstration can be closely related to that of the divine. The primary meaning of the word *divine* is directly related to the concept of God or perfection.[115] This definition has had an important effect upon the concept of the image as a form of demonstration; however, it is the secondary definition of *divine* that is identified most directly with the idea of the demonstration. To divine can also mean to foretell, through inspiration, intuition, or reflection, the shape of future events.[116] Many believe that a divining rod has a magical quality which can foretell the future location of a well. Others may simply credit the individual using the divining rod with the power to observe and interpret the signs of where water might be located. In a similar way, the demonstration allows architects to prophesize the future by interpreting signs and omens. The demonstration then can warn the architect of future problems and can admit marvel, wonder, astonishment, and surprise into the design process.

To come full circle, the divine represents the goddesses, the Muses who held the power of prophesy. The gift of the Muses to architects is the ability to visualize the future, convince others of this future, and then design and build it. Architects' character puts them in a position to be some of the only people able to foretell future environments.

Conclusion

The use of images has always been essential to the character of architects while the role of the Muses to affect inspiration relates to production of these images.

Figure 2.9
Man using divining rod.
Source: CC-PD-MarkPD Old.

The Greek myth of the Muses presents relevant and primal exemplars for each of the associated faculties of imaging, faculties that can constitute a foundation for the architect's relationship with imaging today. The notions of skill and God-given talent can be tied to the abilities of the Muses to encourage and support creative work through random visits. This idea of divine talent is demonstrated today in architects' propensity, "gift," or special talent for displaying their skills in the manipulation of images. The Muses demonstrated the limitations and consequences of imitation through their punishment of the King of Macedon's daughters. Limitations are indeed important, as architects must continuously question the ramifications of intent in their work, and remain mindful that imagery that is misrepresented can be misleading.

The architect as imaginer speaks to the mental impressions that aid in image production, just as the Muses inspired creative imagination in humans. Architects throughout history have been able to expand their imaginations through transforming imagery, a characteristic that has remained constant. Understanding architects' relationships with memory accentuated the importance of the parentage of the Muses. Their mother, Mnemosyne, as the goddess of memory, and Zeus, the father of the gods (assigning all others their roles), provided a "recollection of the world's memories." Architects, as prophesiers, should consider the Muses' relationship with the god Apollo to understand how they can engage the visionary aspects of images. This, perhaps more than the other faculties of the Muses, demonstrates the crucial aspect of architects' character that relates to prediction, representation, and the shaping of the future.

This book, *Building the Architect's Character; Exploration in Traits*, questions whether the character of architects has changed since the ancient Greek period. Certainly, architects of the past used drawings and models to guide construction just as architects do today, although the specific media and technologies might be different. It could be argued that architects still need to draw upon their faculties of memory and imagination to conceive of new forms, even though the parameters of inventive form have been more or less restrictive at various times in history.[117]

Architects of all periods have needed to employ representative media because it is too expensive to build full scale when testing ideas. Visualizing problems is more efficient when using drawings and models. Although architects' use of memory and imagination may not have changed substantially, architectural practice currently requires more drawings. This may be because the contemporary design process has removed many architects from their daily presence on the construction site. It may also reflect a litigious environment in the building industry.

The myth of the Muses becomes important because it analogously offers architects inspiration from the gods. This chapter explored divine inspiration and showed that it has a role in how architects discover new ideas by intuition. The contemporary connotation of divining can be understood in the context of a person who simply has a propensity for foreseeing the future outcome of their actions. Imagery in the form of drawings and models advances architects' vision of the future in the form of building proposals. Here, architects, the creators of these images, are perceived as possessing divine skill. Through their imagery, experimentation, and exploration, architects attempt to achieve divinity. They are always conscious of the past, which helps them to gain a better understanding of the future. As the twentieth-century architect Ludwig Mies van de Rohe wrote, "As an architect you design for the present with an awareness of the past for a future which is essentially unknown." While this future is "unknown" it is architects who perhaps have the best understanding of what its landscape will be, at least through the built form.

The role of architects as influential figures in the creation of the future makes the role of images in the design process increasingly important. Throughout this chapter, the limitations of imaging were introduced, as architects must understand that the images they create hold great power in representing their future proposals. Traditional methods of making images such as drawings and models are still used, although they have their limitations. Other more contemporary methods of imaging have had an important role in furthering the divining nature of images. For instance, 3-D modeling software offers the ability to produce digital manifestations of architects' ideas. Many *Building Information Modeling* (BIM) based workflows can reshape the way architects approach imaging. BIM allows for direct reactions to changing situations. Different systems can be displayed to add a new level of depth to what is represented digitally. In addition to this, the ability to quickly change and edit what is being displayed allows for partners on the team to quickly alternate between phases of the design process. A design decision that deviates from an idea conceived during the schematic phase of development can be changed. Upon completion of a digital model, architects can produce walk-through videos that allow the observer to understand the experience of the modeled space. This allows users to understand, at a very rudimentary level, how people engage with space. It is important to note, however, that this medium, along with other forms of images, has the potential to falsely display what is being conceived.

Just as a chiasm replicates a mirror image, Chapter 4 will explore those character traits of architects that pertain to persuading. Building on the theoretical foundation of Chapter 2, "Imaging," it will consider practical approaches, will discuss how architects use persuasion, and will consider such potential pitfalls as seduction and propaganda. The chapters "Defining" and "Imaging" alluded to the role character traits play in the architect's design process. Chapter 3 will build on this foundation and will focus on those traits that assist architects as they transform, transition, and translate their conceptual thinking into architecture.

Notes

1 *Oxford English Dictionary*, s.v. "talent."
2 Amy T. Peterson and David J. Dunworth, *Mythology in Our Midst: A Guide to Cultural References* (Westport, CT: Greenwood Press, 2004), 121.
3 Julia Forster, *Muses: Revealing the Nature of Inspiration* (Harpenden, UK: Kamera Books, 2007), 14.
4 Robin Hard and H.J. Rose, *The Routledge Handbook of Greek Mythology: Based on H.J. Rose's "Handbook of Greek Mythology"* (London: Routledge, 2004), 205.
5 See Pausanias, *Pausanias Description of Greece*, trans. W.H.S. Jones and H.A. Ormerod (Cambridge, MA: Harvard University Press, 1918).
6 Hesiod in the *Theogony* was the first to indicate the names of the nine goddesses.
7 Hard and Rose, *The Routledge Handbook of Greek Mythology*, 206–207.
8 Hesiod, Homer, and others cite the Muses as the very reason they were able to write poetry.
9 Peterson and Dunworth, *Mythology in Our Midst*, 121–123.
10 Diodorus Siculus, *The Library of History, Volume II*, trans. C.H. Oldfather (Cambridge, MA: Harvard University Press, 1933), 352.
11 Ibid.
12 Ibid.
13 *Dictionary of Greek and Roman Biography and Mythology*, s.v. "Musae."
14 Francesco Dal Co and Guiseppe Mazzariol, *Carlo Scarpa: The Complete Works* (New York: Electa/Rizzoli, 1984), 242.
15 *Oxford English Dictionary*, s.v. "inspiration."
16 David Summers, *Michelangelo and the Language of Art* (Princeton, NJ: Princeton University Press, 1981), 104.
17 Ibid., 104–105.
18 Ibid., 107.
19 Ibid., 108.
20 Murray Wright Bundy, *The Theory of Imagination in Classical and Medieval Thought* (Urbana, IL: University of Illinois Press, 1927), 89.
21 Summers, *Michelangelo and the Language of Art*, 111.
22 Ibid., 129.
23 Ibid., 116.
24 Giorgio Vasari, *Lives of the Artists*, ed. Betty Burroughs (New York: Simon and Schuster, 1946), and Ernst Kris and Otto Kurz, *Legend, Myth and Magic in the Image of the Artist* (New Haven, CT; Yale University Press, 1979) discuss artists with mythical qualities.
25 Most notable is Rudolf and Margot Wittkower, *Born Under Saturn; The Character and Conduct of Artists* (New York and London: W.W. Norton & Company, 1963).
26 Ibid., 98.
27 Ibid.
28 Ibid.
29 Summers, *Michelangelo and the Language of Art*, 119.

30 Ibid.
31 Ibid., 122.
32 Ibid., 103.
33 D.J. Gordon, *The Renaissance Imagination* (Berkeley: University of California Press, 1975), 93.
34 Ibid., 82.
35 Ibid., 81.
36 Ibid., 94.
37 Kris and Kurz, *Legend Myth and Magic in the Image of the Artist*, 58.
38 Vasari, *Lives of the Artists*, 100–101.
39 Ovid, *Metamorphoses*, trans. A.D. Melville; introduction and notes by E.J. Kenney (Oxford, UK: Oxford University Press, 2008), 5.677–678.
40 *Oxford English Dictionary*, s.v. "imitation."
41 Brian Keeble, *Every Man an Artist: Readings in the Traditional Philosophy of Art* (Bloomington, IN: World Wisdom, 2005), 46.
42 W.R. Lethaby, *Architecture, Mysticism and Myth* (Mineola, NY: Dover Publications, 2004), 35–36.
43 Louis Mayeul Chaudon, *Historical and Critical Memoirs of the Life and Writings of M. De Voltaire: Interspersed with Numerous Anecdotes, Poetical Pieces, Epigrams and Bon Mots, Little Known, and Never before Published in English, Relative to the Literati of France* (London: Printed for G.G.J. and J. Robinson, 1786), 290.
44 Ann Handley, *Everybody Writes: Your Go-To Guide to Creating Ridiculously Good Content* (Hoboken, NJ: John Wiley & Sons, 2014), 56.
45 Moshe Barasch, *Theories of Art; From Plato to Winckelmann* (New York and London: New York University Press, 1985), 4–9.
46 John D. Lyons and Stephen G. Nichols, *Mimesis, from Mirror to Method, Augustine to Descartes* (Hanover, NH: Published for Dartmouth College by the University Press of New England, 1982), 2.
47 Peter A. Angeles, *Dictionary of Philosophy* (New York: Barnes & Nobles Books, 1981), 172.
48 Ibid., 172, and Moshe Barasch, *Theories of Art; From Plato to Winckelmann* (New York: New York University Press, 1985), 5, citing Cratylus 432b, d.
49 Plato makes this argument in *Ion*.
50 Barasch, *Theories of Art*, 5.
51 Ibid., 12–13.
52 Ibid., 10.
53 Ibid.
54 Ibid.
55 Ibid., 11.
56 Richard Padovan, *Proportion: Science, Philosophy, Architecture* (London: E & FN Spon, 1999), 5.
57 Vitruvius, *On Architecture*, trans. Frank Granger (Cambridge, MA: Harvard University Press, 2002), 159–167.
58 See Francesco di Giorgio Martini, *Trattati di architettura ingegneria e arte militare (volume 1–2)* (Milano: Il Polifilo, 1967).
59 Juhani Pallasmaa, *Eyes of the Skin: Architecture and the Senses* (Hoboken, NJ: John Wiley and Sons, 2005), 17.
60 Arnold H. Modell, *Imagination and the Meaningful Brain* (Cambridge, MA: A Bradford Book, 2006), 32.
61 W.J.T. Mitchell, *Iconology: Image, Text, Ideology* (Chicago, IL: University of Chicago Press, 1986), 23.

62 Ibid., 24.

63 Forster, *Muses*, 21–23.

64 Edward S. Casey, *Imagining: A Phenomenological Study* (Bloomington, IN: Indiana University Press, 1979), 40. Casey writes that perception is "worked" on by imagination. The basic absorption of stimulation is altered by the mind's use of imagination.

65 Mary Warnock, *Imagination* (Berkeley and Los Angeles, CA: University of California Press, 1970), 193.

66 Casey, *Imagining*, 5.

67 Ibid., 63–86.

68 Ibid., 66.

69 Ibid., 87–102.

70 Ibid., 89

71 Ibid., 106.

72 Ibid., 105.

73 Ibid., 113.

74 Ibid., 17.

75 David Hume, *A Treatise of Human Nature*, ed. L.A. Selby-Bigge (Oxford, UK: Clarendon Press, 1978), 10.

76 Ibid., 11.

77 Warnock, *Imagination*, 16.

78 Casey, *Imagining*, 8.

79 Angeles, *Dictionary of Philosophy*, 2.

80 Hard and Rose, *The Routledge Handbook of Greek Mythology*, 204.

81 Ibid.

82 Peterson and Dunworth, *Mythology in Our Midst*, 121.

83 There are three types of memory: encoding, the registering or processing of information; storage, the recording of information (short or long term); and retrieved, the recall or recollection.

84 Robin Evans, "Translations From Drawing to Building," *AA Files* 12 (Summer, 1986): 6.

85 Frances Yates, *The Art of Memory* (Chicago, IL: University of Chicago Press, 1966), 4.

86 Ibid., 36.

87 Aristotle, *On the Soul, Parva Naturalia*, trans. W.S. Hett *De Anima* (431b2) and *De Memoria* (449b2) (London: Harvard University Press, 1935 or 1957).

88 Plato, *The Republic,* trans. B. Jowett (Roslyn, NY: Walter J. Black, 1941), 128.

89 Aristotle, *De Memoria* (449b2).

90 Yates, *The Art of Memory*, 36.

91 See Edward S. Casey, *Remembering: A Phenomenological Study* (Bloomington and Indianapolis, IN: Indiana University Press, 1987).

92 Yates, *The Art of Memory*, 33; and Casey, *Remembering*, 14.

93 Yates, *The Art of Memory*, 33.

94 Casey, *Remembering*, 14.

95 Ibid.

96 Ibid., 15.

97 Ibid.

98 Ibid., 18.

99 Yates, *The Art of Memory*, 7–12.

100 Ibid., 65.

101 Casey, *Remembering*, 95.

102 Ibid., 96; original emphasis.

103 *Oxford English Dictionary*, s.v. "prophecy."

104 Ibid.

105 *Oxford English Dictionary*, s.v. "intent."

106 Intention should not be confused with the area of philosophy known as "intentionality."

107 Bertram F. Malle and Joshua Knobe, "The Folk Concept of Intentionality," *Journal of Experimental Social Psychology* 33(2) (1996): 101–112.

108 Richard Wollheim, *Art and its Objects* (New York: Harper & Row, 1968), 16.

109 Ibid., 18.

110 Ibid., 17.

111 *Michelangelo Presenting the Model of the Completion of St. Peters to Pope Pius IV*, www.gettyimages.ca/detail/news-photo/michelangelo-presenting-the-model-for-the-completion-of-st-news-photo/148274010?#michelangelo-presenting-the-model-for-the-completion-of-st-peters-to-picture-id148274010, accessed October 17, 2017.

112 Josef Bleicher, *Contemporary Hermeneutics: Hermeneutics as Method, Philosophy and Critique* (New York: Routledge and Kegan Paul, 1980), 11.

113 Vitruvius, *The Ten Books on Architecture*, trans. Morris Hickey Morgan (New York: Dover Publications, 1960), 1.4.9.

114 Albert C. Smith, *Architectural Model as Machine* (Oxford, UK: Architectural Press, 2004), 2.

115 *Oxford English Dictionary*, s.v. "divine," the etymology of the word "divine" comes not only from the Latin *divinus,* meaning pertaining to a deity, but also from the Latin *divinare,* which means to foretell or predict.

116 Ibid.

117 See Spiro Kostof on the role of architects at various periods in history. *The Architect: Chapters in the History of the Profession* (Oakland, CA: University of California Press, 2001).

Chapter 3

Transforming, Transitioning, Translating

Few would disagree that it is in the character of architects to believe that the inhabitants of their buildings should live in a certain way. Every time architects design a wall, roof, entrance, or façade, they are making decisions, and in fact influencing how the inhabitants of a building should use the space. This chapter concerns the characteristics architects require to interpret the changes encountered in the design process, as a building project progresses from conceptual beginnings to construction. The chapter will invoke the Greek myth of Hermes as an allegory. Referencing key character traits of Hermes that can be compared to those required by architects during their design processes, it will explore past traditions to provide examples of issues architects may encounter in contemporary practice. It will conclude by addressing whether these issues are still relevant today.

When employing the design process to create environments, architects attempt to define the undefined. To do this, they use interpretation and critical thinking. Every architect must interpret such things as nature's influence on the building site, the needs of future inhabitants, and what the building represents. Initially, they may not know what the buildings they are designing will look like; but, through design, they can mark out and demonstrate what the final building will be. Architectural theorists have compared the design process to a theory of hermeneutics.[1] Hermeneutics, as described in the Introduction, is primarily a theory of interpretation. Referring to the etymology of hermeneutics, the philosopher Martin Heidegger wrote that the Greek words for interpreting and interpretation—*hermeneuein, hermeneia*—can be traced to the god Hermes.[2] He argued that interpretation connects the past and present in an intersection above and below consciousness. This intertextuality involves listening and then internalizing, in a way that builds upon the writings of earlier thinkers.[3] The intertextual relationship can be compared to interpretation and to the design process. The Greek god Hermes demonstrates qualities of interpretation that can be useful to provide structure for this chapter. An exploration of interpretation in design will set the stage for the discussion in the following chapters of those aspects of architects' decision making that are necessary to persuade and to fabricate.

Because of his role as patron of messengers, inventors, and orators, the Greek god Hermes had many qualities that can assist in a discussion of representational thinking. Although the Greek goddess Hestia has traditionally been identified as the god of architecture, the ancient interpretations limit her to being the god of domestic buildings and of the hearth. The characteristics of Hermes are more

Figure 3.1
**Hermes. Source:
Marie-Lan
Nguyen,
CC-BY-2.5.**

appropriate for comparison to contemporary architects, and we have therefore chosen him to explore the transforming, transitioning, and translating design aspects of architecture. Thomas Bulfinch describes Hermes' main characteristics:

> Mercury [Hermes] was the son of Jupiter [Zeus] and Maia [one of the Pleaides]. He presided over commerce, wrestling, and other gymnastic exercises, even over thieving, and everything, in short, which required skill and dexterity. He was the messenger of Jupiter and wore a winged cap and winged shoes. He bore in his hand a rod entwined with two serpents, called the caduceus.[4]

Traditionally, many of Hermes' qualities can be seen as similar to those of architects, and as conducive to their design processes. To construct buildings with intention, architects should be able to translate ideas into form, be learned, be able to imbue their buildings with meaning, be able to understand historic references, be able to utilize construction methods, and be creative regarding a vision of the future. To avoid the pitfalls of theory without practice, as described by Vitruvius, architects require character to guide the transforming, transitioning, and translating of ideas, from being formless to demonstrating meaning through form.[5]

The organization of this chapter, based on Hermes' character traits, will address some of the changes we view in current architectural design processes. As an allegory or sustained metaphor, each characteristic presented in the chapter references and explores qualities ascribed to Hermes; each parallels the transforming, transitioning, or translating required in architecture with an aspect of Hermes' multifaceted role as *messenger*, *traveler*, *thief*, *magician*, and *inventor*.

Transforming, transitioning, and translating are fundamental to any design process. From the first definitions discovered through design to the fabrication of the building, transition facilitates innovation and invention. The word *transition* references the passage from one condition, action, or place to another.[6] Similar to transmutation, transition suggests a change in nature, properties, appearance, or form. It describes the movement in the state of something or a change in location. This change can be physical or conceptual, and is demonstrated in the manipulation of materials and concepts in design processes. A definition of *transformation* also focuses on change, especially the change in appearance or character of something, and especially the operation of changing.[7]

More importantly to architecture, the change evident in transformation is often an alteration in condition. It is inherently the role of architects to transform ideas or clients' wishes into physical forms; these, in turn, transform our environment. The word *translation*, additionally, expresses the prefix *trans*, or across, but adds the dimension of conveyance or interpretation, turning one language into another while still retaining meaning.[8] By using the verb form of these words, our intention is to emphasize the action of the design process as used by architects to manipulate media when moving ideas into form.

Chapter 1 established the connections between defining, designing, and playing as ways to mark out boundaries. It is important to recognize that the actions of play are critical to transforming, transitioning, and translating, since play is the medium of change. To transform something, on a practical level, means to manipulate that thing. Play epitomizes this action since *to play* encourages the distortion necessary for change. The definitions of play discussed in Chapter 1 included the "give and take" of action and reaction, defining, stretching boundaries, and being engrossed in the action of play. To transition implies a movement that necessitates an action, a deliberate intention to change something into another state or place. Transforming, transitioning, and translating are not passive: they require critical thinking, comparison, analysis, and, crucially, judgment. Design in itself is an act of transforming, transitioning, and translating that can be viewed as supportive of play. Chapter 2 addressed the qualities of imaging. It discussed how architectural imaging requires interpreting, translating, and manipulating images in the mind as well as those produced by artists and architects. This transitioning and transforming of images is also distinctive of visual play.

Establishing character that assists judgment in architecture is not easy, especially when the boundaries (rules) for decision making are not clear or are continuously changing. Judgment can also emerge from the realization that there is very little truth and that rules can be broken. Judgment usually depends on knowledge, and knowledge may require many years to acquire. One decision based in theory may differ drastically from its counterpart in practice. Thus, *crossing* between theory (Chapter 1 "Defining" and Chapter 2 "Imaging") to practice (Chapter 4 "Persuading" and Chapter 5 "Fabricating") needs transforming, transitioning, and translating to become fully understood.

Architect as Messenger

Architectural communication requires some amount of translation. The Greek god Hermes is well known for his role as a divine messenger. He was a god who could easily move between the worlds of the mortal and divine, serving as the messenger of the gods. Homer, in *The Odyssey*, declares, "Hermes, you are always our messenger."[9] Hermes was considered skilled with eloquent or graceful speech.[10] Consistent with his abilities as orator were his skills of persuasion. In some texts, he is called the herald of the gods.[11] Being a herald expands the definition of mere messenger, since heralding holds connotations of proclamation, prediction, or advocacy.[12] Being a messenger, or herald, is certainly a role familiar to architects. They communicate with eloquent speech to many partners in the design and construction processes, and most believe they use their buildings to herald in some way.

It is in the character of architects to be messengers. A messenger can be defined as "one who carries or goes on an errand. . .the bearer of a specified message."[13] The philosopher Marshall McLuhan, when speaking about contemporary culture, wrote that "the medium is the message."[14] Traditionally, architects have served as messengers, since buildings serve as a medium of communication. If architecture (as differentiated from mere building) is the medium of the message, how definitive can that message be in conveying meaning? Historically, architecture of various periods has presented messages more or less literally. There was not any doubt that the monuments of the Egyptians conveyed the message of the power of the Pharaoh. In more contemporary architecture, we are reminded of the book *Learning from Las Vegas* by Robert Venturi, Denise Scott Brown, and Steven Izenour; the authors categorize buildings as either "ducks" or "decorated sheds" in their questioning of various degrees of literalness.[15] Deconstructive philosophy, post-structuralism, and deconstruction in architecture questioned the role of meaning and taught that meaning is neither symbolic nor like language.[16]

Considering world architecture, there may be confusion about the meaning of the message of contemporary buildings. With globalization, architecture, especially in large cities, has become somewhat homogeneous; it is more corporate, flashier, and non-contextual. All this may be a result of the fast-track

Figure 3.2
Messenger.
Source:
CC-PD-MarkPD-old-70-1923.

construction of buildings by developers, the flow of architects across borders, and the rise of international corporations with the result being that buildings in Beijing often look like those in New York City.

Referencing McLuhan, architecture is a medium of culture, as it reflects societies' ideals and aspirations. Currently, avant-garde architects are experimenting with digital fabrication using parametrics. The computational software that allows digital images to be directly connected with fabrication was originally developed by the military and the aerospace industry.[17] This experimentation, due in large part to the availability of software, assumes an attitude of using it "because we can," and possibly questions what media architects use to *make* meaning. It may lead to the question of whether or not buildings by such contemporary architects as Zaha Hadid lose meaning because of the distancing caused by digital technology—although she clearly begins with conceptual notions. Currently, architects should question the relationship between the medium and the message. If they assume the role of Hermes (along with the Greek goddess of seduction, Peitho) who predicts or persuades, it is important to ask what is being communicated? If the buildings being built today are too homogeneous, are we losing our critical view—possibly losing faith in how to deliver the message or even what the message is? The persuasive qualities of digital fabrication, such as maximum efficiency, may become too seductive when making a choice between relatively safe solutions or experimentation.

Recently, several architects have been exploring the message of architecture. The *Blur Building* designed by the office of Diller, Scofidio, and Renfro for the Swiss EXPO 2002 at the base of Lake Neuchatel in Yverdon-les-Bains, Switzerland, questions the very definition of architecture. As a project with a less defined function, the pavilion exhibits a strong conceptual intention and a willingness to experiment. It asks if a building can be scaleless, formless, massless, colorless, dimensionless, weightless, odorless, centerless, feature-less, depth-less, meaningless, spaceless, timeless, and surfaceless.[18] As a construction of pipes over a lake, the *building* envelops visitors in a cloud of mist demonstrating a non-traditional construction material. The resulting pavilion provocatively pushes the boundaries of architectural form and questions the definition of what constitutes a building.

It is important to briefly explore an aspect of the definition of the term *messenger* that may not be completely clear from a dictionary definition. Referencing the study of semiotics, an architectural message, in most cases, is not a symbol.[19] A message can implement either passive or active aspects of

Figure 3.3
The Blur Building, Pavillion for Swiss EXPO, architects Diller, Renfro, and Scofidio, 2002 (Yverdon-les-Bains, Switzerland). Source: Norbert Aepli, CC-BY-2.5 Self-published work.

communication. In a passive mode, a message conveys information in a neutral manner. Conversely, a message can also be active and may be considered in the light of Hermes' role as herald. It can be convincing, exhibit an argument, be enhanced with active persuasion, or be intentionally expressive. Architects' messages are active forms of communication and demonstrate more complex concepts than mere information. Thus, it is nearly impossible not to imbue the architectural message with intention. Demonstration might be the key word here since to demonstrate implies a greater role than to convey. With definitive and persuasive communication, it is important to remember that Hermes, besides being a graceful orator, was attributed with being a liar.[20] The intensity of persuasion, as a rhetorical technique, may lead to a falsehood, so it is important for architects to be conscious of what their messages convey.

It is crucial to realize (as in any form of art) that the intended message of the artifact may not be perceived by the observer. Possibly this statement is obvious and unnecessary, but architects may ask what level of intended *message* is important. For example, it may be impossible to convey elaborate philosophical arguments, while emotional experiences may be relatively easier to construct. Several architects have made the experiential aspects of spaces critical to their buildings. Those displaying extreme emotion, such as Peter Zumthor's *Therme Vals* in Graubünden, Switzerland, make it easier to understand how architects transform concepts into architectural form through the use of phenomenology. Zumthor employs textured building materials such as rough-formed concrete to suggest a natural environment. The primary bath is window-less, providing a cave-like atmosphere. The entire building being partially submerged in a hillside supports a cave analogy. In the bathing rooms, Zumthor controls the amount, diffusion, and direction of light to create atmosphere. He accomplishes this by using narrow slit windows on the roof to direct light from above. Zumthor also installed lights under the water to create an eerie glow in the baths. The emotional *message*, which takes on poetic dimensions, is one that is less easy to define. A poem, although (usually) tightly structured in its format, uses words in combinations that make the meaning open-ended. This ambiguity transfers much of the interpretation and translation of the message to the reader.

The messenger aspect of architects' character may also involve translation. Translators of language must convert combinations of words into a different language, choosing phrases with the closest meanings. They must understand the nuances of the two languages to find a comparable meaning, although locating identical meaning is nearly impossible. The work of architects is to translate messages into physical form or artifacts of culture; they must avoid the use of symbolism or overly literal terms. Even though architects or architectural students identify *concepts* to begin a design process, how these concepts are conveyed through the final design varies widely.

A consideration of the qualities of Hermes, the messenger, as they relate to the character of architects requires a knowledge of culture and human nature. Architects gain this knowledge through education. Travel gives architects a repertoire of experiences, a mental archive of spaces, to inform their intention.

Architect as Traveler

To develop their character, architects must visit notable buildings to learn to design sensitive architecture. As a god, Hermes traveled easily between the heavens and the earth, transitioning from one place to another. He exemplifies not only transition, but also transactions, between realms, as he mediated between the gods and human beings, the conscious and unconscious, life and the afterlife, and the visible and invisible. Hermes was considered a god of roads, crossroads, thresholds, and boundaries as he presided over all transactions at borders.[21] Thus, Hermes was the quintessential traveler and those who travel learn from the experience. As the author from Classical Greece Euripides wrote, "experience, travel—these are an education in themselves."

Hermes was also considered the god of wisdom, eloquence, memory, and learning, and referencing the previous section concerning the messenger, also the god of language, writing, crafty wiles, and cunning, all useful skills for a traveler.[22] While these may seem on the surface to be a great many disconnected skills, they all speak of a learned person who continues to search for knowledge and then conveys it in the act of transformation or translation. As the writer Pat Conroy states, "once you have traveled, the voyage never ends. . .the mind can never break off from the journey."[23] This may be why Hermes was also the god of searches.[24]

It appears that Hermes was constantly adapting to assume his many roles. It is interesting that, in addition to being the god of roads and travelers, Hermes was also the god of hospitality.[25] Architects are typically a form of host, creating a hospitable environment where the inhabitants can be sheltered. Again, in ancient Greek mythology, it was Hestia, not Hermes, who was the god of building. Hestia was a virgin goddess of the hearth, the right ordering of domesticity, the family, and the state.[26] Her role may have been quite different from that of current architects. In Greek society, architects were primarily master craftsmen and not well educated. As reflective of this, Plato believed that architects, as well as other creative artists, were mere makers of images, fabricators or manufacturers of shadows and illusions, and purveyors of make-believe. He placed them and their

Figure 3.4
**Travelers.
Source:
Bibliothèque
national de
France,
CC-BY-2.0.**

work in the lowest level of his divided line of knowledge.[27] Vitruvius attempted to rectify the situation described by Plato when he wrote about the necessity of education for the architect. Vitruvius wanted to find a balance between theory, the area concerning education and knowledge, and practice, the area concerning the craft of construction. He wrote that an educated architect

> . . .must have both a natural gift and also readiness to learn. . .He should be a man of letters, a skillful draughtsman, a mathematician, familiar with scientific inquiries, a diligent student of philosophy, acquainted with music; not ignorant of medicine, learned in the responses of jurisconsults, familiar with astronomy and astronomical calculations.[28]

The Renaissance architect Leon Battista Alberti reiterated the need for education and wrote that architects were craftsmen who could read Latin.[29] During this period, the ability to read Latin was the sign of an educated person, and the requirement for an architect to be an educated craftsman remains relevant today. Without an understanding of construction, architects are not complete, and their buildings will not be successful. However, the architect without a solid education cannot hope to develop an architectural theory that is not merely illusion.

The need for architects to have the knowledge and learning that comes from travel is especially true with the globalization of architecture and the current pervasiveness of technology. As described earlier, globalization is the concept that recognizes the increase in global relationships between culture, people, and economic activity. The concept brings forward a new interpretation of the world. Architects are becoming increasingly more global since boundaries between countries are more easily crossed, and distances become shorter through convenient and inexpensive modes of transportation. Travel has always been part of architects' tradition. For instance, the Grand Tour undertaken by Beaux-Arts students allowed them to gain new knowledge and insight. The architecture of the twenty-first century is also becoming increasingly international, because architects can travel in ways other than physically visiting a place. The Internet has made the world more accessible, and software has been developed which allows for the exploration of foreign locations from virtually anywhere. Architects can conduct business meetings while sitting great distances away from clients or partners. Architectural projects can now be completed without physically traveling to a construction site. *Building Information Modeling* (BIM) supports architects as they model an idea or render an image, and send it to someone on the other side of the world. Modern technology gives architects the ability to share computer screens and to give design and construction partners the same amount of control as if they were simply sitting across the table. While technology enables architectural practice, it may also disable our experience. Architects might avoid traveling the globe when places can be *experienced* through the Internet. Alternative means of learning, although providing some notions of a place, can never fully capture the impact of architecture's ability to address all of the bodily senses. While we become more global as a society, perhaps we become less globalized and more insular as individuals.

Experiencing new places through travel also provides insight into an architect's culture and context. The work of the early twentieth-century Catalan architect Antonio Gaudí offers an example. Studying this architect's buildings from photographs in books suggests his architecture is exaggerated and extreme. When viewed in comparison to structures in other Western cities, Gaudí's fluid wave-like forms can appear strange and unusual. We can consider that Gaudí's approach was actually quite classical and reflected his conservative religious outlook. A trip to Barcelona helps the visitor to place his buildings in the context of Spanish shipbuilding, the Islamic architectural influence on the Iberian Peninsula, and Catalan cultural tradition. On closer inspection, we see that his anthropomorphic structural systems are the results of engineering diagrams and that they draw inspiration from forms in nature such as seashells. The experience of a visit to Barcelona gives architects a comprehensive view of Gaudí's work and guides a deeper understanding of the intentions in his design.

While a traveler, Hermes was also a guide. In this capacity, he guided souls to the afterlife, and there may in the architect's character be a comparison to this role.[30] Ultimately, he was responsible for transferring and translating information, much like architects who are responsible for organizing a design team. It is in the character of architects to travel, to bring a global perspective to their work, and to translate what is learned into new compositions.

In this increasingly globalized world, architects have the ability to easily travel and learn from their experiences. There is an old saying, attributed to the Prophet Mohammed: "Do not tell me how educated you are, tell me how much you traveled." Travel offers architects a repertoire of experiences for their design process, a mental archive of spaces like a Rolodex of precedents that can be called upon

Figure 3.5
Architecture must be experienced first-hand through travel. Source: Albert Smith, CC-BY-SA-2.5 Self-published work.

when needed, because it is hard to imagine (and subsequently make) what one has not seen.

Architect as Thief

Traditionally, architects have looked to precedent for inspiration. Hermes was portrayed in Greek mythology as a liar and a thief who used deceit to create illusions.[31] He was described as "blandly cunning, a robber, a cattle rustler, a bringer of dreams, as watcher by night, a thief at the gates."[32] He could not be bound or captured and, thus, was named the "prince of robbers."[33] This role is similar to that of Prometheus, the most famous thief in Greek mythology. The god Hermes invented fire, and the mortal Prometheus stole this technology from the gods and gave it to humans. Both thieves are thus involved in the mythical beginning of technology.[34] (The theft of technology from the gods will be revisited in Chapter 5.) A thief is defined as someone who takes the property of others by stealth.[35] If the theft of property involves the physical transference of something from one place to another, then architects can be seen as thieves who transfer ideas across contexts.[36]

Throughout history, architects have studied buildings from previous periods as precedents. They assume the role of thieves early in the design process as they deconstruct images of historic buildings, analyze constituent elements, identify solutions that are timeless, and apply them in their work, either deliberately or subconsciously.[37] Historical examples demonstrate the varying degrees of

Figure 3.6
Prometheus steals Fire from Apollo's Sun chariot,
Giuseppe Collignon, 1814, Collection of Palazzo Pitti (Florence, Italy).
Source: Palazzo Pitti, CC-PD-100, PD-Art (PD-old-auto).

Transforming, Transitioning, Translating

influence that precedent has had on the architectural outcome. For instance, the form of Greek temples was strictly based on previous temple construction. The builders reproduced the basic temple form from one building to the next, altering secondary details such as the number of columns and steps.[38] These builders retained the most significant elements while incrementally expanding on these elements. These later iterations led to new interpretations such as thinner columns and a refinement called *entasis*.[39]

The use of precedents is still integral to architectural design. Understanding through analysis is a learning process that enriches architects' design vocabulary by extracting ideas that accumulate into a collection of knowledge. When architects are faced with a design problem, these ideas can be revisited and recomposed into a new solution.[40] The more architects study precedents, the larger their frame of reference becomes.[41]

Architects rarely invent anything completely new, since most of what exists today is rooted in history.[42] Architects who study precedent can avoid unnecessary failures by employing solutions that have been tested over time.[43] For example, the failure of the *Pruitt-Igoe housing project* in St. Louis, Missouri, served as a warning for urban planners and architects.[44] It resulted in a shift in recent years away from the rational, isolated tower-in-the-park planning model to more mixed-use, diverse, and human-scale neighborhoods. Undeniably, more suitable historical precedents, such as Italian towns, have influenced the contemporary city, and have led to the use of such aspects as walkability and sociability which transcend time and place.[45] Accumulated knowledge enables architects to build on previous successes, a process that recalls the legend of Hermes' resourcefulness.[46] Similarly, the scientist Isaac Newton's famous phrase references the evolution of

Figure 3.7
The demolition of the Pruitt-Igoe housing project, 1972–1976 (St. Louis, Missouri).
Source: U.S. Department of Housing and Urban Development, PD US HUD.

65

knowledge: "If I have seen further, it is by standing on the shoulders of giants." Architects, inspired by precedents, can create synergy.[47]

Designers should be mindful of the way they use precedent, as access to previously existing ideas can produce both positive and negative results. We are reminded that after Prometheus had given humans fire, the Greek god Zeus sent Pandora with a box for Prometheus' brother, Epimetheus. Pandora opened the box, and troubles were released into the world and, in this way, Zeus gained revenge on humankind.[48] Self-reflexivity emerges as a controversial practice when designers fixate on certain ideas of their own. For example, architect Frank Gehry is known for his curvilinear, expressive, and sculptural forms. He possesses a strong personal architectural language that reappears in many of his designs. The imagery of boats and sails, for example, has been represented in similar ways in both the *Walt Disney Concert Hall* in Los Angeles and in the *Guggenheim Museum* in Bilbao. However, according to Gehry, the reappearance of the form was never intentional.[49] A personal architectural vocabulary has advantages and disadvantages.[50] During initial design phases, Gehry produces many sketches as a way to clarify his ideas.[51] It is at this stage that his vocabulary may subconsciously guide him to sketch in a consistent language. Gehry places importance on his personal design signature; by being true to himself, he can foster the most compelling designs.[52] On the one hand, his personal language is revered by clients who value his ability to create strong imagery. On the other hand, while Gehry recognizes the importance of evolving his design language to avoid repetition, many of his design elements manifest themselves repeatedly.[53] His signature leads him to create products that appear to be repetitive, even if their intentions, circumstances,

Figure 3.8
Exterior Guggenheim Museum Bilbao, architect Frank Gehry, 1997 (Bilbao, Spain). Source: Tony Hisgett, CC-BY-2.0.

and processes were very different. This raises the question of whether or not architects should confine themselves to a personal style.

It is logical that architects through a design process reference their own works, whether intentionally or subconsciously, as they try to evolve and perfect certain ideas through testing them in different contexts. The consistency provided by a personal language or preference, it might be argued, can lead to successful creations. However, the use of one's own works as precedents should not confine the architect to territories that had been previously explored. Architects should critically reflect on their previous work, and be conscious of the influence of their personal language on the evolution of their design strategies. Being a thief, in this context, is not a negative trait. However, architects must recognize that while developing the *thief* characteristic is necessary to their work, they must be judicious in its use. As we have seen, architects, like Hermes, can be compared to thieves since they rely on precedents; this thievery can successfully facilitate the making of architecture that transforms an idea into a physical reality.

Architect as Magician

Architects make places for people to live and work and, to do this, they attempt to control the forces of the environment. The myth of Hermes has been connected to the ideas of making and magic since he was credited with being dexterous. He was skilled in manual construction, as evidenced by the fact that he was responsible for making dice and musical instruments, in particular, the lyre. Greek mythology relates that from his birth, Hermes began to make things. As a child, he found a turtle; he turned it upside-down, emptied its shell and covered its top part with stretched calfskin. He secured seven strings to the shell (from sheep intestines) to produce a wonderful musical instrument. The child Hermes then used a stick and started improvising, singing about the love of his father and mother.[54]

Characteristics that architects most have in common with Hermes are their skill, dexterity, and ability to construct. The architect Ludwig Mies van der Rohe described the fundamental aspects of building when he wrote, "architecture starts when you carefully put two bricks together. There it begins."[55] To *make* is defined as to cause to happen or appear; to bring into being by forming, shaping, or altering material; to lay out and construct; to carry out.[56] The word has connotations of creativity or the ability to bring forth something from nothing. The etymology of *make* emerges from the Old English *macian*, to form, construct, do, prepare, arrange, cause; behave, fare, or transform.[57] The act of making implies *by the hand* and *making* can indeed be viewed as the transformation of materials into meaningful and useful objects, and into constructed human habitation.

The ability to construct has historically been revered by society. For example, the Egyptian architect Imhotep was bestowed with the titles of healer, scribe, astronomer, magician, and architect.[58] However, architects have not enjoyed elevated positions in all historical periods and certainly did not in ancient Greece. Medieval and Gothic craftsmen may not have been the intellectual guides for buildings of their time, but they were those who organized activities and labored

Figure 3.9
The Magician.
Source: CC-By-SA 3.0.

to complete projects.[59] Although craftsmen are considered uneducated in the traditional sense of the word, they are nevertheless the ones who are closest to the construction process and who understand the nature of materials. We may recall Plato's designation of those who imitate. The user is the one who knows how something should function, the maker understands that thing through construction, and the imitator is ignorant.[60] As the role of the master craftsman evolved, questions arose as to who intends and foresees the future of a building, as opposed to who crafts it. As an example of their shifting responsibility, at the beginning of the Gothic period in France, Abbot Suger defined the architectural intention of the *Basilica of Saint Denis*, in contrast to the craftsmen who constructed it.[61]

Hermes was also described as crafty. For the ancient Greeks, this referred to his skills in craft.[62] The definition of craft includes an activity that involves making something in a skillful way by using your hands.[63] This definition can be extended to include a job or activity that requires special skill, but could also refer to skill in planning, making, or executing. The word *craft* once referred to power, physical strength, and might, but evolved in Old English into skill, dexterity, art, or talent.[64]

A scholar of ancient Greece, Norman Oliver Brown introduced a relationship between craft and magic by relating that the character of Hermes included stealthiness, cunning, and being a trickster—traits he feels are associated with magicians.[65] Also linking magic with making, the French sociologist and anthropologist Marcel Mauss connected a historic interpretation of cultural magic to the supernatural, concluding that powers could be conjured to guarantee a desired end.[66]

> However, human skill can also be creative, and the actions of craftsmen are known to be effective. From this point of view, the greater part of the human race has always had difficulty in distinguishing techniques from rites. Moreover, there is probably not a single activity which artists and craftsmen perform which is not believed to be within the capacity of the magician. It is because their ends are similar that they are found in natural association and constantly join forces.[67]

In an attempt to control nature, humans used ritual and superstition to determine the outcome of chance or fate, or to forecast future events: "Magic is essentially the art of doing things, and magicians have always taken advantage of their know-how, their dexterity, their manual skill."[68] With the profession of architecture emerging from a craft tradition, architects, as well as a general population, may find that magic helps define the analogies and metaphors that explain their world. This is not to suggest that the long and involved process of designing and building a structure can be made to suddenly appear out of "thin air." Rather, we are referring to the aspects of the design process that compare magic and making. We are evoking a historic definition of magic defined as the art of producing a desired effect to help control the forces of nature. This understanding of magic compares architects to magicians in regard to their design process. The process that informs the eventual *making* requires dexterity of hand and also magical thinking.

Since dwellings were first constructed, humans have tried to control nature to create places for habitation. The characteristic of the architect as maker includes the ability to transform materials into shelters to protect humans from the elements, and also the control of spirits, or unknown forces that can frighten.[69] The concept of controlling nature also may be extended to include material manipulation in architectural construction.

Hermes knew craft, but he was also known to be crafty. A contemporary interpretation of *crafty* has dubious connotations, and may refer to someone as a trickster, as a magician, and may imply deception. Consistent with the belief that controlling nature involves the manipulation of materials, we are reminded of the Modernist architect Louis Kahn who asked, what does a brick want to be? He was alluding to the fact that masonry lends itself to making arches since it works well in compression. The current practice of hanging brick on façades acts against these principles. We may ask if contemporary architects are being dishonest by using brick and other materials in ways that are inconsistent with their properties. A case in point is the *Caixa Forum* in Madrid designed by the architects Herzog and De Meuron. This beautiful brick and steel building reuses a historic façade lifted off the ground to create a first-floor entrance void. The building seems to float, and the abundant use of corten steel and terracotta-colored brick is contrasted by an underside of stainless steel and a white terrazzo staircase. On the one hand, the beautiful color and textural palette of materials are striking; on the other hand, the raising of the façade makes the visitor conscious of the historical brick hanging above the ground plane. Structurally innovative, the building expresses the strong concept of a floating mass entered from beneath. However, it also raises the question of appropriate use of masonry.

The role of architects as craftsmen has evolved and we may question if the practice of architecture has changed from those who construct to those who draw. We suggest that Hermes' caduceus could be seen as a magician's wand and might

Figure 3.10
Entrance Condition to the Caixa Forum Madrid, architects Herzog and De Meuron, 2007 (Madrid, Spain). Source: Albert Smith, CC-BY-SA-2.5 Self-published work.

also be considered a drawing tool (stylus). As stated earlier, the characteristic most associated with architects is their dexterity and their ability to construct, especially to construct on paper, remembering that to *make* is defined as to cause to happen or appear. The pencil is about *doing* since it facilitates designing, and what appears on the paper has also been viewed by some as similar to magic. A contemporary architect, coming from a tradition of doing and making, needs to be proficient in drawing, to be able to give buildings meaning, to design, and to have the knowledge of the builder who oversees construction.

The Pritzker Prize-winning architect Renzo Piano is known for being involved in all stages of design and construction. He believes in the combination of craft and technology and seeks to establish a balance between available local materials and those that are appropriate to express his intent, and also between the conventional and the innovative.[70] We asked earlier if architects, because of specialization, are currently losing their connection with making. Possibly new technologies are reconnecting architects to construction since current practices of fabrication, in particular, parametric modeling, may be redefining construction methods. Frank Gehry's use of CATIA is an instance where utilizing software makes an immediate and direct connection between drawings and factory production.[71] Future trends may include the fabrication of building components becoming a new definition of making.

The distance, or separation, that arises from simulation may raise ethical questions concerning architects' control of, or involvement in, the design process. The distancing through the computer in a scale-less environment may not provide the same tactile qualities that were necessary to the traditional craftsman. Transforming steel, wood, glass, and concrete into creative and inspiring spaces requires an understanding both of technology and of methods of assemblage. This may mean that it is in the character of architects to be makers, magicians, and also inventors.

Architect as Inventor

Architects' character positions them to be inventors; they have the intelligence that accompanies creativity. It is said that Hermes created the first lyre, fashioned the syrinx, and developed sports, the alphabet, the calendar, and numbers. As an infant, he produced fire and fire sticks. Without Hermes, there would be no olives since he receives credit for the cultivation of the olive tree, and he was also the inventor of arts and writing.[72] An inventor such as Hermes is the originator of an idea. The term originates from the Latin verb *invenire*, that is, to contrive, to come upon, or to devise.[73] Thus, to invent is to create or design something that has not existed before.

The act of inventing transforms an abstract idea into its physical manifestation. This often involves a critical (eureka) moment where one concept informs another through association. To bridge the gap between the invisible and the visible, architects first disassemble, analyze, and re-interpret previously existing ideas. The concepts are then reassembled and synthesized into a fresh idea based on new circumstances. These actions coincide with architects' responsibilities as those who plan for the future using creations that stem from the past and engage the present. Envisioning the future involves risks, which raises ethical questions about the validity of architectural interventions.

The process of transformation, through invention, is indispensable to architectural design. While the craftsman possesses the practical skills required to construct, architects conceive the ideas and methods that give rise to the construction. The difference can be demonstrated by the different roles assumed by Greek builders in contrast to architects of the Renaissance. As mentioned earlier, ancient Greek architects did not conceive of the designs for their buildings. Instead, they followed traditions established by master masons, resulting in little variation. Renaissance architects, by contrast, were educated in craftsmanship and intellectual fields. They designed their buildings and embedded their architecture with meaning, which consequently affected every detail of the creation.[74] The intellectual act of invention thus distinguishes the art of architecture from mere construction and produces buildings that are a result of conscious decisions.

Architects today have inherited the role of the inventor and, thus, are educated craftsmen who are well versed in both theory and practice. They tend to seek unique solutions as a result of being confronted by varying contextual influences. To use a Modernist architect to illustrate: Le Corbusier's sketchbooks are a collection of ideas that he had encountered during his lifetime. These ideas constitute an inventory of architectural concepts that were selectively re-interpreted to invent new solutions.[75] Le Corbusier's fondness for rationality in Greek architecture, for example, encouraged him to analyze its underlying order. He then re-interpreted the mathematical relationships and invented the Modular, which he employed to introduce rationality to his architecture.[76] Thus, he made use of history to provoke a new way of thinking.

For architects to be inventive, they must also be sensitive to current social, cultural, environmental, and technological trends. Furthermore, they must be aware of the implications of these trends, which often represent shifts in values. All these dynamic forces stimulate new sets of the framework under which invention takes place. Architects as inventors envision the future by building what no one has seen before. As US President Abraham Lincoln said, "The best way to predict the future is to create it." This quote captures the unique and proactive role that architects play in shaping the future. Again, this role can be compared to that of a soothsayer, who has the power to foretell future events.[77] Like Hermes, whose inventions ranged from the small—the lyre—to the all-encompassing—arts and writing—architects are involved in planning for the future, a task that involves the creation of small-scale objects as well as of buildings and cities.

The development of cities in the early twentieth century highlights the active involvement of architects as visionaries in city planning. In Milan, Italy, new industries were rapidly transforming the cityscape. The Italian architect Antonio Sant'Elia revealed his plan of the *New City* (*Città Nuova*, 1914) as a response to the changing urban environment. He envisioned a city populated with stepped-back high-rise buildings, housing, offices, shops, and residences. He also designed train stations, airports, and power stations, all of which shared similar sleek futurist

Figure 3.11 **Futuristic drawings of power station, Antonio Sant'Elia, 1914.** Source: CC-PD-MarkAuthor, PD-Art (PD-old-auto).

forms. Sant'Elia was anticipating a rapid and complex transportation system, not unlike those found in a modern metropolis.[78]

Sant'Elia's revolutionary designs synthesized influences from a variety of precedents, both inside and outside architecture and urbanism. His *Città Nuova* was influenced by Henri Sauvage, a French architect who had worked with this typology since the early 1900s.[79] Sant'Elia also referenced the skyscrapers in New York for their unique verticality. His integration of streets, roads, and tracks may have been influenced by Otto Wagner's design for Vienna in 1905. Sant'Elia was well aware of the technological advancements of his time. For instance, his treatment of elevators as a separate element could have been influenced by the design of tourist elevators in the mountains of Lake Como, as well as by the exterior elevator shafts built in exposed steel structures in factories around Milan.[80] In the end, the design of his New City was never fully realized. One large drawback was the fact that the proposal was out of context since it rejected the existing urban fabric as well as the natural landscape. Also, the lack of scale figures on his drawings prevented a realistic reading of the design.[81] We cannot say, however, that his proposals had no merits. Sant'Elia's experiment with the typology of stepped-back apartments resulted in an improvement in circulation and natural lighting. These refinements later influenced the *Rue des Amirax* completed by Sauvage in 1922, which subsequently impacted housing of the century and beyond.[82]

It can be seen that while architectural visions are susceptible to failure, they can also have positive influences on the built environment. Architects interpret environmental, cultural, and social factors to formulate educated guesses about the future.[83] On the one hand, there are always risks involved in anticipating something that does not yet exist. On the other hand, educated guesses may be the only way through which architects can respond to the uncertainties that lie ahead. A saying attributed to Pericles expresses this situation well: "It is not a matter of correctly predicting the future, but of being prepared for it." In the end, architects may have to choose to adopt a more cautionary approach or, conversely, to intervene with a more progressive model. There is never a single correct response to situations that arise, and it is architects' character that will most strongly influence what decisions they make.

Conclusion

As mentioned earlier, myths attempt to explain events in practical life as well as the existing practices of culture. Myths such as that of Hermes can be considered allegories and can be seen as presenting a *chart* of Western social customs and beliefs. The ancient Greek myth of Hermes was referenced, through analogy, to present five key characteristics of the god that may prove useful to the study of the character of architects. As stated in the Introduction, the character of someone refers to his or her nature, ethical stance, or persona. The consideration of the character of the messenger addressed the abilities of architects to communicate and to persuade concepts regarding the unknown and the undefined, and to recognize that these require translation of ideas into form. The architect as traveler demonstrated the importance of learning gained from experience in an increasingly globalized world. It expressed the importance of architects being able to transform themselves through education to address various cultural issues in the design process. The analogy of the architect as thief exposes architects as borrowers from other sources. Appropriating concepts or forms through the use of precedent, architects transfer and translate these into new constructs. A common characteristic of architects is that they construct things. They are makers who transform materials into habitations and, in doing so, reference traditions of craftsmanship. Architects have always been in the enviable position of being able to invent, to use technology to transform the environment. Most importantly, it is the act of inventing that envisions the future.

Architects have an affinity for Hermes. Even though he had perceived faults (he was a liar and a thief), considering his character is still valid because he kept the welfare of humans and the world, in general, as a priority. Hermes was well aware of worlds that humans, while curious, could not yet understand. Walter F. Otto calls him affable, ingenious, and lucky, and wrote, "Hermes, 'the friendliest of the gods to men,' is a genuine Olympian."[84] The psychologist Murray Stein remarks that the god's character is creative and like a magician's, and that he creates space and especially transitional space—that is, spaces of the psyche.[85] It is interesting to note that Hermes, who traveled between boundaries, is cast in a fundamentally different role than that of the Roman god Janus, who defended existing borders. Given the absence of a comparable god in the ancient Greek pantheon, Janus is important to a discussion of transforming, transitioning, and translating. As the "porter of Heaven," Janus' prominent feature is a head with two faces, one looking forward and the other backward, and thus he represented past and future. Some authors have identified him with the concepts of time and movement, and it is said that Janus presided over the beginning and end of conflict.[86] Representing the threshold, or the place between, he was associated with gates, doors, and passages.[87] Janus may suggest ways of thinking about this transitional chapter. However, we propose that the architect's character is more like Hermes than Janus. We are in agreement with Murray Stein that Hermes was not the guardian of gates but, rather, he stood at boundaries to define space and, in this way, created architectural space.[88] Space-defining boundaries can always be interpreted and, when doing so, architects must rely on their best judgment and on educated guesses as they move between worlds, to transform, transition, and translate in a design process.

As architects travel across borders, they also mark out and define the boundaries of their cosmos through buildings. For architects, the boundaries of their cosmos are not static but are in constant flux, and therefore the boundaries that architects play within are also in transition. Architects are usually not gods, although some people see them this way, and the boundaries established by humans are not perfect and must always be open to criticism. The problem for architects, however, is that they must apply rules and mark boundaries to critique projects and to identify their good or poor attributes. For this reason, architects

Figure 3.12
**Statue of Janus' two faces upon one head.
Source: Vatican Museum, CC-BY-SA-3.0, 2.5, 2.0, 1.0.**

need character to understand, accept, or even create rules within which to function. They need to learn, travel, experience, and play to establish the character essential to their work. The five characteristics discussed in this chapter can assist in the definition of good judgment, and can thus help architects to interpret for themselves.

The characteristics of architects discussed in this chapter, and compared to those of Hermes, remain relevant today and offer a way to portend the future of the discipline. Like a chiasmus, the myth of Hermes provides a useful allegory to guide architects as they cross between the past, present, and future of their discipline. The two sides, the past and the future, are not disparate from each other, but rather are continually intertwined, as each can impact the positives and negatives of critical decision making. Hermes' distinctive wand, the caduceus, reveals through its use of intertwined snakes that he is the intermediary between worlds—above and below, gods and humans, past and future. Architects, as mediators, should ask if we can, in the guise of Hermes, still pass between the past and the future. Do we still have the ability to bring messages from the gods— or are we only interested in the rational and the scientific? Most importantly, Hermes is still relevant as an analogy for architects and their architecture today. This analogy not only remains appropriate, but is, in fact, critical for the future of architecture.

Notes

1   For research in this area, see Adrian Snodgrass and Richard Coyne, "Models, Metaphors and the Hermeneutics of Designing," *Design Issues* 9(1) (Autumn, 1992): 56–74.

2   Martin Heidegger, "A Dialogue on Language: Between a Japanese and an Inquirer," in *On the Way to Language*, trans. Peter D. Hertz (New York: Harper & Row, 1970), 29; ". . .hermeneutics means neither the theory of the art of interpretation nor interpretation itself, but rather the attempt first of all to define the nature of interpretation on hermeneutic grounds" (ibid., 11).

3   See Heidegger, *On the Way to Language*; Josef Bleicher, *Contemporary Hermeneutics: Hermeneutics as Method, Philosophy and Critique* (London and Boston, MA: Routledge and Kegan Paul, 1980); and Robert Mugerauer, *Interpreting Environment; Tradition, Deconstruction, Hermeneutics* (Austin, TX: The University of Texas Press, 1995).

4   Thomas Bulfinch, *The Age of Fable or the Beauties of Mythology* (New York: The Heritage Press, 1942), 9.

5   Manfredo Tafuri, *The Sphere, and the Labyrinth: Avant-Gardes and Architecture From Piranesi to the 1970s* (Cambridge, MA: MIT Press, 1987), 25–54.

6   *Oxford English Dictionary*, s.v. "transition."

7   *Oxford English Dictionary*, s.v. "transformation."

8   *Oxford English Dictionary*, s.v. "translation."

9   Homer, *The Odyssey*, trans. Walter Shewring, Introduction by G.S. Kirk, Oxford World's Classics (Oxford, UK: Oxford University Press, 2008), 5.28 ff.

10 See *The Hymns of Orpheus*, trans. Thomas Taylor (1972) (Philadelphia PA: University of Pennsylvania Press, 1999), Hymn 27.

11 See Hesiod, *Hesiod, the Homeric Hymns, and Homerica*, trans. Hugh G. Evelyn-White, Loeb Classical Library No. 57 (Cambridge, MA: Harvard University Press, 1914), "The Astronomy Frag1" in *Scholiast on Pindars' Nemean Ode 2.16*.

12 *Oxford English Dictionary*, s.v. "herald."

13 *Oxford English Dictionary*, s.v. "messenger."

14 See Marshall McLuhan, *Understanding Media: The Extensions of Man* (New York: McGraw-Hill, 1964).

15 See Robert Venturi, Denise Scott Brown, and Steven Izenour, *Learning from Las Vegas* (Cambridge, MA: MIT Press, 1972).

16 Robin Evans, "Translations from Drawing to Building," *AA Files* 12 (1986): 3–18.

17 See Nick Dunn, *Digital Fabrication in Architecture* (London: Lawrence King, 2012).

18 Notes on a sketch by Elizabeth Diller. See Kendra Schank Smith, *Architect's Drawings: A Selection of Sketches by World Famous Architects through History* (Oxford, UK: Elsevier, 2005), 224–225.

19 See Charles Sanders Peirce, *Philosophical Writings of Peirce* (New York: Dover Publications, 1995).

20 Plato, *Cratylus,* trans. Harold North Fowler (London: Heinemann; Cambridge, MA: Harvard University Press, 1914), 400d and 40a ff.

21 Walter F. Otto, The Homeric Gods: The Spiritual Significance of Greek Religion, trans. Moses Hadas (New York: Pantheon, 1954), 114.

22 Ibid., 104–106.

23 Pat Conroy, *The Prince of Tides* (New York: Dial Press Trade Paperback, 2002).

24 Aeschylus wrote in *The Eumenides* that Hermes is the god of searches and those who seek things lost or stolen: Aeschylus, *Aeschylus in Two Volumes, Volume II Agamemnon Libation-Bearers Eumenides Fragments*, trans. Herbert Weir Smyth (New York: William Heinemann/G.P. Putnam's Sons, 1936), 919 ff.

25 Homer, *The Iliad*, trans. Richmond Lattimore (Chicago, IL: University of Chicago Press, 2011), 24 334 ff; Aeschylus, *The Eumenides*, 89 ff.

26 Bulfinch, *The Age of Fable or the Beauties of Mythology*, 12.

27 Moshe Barasch, *Theories of Art, from Plato to Winckelmann* (New York: New York University Press, 1985), 23. To Plato, the poet and the musician are inspired, and inspiration is transmitted even to the bards who only recite the poet's songs, but sculptors and painters are seen as working solely according to the established rules of mechanics.

28 Vitruvius, *On Architecture*, trans. Frank Granger (Cambridge, MA: Harvard University Press, 1931), 7–9.

29 See Leon Battista Alberti, *On the Art of Building in Ten Books*, trans. Joseph Rykwert (Cambridge, MA: MIT Press, 1988).

30 Otto, *The Homeric Gods*, 114. Walter F. Otto writes that part of Hermes' role as a guide emerges from the heaps of stones used as road markers called *hermaion* which bear his name.

31 See Norman O. Brown, *Hermes the Thief: The Evolution of a Myth* (Great Barrington, MA: Lindisfarne Press, 1990).

32 Hesiod, *Hesiod, the Homeric Hymns, and Homerica*, "Hymn 4 to Hermes," 14 ff.

33 Ibid., 282 ff.

34 Bulfinch, *The Age of Fable or the Beauties of Mythology*, 16–18.

35 *Oxford English Dictionary*, s.v. "thief."

36 Ibid.

37 Roger H. Clark and Michael Pause, *Precedents in Architecture: Analytic Diagrams, Formative Ideas, and Parts* (Hoboken, NJ: John Wiley & Sons, 2005), v.

38 See Spiro Kostof, ed., *The Architect: Chapters in the History of the Profession* (New York: Oxford University Press, 1977).

39 Entasis is the intentional convexity of a column's shaft employed to adjust for an optical illusion.

40 Clark and Pause, *Precedents in Architecture*, v.

41 Herman Hertzberger, *Space, and the Architect: Lessons for Students in Architecture 2* (Rotterdam: nai010 publishers, 2013), 38.

42 Peter Zumthor, *Thinking Architecture* (Basel, Switzerland: Birkhäuser, 1999), 21–22.

43 Clark and Pause, *Precedents in Architecture*, v.

44 Charles Jencks, *The Language of Post-Modern Architecture* (New York: Rizzoli, 1984). The *Pruitt-Igoe housing project* was one of the first demolitions of modernist architecture; postmodern architectural historian Charles Jencks called its destruction "the day Modern architecture died."

45 See Giulio Carlo Argan, *The Renaissance City* (New York: Braziller, 1969), and Gary B. Cohan and Franz A.J. Szabo, *Embodiment of Power: Building Baroque Cities in Europe* (New York: Berghahn Books, 2008).

46 Otto, *The Homeric Gods*, 106.

47 Generally attributed to Isaac Newton.

48 Bulfinch, *The Age of Fable or the Beauties of Mythology*, 16–18.

49 Barbara Isenberg, *Conversation with Gehry* (New York: Alfred A. Knopf, 2009), 276–277.

50 Ibid., 253.

51 Ibid., 186.

52 Ibid., 291.

53 Ibid., 290–291.

54 Versions of this story can be found in: Pausanias, *Description of Greece*, trans. W.H.S. Jones, Loeb Classical Library No. 93 (Cambridge, MA: Harvard University Press, 1918); Philostratus the Elder, *Imagines*, trans. Arthur Fairbank, Loeb Classical Library No. 256 (Cambridge, MA: Harvard University Press, 1931); and Gaius Julius Hyginus, *Astronomica*, trans. Mary Grant *(Theoi Greek Mythology*, www.theoi.com).

55 See Joseph Demakis, *The Ultimate Book of Quotations* (Raleigh, NC: Lulu Enterprises, 2012), 11.

56 *Oxford English Dictionary*, s.v. "make."

57 Ibid.

58 E. Baldwin Smith, *Egyptian Architecture as Cultural Expression* (New York: D. Appleton-Century Co., Inc, 1938), 61.

59 See Kostof, *The Architect*.

60 Hazard Adams, ed., *Critical Theory Since Plato* (New York: Harcourt Brace Jovanovich, 1971), 35–39.

61 See Erwin Panofsky, *Gothic Architecture and Scholasticism* (New York: A Meridian Book, 1973).

62 Otto, *The Homeric Gods*, 106.

63 *Oxford English Dictionary*, s.v. "craft."

64 Ibid.

65 Brown, *Hermes the Thief*, 12–18.

66 Marcel Mauss, *A General Theory of Magic* (New York and London: W.W. Norton & Company, 1972), 18–22, 33.

67 Ibid., 19.

68 Ibid., 141.

69 See E.H. Gombrich, *The Story of Art* (Englewood Cliff, NJ: Prentice-Hall, Inc., 1984).

70 Peter Buchanan, *Renzo Piano Building Workshop; Complete Works, Volume Four* (London: Phaidon Press, 2000), 15. "Piano is concerned more fundamentally with process and equilibrium. For instance, with deciding what ways of doing things (use of materials, technology, craft, and form) should be local in source and/or associations, and

71 CATIA is an acronym for Computer Aided Three-dimensional Interactive Application. It was first developed in 1977 by the French aircraft manufacturer Avions Marcel Dassault.

72 *Greek Myth Index*, s.v. "Hermes," www.mythindex.com/greek-mythology/H/Hermes.html, accessed August 21, 2015; Ron Leadbetter, "Hermes," *Encyclopedia Mythica*, last modified February 8, 2006, www.pantheon.org/articles/h/hermes.html, accessed August 21, 2015.

73 *Oxford English Dictionary*, s.v. "invent."

74 See Kostof, *The Architect*.

75 Hertzberger, *Space, and the Architect*, 41–47.

76 See Le Corbusier, *Towards a New Architecture*, trans. Frederick Etchells (New York: Dover Publications, 1986).

77 *Oxford English Dictionary*, s.v. "soothsayer."

78 Esther Da Costa Meyer, *The Works of Antonio Sant'Elia* (New Haven, CT: Yale University Press, 1995), 110–117.

79 Ibid., 115.

80 Ibid., 114, 118–119, 133.

81 Ibid., 138.

82 Ibid., 115.

83 We are using the term "educated guess" when referring to abductive reasoning. See Umberto Eco and Thomas A. Sebeok, eds., *The Sign of Three* (Bloomington and Indianapolis, IN: Indiana University Press, 1983).

84 Otto, *The Homeric Gods*, 104–105.

85 Murray Stein, "Hermes and the Creation of Space," *Quadrant* 29(2) (1999): 5–6.

86 Bulfinch, *The Age of Fable or the Beauties of Mythology*, 12–13.

87 Ibid., and James George Frazer, *The Golden Bough: A Study in Magic and Religion* (New York: Collier Books, 1922), 190–192.

88 Stein, "Hermes and the Creation of Space," 4–6.

Chapter 4

Persuading

It is important to understand the persuasive character of architects and their buildings since both have significant consequences for society. Architects usually have acute verbal and written skills, valuable since they must continually explain their concepts and reasoning, and must communicate with everyone involved in the construction of a building. They have traditionally used forms of visually persuasive media to design their future buildings and to convince their clients (the future inhabitants) of the merits of their proposals. Specifically, the explanatory drawings, models, and renderings illustrate a personal dialogue in the design process, since they convey architects' intentions and persuade others. Architects believe in their design media because these images emerge from their whole being: their hands, memories, imagination, and intellect.

The myths that tell the story of Peitho may offer insight into the character of architects in regard to their capacity to use persuasion in conveying their ideas both verbally and visually through design. Peitho was the Greek goddess who personified persuasion and seduction. This chapter discusses the persuasive qualities of architects' design processes, presentations, and completed buildings to explore how it is part of architects' character to effectively persuade: as a *rhetorician*, *persuader*, *seeker of beauty and truth*, *seducer*, and *developer of trust*.

Architectural media used for presentation (sketches, models, and renderings in contrast with construction documents) have an incredible power to seduce and persuade, and therefore are vehicles for the presentation of convincing arguments. The architectural theorist Garrit Confurius conveyed how the discipline of architecture is historically propagandistic in its formulation: "this includes contemporary architecture's peculiar reliance on commentary, in photo series and happenings. . .as well as in the presence of seductive computer representation, with their power of persuasion."[1] Architects employ media in design processes as a trusted means to think through design, encourage dialogue, and help envision the future building.[2] A completed building, as a powerful experiential medium, also can persuade clients and inhabitants. In current society, architects cannot construct buildings alone; they require clients, the general public, financing, zoning boards, consultants, contractors, and subcontractors, to name just a few of the participants in a building process. With this range of partners, architects can, or some may say, are required to have in their character the ability to be persuasive since they must convince others of the validity of their ideas. Thus, the employment of verbal, written, and visual persuasion is immensely important to architects' character and, when used effectively, can be a powerful skill.

Figure 4.1
Pietho as depicted in a Roman fresco (Pompeii, Italy). Source: Museo Archeologico Nazionale, CC-PD-MarkPD-old.

Greek mythology ties persuasion to seduction and Peitho is central to this theme. Pausanias wrote that after Athens had been unified, Theseus created a cult of Aphrodite, Pandemos, and Peitho on the slope of the Acropolis in Athens. While much is written about Aphrodite, the goddess of love and beauty, less is known of her attendant Peitho. However, Peitho's closeness to Aphrodite and specifically the fact that she is often present at scenes relating to marriage demonstrates their connection. In a painting by Polygnotos, she is portrayed beside Himeros, the goddess of desire.[3] As a minor god, she is a background figure, somewhat mysterious and working from the shadows. But her presence in different stories always reinforces their themes. For example, in *The Iliad*, the power of Peitho is demonstrated in the narrative of the Deception of Zeus, and she also appears in the background of a first-century relief depicting the story of the abduction/seduction of Helen of Troy.[4] Peitho was often associated with inducement and rape. The discussion of rape in Greek mythology may add another dimension to the word persuasion since *rape* can mean not only a sexual violation but also to spoil or destroy a place, to take by force (coerce), ravish, or violate.[5]

The very name *Peitho* descends from the ancient Greek verb that means to persuade or prevail. For the ancient Greeks, the concepts of persuasion and faith were much the same. Archaeologist Amy C. Smith writes:

> With this in mind it is possible to understand Peitho as utterly a civic as well as personal virtue, the consensual force that joins people together in civilized society, through trust and faith in each other, as well as the persuasiveness, inducement, and obedience of individuals.[6]

These connections are logical because, in ancient Greece, marriage was a negotiation, with the groom's ability to persuade often determining a successful outcome. Seduction is often dependent upon the compelling attributes of beauty, and this may be a reason why Peitho was closely connected to Aphrodite.[7] It may also help explain why the connection between persuasion and love (or desire) was prominent in ancient Greek culture.

The meaning of the word persuasion is intrinsically linked to the ideas of seduction and propaganda, both of which can be employed to improve society but can also contain elements of deception. Because of the negative connotations of seduction, it is worth noting that ancient Greek historians also connect Peitho, through parentage, to Hermes, and she also had family ties to Ate. Both Hermes and Ate were notorious for deception, and both were considered trickster gods. Along with Hermes, Peitho has been perceived as having goodwill towards humans; she was, after all, one of the Charities. As goddess of persuasion and seduction, Peitho helps inform a discussion of verbal and visual rhetoric.

Architect as Rhetorician

It is in the character of architects to clearly articulate reasoning in their verbal and visual communication. As stated earlier, architects must convince others, and of course themselves, that their decisions are correct, so knowledge of argument is crucial. The fact that ancient Greek society had one goddess, Peitho, responsible for influencing persuasion reflects the importance they placed upon the power to persuade. By definition, to persuade is to urge, bring over, or induce.[8] It is considered to be a rational action that involves convincing, reasoning, and factual information. The Greek philosopher Aristotle established the foundation of persuasion in his book entitled *The Art of Rhetoric*. Rhetoric, as a study, stems from the Greek *hretorike* meaning "the art of oratory." It is defined as the art of expression, persuasive speech, and argumentation, and is also considered the art of using eloquent language to impress as well as to persuade.[9] We are reminded that Vitruvius addressed his treatise *On Architecture* to Caesar Augustus because this document was meant to enlighten the emperor at the same time as it represented an explanation of Roman contemporary architectural practice. The purpose here is not to present an in-depth study of rhetoric as much as to introduce rhetoric as a mode of comparison necessary for understanding the persuasive properties of architecture and design media.

Since buildings and media used for design are physical artifacts, it is important to discuss how visual images communicate, as opposed to verbal or other kinds of messages. Visual rhetoric emphasizes images as sensory expressions of cultural meaning, rather than being purely aesthetic. It is a form of communication that uses images to construct an argument. Lee Morrissey references Karsten Harries to connect rhetoric and architecture:

> . . .on one level, the distinction between building and architecture depends on a metaphor, a "sign." However, on another level, it could be said that architecture is the rhetoric of building, meaning both that the difference

between a "mere" building and successful "architecture" is rhetorical, and that architecture, as a study, has become the preferred discourse of building.[10]

It is necessary to comprehend rhetoric as a historical and philosophical tradition to fully understand how it affects architecture and architectural media. In the fifth century BCE, it was established that there was very little truth but that all argument was dependent upon persuasion. To construct a successful speech (argument) became "a complex art of great power."[11] Elocution could be taught and practiced, and speeches could be divided into parts, memorized, and delivered with great eloquence. In a well-known story, the ancient Greek orator Demosthenes was said to have practiced elocution to the waves with pebbles in his mouth, to improve his pronunciation and rhetorical delivery. Thus, rhetoric, particularly in the form of public speaking, was considered integral to business, governmental, and civic

Figure 4.2
Demosthenes practicing oratory. Source: CC-PD-100, PD-Art (PD-old-auto).

affairs.[12] As compared to the profession of architecture, the public and business aspects of argument may translate into the ability to construct buildings in a cultural context. For this reason, it is essential that architects understand the properties of rhetoric.

In *The Art of Rhetoric*, "Aristotle defines rhetoric as the art of discovering the means of persuasion available for any subject."[13] He identified three aspects of persuasion: *logos* (reasoning), *ethos* (character and dwelling), and *pathos* (emotion), and claimed that these three classical tactics ensured a complete and convincing argument.[14] It is known that Vitruvius was well versed in classical Greek culture. Although it is not possible to know definitively Vitruvius' intention, it is likely that when describing the terms *firmitas*, *utilitas*, and *venustas* he was referencing the three parts of rhetoric.[15] This point can be argued since he believed that the incorporation of *firmness*, *commodity*, and *delight* would result in the embodiment of a complete, unified, and successful building.[16] To better understand this characteristic of architects as rhetoricians, we must explore *firmness*, *commodity*, and *delight* as compared to *logos*, *ethos*, *and pathos*.[17]

The ancient Greek meaning of *logos* was loosely translated as "I say."[18] Heraclitus (535–475 BCE) brought attention to the concept of logos when he contemplated internal truth, finding logos to be the unchangeable and eternal concept around which all other responses are in flux. He believed the concept of logos to be simultaneously ungraspable by humans due to its vastness, and yet inescapable by humans due to its pervasiveness.[19] Following Heraclitus, the Stoics of the third century BCE came to associate logos with "the eternal truth or soul," that which remains beyond the material world.[20] On the other hand, Sophists such as Gorgias, who focused on intellectualism and the communication of wisdom, took a different position. He defined logos as discourse. The meaning of logos developed into *word*, *account*, or *reason*, and was established by Aristotle in his treatise as one of the key elements of a rhetorical argument. Logos is, in fact, the

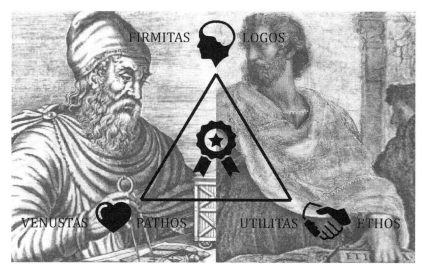

Figure 4.3 **Firmness, commodity, and delight compared to logos, ethos, and pathos,** adapted from *The School of Athens* by Raphael, 1509–1511 (Apostolic Palace, Vatican City). Source: Jason Brijraj, CC-BY-SA-2.5 Self-published work.

reasoning behind an argument. Vitruvius' term *firmness* has been translated to mean durability or strength; it connotes something that is steadfast or stable. The term logos can be compared to the rational qualities of architecture.

Reasoning or rational thought can guide a project. However, to design a well-balanced building that enhances humans' lives, it is critical to understand that reasoning alone cannot provide inspired architecture. In the study of rhetoric, ethos is viewed as the appeal based on the reputation, the character of the speaker.[21] As discussed earlier, ethos has been connected to dwelling and inhabitation. It has its origins in Aristotle's writings which described human beings as political creatures designed by nature to live with others.[22] More recently, societies' *ethos* has been described, by the theorist Karsten Harries, as the attempt to shape time and space by building a dwelling place. He also suggests that "to build is to help decide how man is to dwell on the earth or indeed whether he is to dwell on it at all, rather than drift aimlessly across it."[23] To expand on a definition of ethos, architectural ethics writer Gregory Caicco describes the related word ethics as pertaining to the relationship of humans to all the living and non-living things within a particular setting, a *place*.[24] This relationship emphasizes the importance of architects' occupation as placemakers and the consequent importance of understanding place-makers' character. The ability to make places may be related to Vitruvius' term *commodity* (*utilitas* is often translated as utility or convenience) and may establish architects' role in designing useful places.

The concept of *pathos* may be compared to the third and last aspect of Vitruvius' *complete* building and has been translated as grace, beauty, or delight. In ancient Greek texts, pathos was commonly defined as *emotion* or *suffering* and was found throughout the works of both Aristotle and Homer in discussions of tragedy in Greek literature. The term was primarily used to describe tragic situations concerning a family, with the intended effect of evoking pity, sympathy, or fear from the audience. For example, it was the use of pathos that evoked the feeling of pity for an agonizing Heracles in *Trachiniae* by Sophocles and sympathy for the pain of Oedipus in *Oedipus Tyrannus*. Pathos can be a means of inducing emotion, and of allowing audiences to identify their ultimate fate with that of the characters. Aristotle's writings assert that pathos is necessary for the understanding of a particular story, argument, or explanation where "pathos may be used independently to win assent or conviction. . .[however, the]. . .effective and proper use is by being brought together in deductive and inductive argumentation" with both ethos and logos.[25]

The architects Juhani Pallasmaa and Alberto Pérez-Gómez connect architecture to pathos when they claim that buildings must be tied to the human spirit, to the "enigma of life."[26] The architect Arthur Erikson once stated, "buildings that move the spirit have always been rare. In every case, they are unique, poetic, products of the heart."[27] Thus pathos may be seen as being embodied in the *beauty*, *grace*, or *delight* of a building. It is in a balance of logos, ethos, and pathos where true meaningful architecture may develop. Architects must assume the role of rhetorician; they must practice the art of oratory, and skillfully present the necessary components of an argument. Taking guidance from Peitho, they must have amongst their characteristics the ability to persuade.

Architect as Persuader

Buildings can be comprehended as similar to verbal arguments in the sense that both can be used to persuade. Barbara Breitenberger, when discussing the goddess Peitho, writes that while persuasion through words is Hermes' domain, Peitho is more about visual persuasion.[28] The myth of Peitho has been told not only verbally and in writing, but also visually through media such as statues representing her and temples dedicated to her. Architects use media such as drawings and models to explore concepts and to persuade others to their views because they are easily manipulated media in a design process. Pertaining to a completed construction, architects cannot stand in front of their buildings to verbally explain their intentions; instead, the buildings must assume this task. Buildings can visually represent the persuasive rhetoric determined by architects. Often this is accomplished through the use of metaphors. Again, a metaphor is a figure of speech in which a word or phrase usually applied to one object or idea is applied to another to which it is not applicable, in order to suggest a likeness between them.[29] A good example of how architecture has historically represented meaning is offered by the six female figures that support the entablature of the Caryatid porch on the *Erechtheion* at the Acropolis in Athens. Vitruvius wrote that the Caryatids represent a captured people, and their bodies carry a heavy burden of slavery. The narrative of their communities' capture becomes a visual metaphor. This story contains interesting analogies. Here, the load of the roof resting on the heads of the Caryatid women presents an analogy of their bodies to columns. The statues' shape also demonstrates the historical analogy of the human body to a column (with the head as the capital, the shaft as the torso, and the base as feet).

Figure 4.4
Replicas of Caryatids from the Erechtheion, northern side of the Acropolis, 406 BCE (Athens, Greece). Source: CC-BY-SA-2.5.

It may be difficult to compare vision and language as they use such different faculties of the mind. The question may arise: why use rhetoric to explore architectural media and persuasion? The comparison of architectural images to rhetoric is contingent upon their persuasive qualities rather than upon any performance of rhetoric. A discussion of the *language of persuasion* might be timely, as philosophers and architectural theorists have recently questioned how architecture can be comprehended as a *text*, specifically in the context of "perception, interpretation, and production of works of art."[30] Although it might be inaccurate to say images are *like* language, it is nevertheless possible to imagine that their visual persuasion can be interpreted as an argument.[31] It is also possible to understand how images can be convincing, recalling the famous adage "seeing is believing."

The consideration of architecture as a *sign* leads to the questioning of buildings as indicators of meaning.[32] Since the time of Vitruvius, architectural theory has borrowed terms from the vocabulary of classical rhetoric to articulate some of the conditions under which architecture could communicate meaning; that it could do so naturally implies that architecture is a sort of language.[33] Most architectural theoreticians believe that buildings cannot be read symbolically as a *text*, but that they must be interpreted. These buildings can use such techniques as sign and metaphor to convey conceptual ideas; some are elusive and others are more explicit.[34] The philosopher Umberto Eco elucidates this position when he explains that while meaning in communication can be definitive, there are cases where it is ambiguous and subject to interpretation:

> The universe of visual communications reminds us that we communicate both on the basis of *strong* codes (such as language) and indeed *very strong* ones (such as the Morse code) and on the basis of *weak* ones, which are barely defined and continuously changing, and in which the free variants prevail over the pertinent features.[35]

The imagination is also important at this juncture since conceptual thinking requires the associative qualities of imagination in order to understand metaphorical meanings. If buildings present themselves as they were proposed, the question of a medium acting as a sign may not be in doubt:

> The communicative functions of the architectural drawing could be defined, based on the work of Roman Jakobson, like linguistic phenomena, in three ways. To the extent that they represent a state of affairs, the drawings are *signs for something*. If they provide information about particular characteristics of the drawer, they are an *expression of their education*, *handwriting*, perhaps even of *their temperament*, even *mood* on a given day. Thirdly, drawings refer to an observer: they want something, they challenge the observer to use them, and this means producing, comparing, measuring, or remembering something according to the information they provide. One can distinguish, thus, between three functions of "drawings as language": representational, expressive, and appellative.[36]

This discussion of media as compared to language is important to understanding architectural images, which may be representational and *stand for* something else. Media can also be expressive, appeal to emotions, be poetic, and communicate things difficult to convey in language. Architectural media reveal the appellative (in Latin *appellare*—to call) in their attempt to conjure persuasion and argument by appealing to the observer using *measuring* analogies and *remembering* abstractions that may be metaphorical.

Theorists have found a relationship between form and the meaning displayed in rhetoric.[37] The rhetorician Lee Morrissey in his article "Toward a Rhetoric of Architecture" writes, "form can be apprehended as content; both form and content are rhetorical; moreover, it is precisely because form is rhetorical that it can be 'apprehended as content' or that there can be a 'content of the form.'"[38] Building upon this concept, Lee Morrissey feels that an "aesthetic component" is found in rhetoric, such that architecture consists of building with metaphor.[39] Aristotle writes in *Poetics*, "The greatest thing by far is to have a command of metaphor. This alone cannot be imparted by another; it is the mark of genius, for to make good metaphors implies an eye for resemblances."[40] Manfredo Tafuri in *The Sphere and the Labyrinth*, when discussing the polemic of the late Renaissance architect/artist Giovanni Battista Piranesi's *Carceri* etchings, finds a political and social argument.[41] For Tafuri, the underground fantasies refer to a bureaucratic government or repressive society. The graphic technique of etching supports this theory since it causes various elements in the image to become less focused and even fade into nothingness. The many vanishing points that can be found within the same frame make the viewer feel off-balance. The pulsating parallel lines of the etching technique present a nervous uncertainty to the oppressive spaces. Giving the observer little sense of orientation, the omnipresent light is never consistent in its direction—possibly implying the ever-present observance of a panopticon. It is possible to conclude that these images persuade an attitude or atmosphere, whether it be a contextual condition, narrative, or argument.

The Constructivist designer Vladimir Tatlin's model for the *Monument to the Third International* provides an example of a medium that conveys analogical and metaphorical meaning. The tower was designed in the early days of the Russian Revolution, a dangerous and chaotic time. The *maquette* presented a theoretical position of the new and developing paradigm of communism, and also raised the issue of conflict between the technical and ideological aspects of architecture. As an analogy, the model demonstrated symbolic messages, for instance: the floors that rotated once per year, the executive committee meeting room that rotated once per month, and the information office that rotated once per day. This project was a measure of the collective will of the Soviet people, and at the same time it served as "a social alembic for distilling this will and projecting it back to the masses."[42] Tatlin's model, referencing astrology, alchemy, and the human body, also operated as a lever, or an *Axis Mundi*, creating a fixed point for future orientation. As a lever to move the world, the model was a reference standard representing the will of the people.[43]

It is in the character of architects to use their design media and buildings to persuade others of a belief system. The subjective qualities of analogy and metaphor in persuasion lead to a discussion of the nature of beauty and truth.

Persuading

Figure 4.5
The Drawbridge, Le Carceri d'Invenzione series, Giovanni Battista Piranesi, 1750. Source: The Drawbridge, CC-PD-MarkAuthor, PD.

Architect as Seeker of Beauty and Truth

Just as architects design their architecture with associative qualities to be persuasive, it is typically a goal for architecture to be beautiful and truthful. Earlier in this chapter, *firmitas*, one of Vitruvius' three principles, was related to rational thought in rhetoric. In contrast to *firmitas*, the term *venustas* encapsulates the essence of beauty or delight in architecture. This notion of delight, when embedded in the built form, can produce emotion or often pathos. As persuasive arguments, buildings should, as Aristotle purports, reflect pathos as well as logos. The interpretation of *venustas* in architecture has initiated discussions concerning how to design beautiful buildings. As aesthetic philosophers have historically connected beauty

89

Figure 4.6
Model of the monument for the Third International (*Maquette du Monument a la Troisiem internationale*), **Centre Pompidou Metz, Vladimir Tatlin, 1919–1920** (Paris, France). Source: Centre Pompidou Metz, CC-BY-2.0 Generic.

with truth, architects should be skilled in the integration of both these qualities into their architecture:

> The importance of truth and beauty is apparent throughout many Greek myths, as anything seen as less than perfect was rejected by society. Again, we return to Aphrodite, the Greek goddess of beauty, love, and desire, who personifies the ideas of beauty. She was desired by many of the gods and often depicted as nude as to express her ideal female figure. Peitho may have been depicted as the attendant of Aphrodite (the quintessential expression of beauty) in order to reinforce the connection between love and persuasion.[44]

The aesthetic philosopher George Santayana begins his book *The Sense of Beauty* with a statement connecting beauty, truth, and good: "We know on excellent authority that beauty is truth, that it is the expression of the ideal, the symbol of divine perfection, and the sensible manifestation of the good."[45] Santayana concurs with Socrates in his belief that measurement and symmetry were closely associated with beauty. The Greek philosopher Plotinus suggested beauty could be found in the virtues such as righteousness, and also in the divine intellect and ideal form.[46] Although taking a slightly different approach from Socrates, he proposed that unity, harmony, and craftsmanship are instrumental components of beauty. Things that are concordant and congenial are also beautiful, and beauty is synonymous with good.[47] The equation of beauty with the concept of *good* has been a common theme throughout history.

Augustine of Hippo agreed with the ancient Greeks and wrote that beauty is "unity, number, equality, proportion and order."[48] This concept recurs in the works of Leon Battista Alberti. This is not surprising since the Renaissance constitutes a philosophical reflection of re-discovered ancient Greek beliefs. Again reiterating Vitruvius, Alberti believed that beauty is associated with proportion and stems from the sum of the parts to make a whole. He viewed ideal beauty in terms of proportion, stating that "I shall define Beauty to a Harmony of all the Parts, in whatsoever Subject it appears, fitted together with such Proportion and Connection, that nothing could be added, diminished or altered, but for the Worse."[49] The belief of architects and designers that beauty lies in the completeness of the whole persists in contemporary thought.

The construction of Greek temples demonstrates the importance placed on beauty in Greek culture. The temples "exhibit certain ideal proportions in the relation of part to part; and indeed, in the construction of the temple, precise mathematical measurements are taken to essential these proportions."[50] The most prominent of Greek architectural work, the *Parthenon*, displays this phenomenon. Built for the Greek goddess Athena, the temple once housed a great statue of the goddess as its focal point. The statue's pedestal was used as a proportioning device for the rest of the temple. Its width of 21,731mm directly translates to the temple's width of 21,733.5m.[51] The Greeks' equation of truth with rationality influenced their utilization of devices such as measurement and proportion; they translated these symbols of beauty directly into built form. As a way to produce beautiful buildings, they introduced spirit and emotion into the realm of the rational, or *logos*.[52]

The attempt to connect truth and measure has been a theme through history. For example, the philosopher René Descartes believed in the superiority of the mathematical scale model as a means for measuring.[53] He wrote, "Of all who have sought for the truth in the sciences, it has been the mathematicians alone who have been able to succeed in producing reasons which are evident and certain."[54] He believed that all situations in human life (which could include architecture), and all problems facing humankind, could be solved by applying the

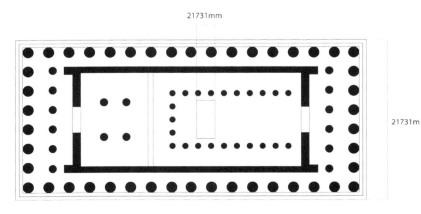

Figure 4.7 **Plan of the Parthenon showing proportional relationships. Source: Jason Brijraj, CC-BY-SA-2.5 Self-published work.**

infallible, all-encompassing laws of mathematics. In the eighteenth century, the concept of truth in architecture took a different approach when the *truth* of a building was not necessarily dependent upon its being beautiful. In *The Lamp of Truth*, John Ruskin presented seven fundamental principles of architecture: sacrifice, truth, power, beauty, life, memory, and obedience.[55] He defined how buildings could be truthful, and argued that truthful buildings should not use materials or structures other than those that were true. For instance, he deplored the use of applied decoration to mask the *truth* of the structure. In his interpretation, it was deceitful to paint surfaces to make them different from what they were originally. However, the definition of truth has changed since Ruskin presented his view.

The Modernist architect Le Corbusier was able to express his interpretation of truth with the *Carpenter Center for Visual Arts* built in 1963. He employed concrete throughout the building, and let its various textures demonstrate, as opposed to hiding, the nature of this construction material. The minimal use of ornamentation suggests that the beauty of the project is sufficiently displayed by the form of the concrete. For Le Corbusier, the truth in materials was displayed with clean, elegant lines to produce a building that is *beautiful*. However, honesty in systems does not always guarantee a beautiful building.

Boston City Hall, also built during the 1960s, presents a similar approach towards truth in materials, as it uses concrete as a primary building material, provides minimal ornamentation, and does not hide the structure. However, this building is regarded by some as one of the most unattractive buildings of the *Brutalist* era and is despised by a majority of Bostonians. It is an example of a truthful building being considered unsuccessful by its community. Sometimes

Figure 4.8
Exterior of the Carpenter Center for the Visual Arts, architect Le Corbusier, 1963 (Cambridge, Massachusetts).
Source: Daderot, Self-published work PD-self.

Persuading

Figure 4.9 Exterior of Boston City Hall, architects Gerhard Kallmann and Michael McKinnell, 1968 (Boston, Massachusetts). Source: Daniel Schwen, CC-BY-SA-4.0.

constructions are initially unpopular, for instance the *Eiffel Tower*, but communities grow to appreciate them.

If styles and fashions change, definitions will also change, resulting in paradigm shifts. Like definitions, what is true and beautiful may not be static, and discerning the difference between popular and truthful may not be possible. A building that is not truthful can still be perceived as beautiful. Often projects designed by students of architecture demonstrate this concept. Students may use beauty independently of truth to persuade their audience that what they are presenting is the truth. For example, a digital rendering illustrating a light-filled space can become a great instrument of persuasion, even though this lighting situation may not be possible in reality. The sheer beauty of the image may persuade viewers to disregard the truth of the scenario.

Seductive rendering reveals a potential divide between truth and beauty and demonstrates the importance of further discussion of these two principles and their effects on persuasion. To define *beauty* with such concepts as truth can enhance a person's perception of a building, but it does not establish whether a building is truly beautiful or not. What constitutes a beautiful building can be interpreted in many different ways by different people, and what is truly beautiful cannot be limited to one definition. Alberto Pérez-Gómez writes about architecture and its relationship to beauty as an immeasurable element: "An expressed intention can never fully predict the work's meaning, and *others* decide its destiny and its final significance."[56]

It is critical to discuss the relationship between Peitho and Aphrodite. Aristotle implied that there is very little truth and that rhetoric is the convincing argument that persuades regarding a point of view. Aphrodite was said to be beautiful in the context of Greek society, but the role of Peitho (as her presence at Aphrodite's side might suggest) was to persuade others of that assertion. Although rhetoric concerns persuasion, what we persuade people to believe is

93

important. Architects can persuade society of what is beautiful, and this is a huge responsibility in the search for ultimate truth and relative permanence. The truth of a building is in some ways dependent upon our beliefs. As Pérez-Gómez states, "Our love of beauty is our desire to be whole, beauty transcends the contradiction of necessity and superfluity; it is both necessary for reproduction and crucial for our spiritual *well-being*, the defining characteristic of our humanity."[57] It is a characteristic of architects to search for beauty and truth, and not to just adhere to what is popular. Architects must recognize their power to influence what a society builds, but should also consider the responsibilities associated with it.

Architect as Seducer

Architects are continually put in situations where they are required to persuade, but what are their roles regarding seduction? In Greek mythology, Peitho was the personification of erotic persuasion, and she was known as the goddess of seduction.[58] Seduction can be defined as the ability to persuade someone to do something, to guide, tempt, entice, or beguile.[59] To be seduced can also mean to be led astray in conduct or belief, or to draw away from the right or intended course of action into a wrong one.[60] This definition implies that persuasion may also have negative connotations since to seduce is to persuade with the intent of disloyalty or false promises. The words *beguile* and *entice* remind us of seduction's association with magic. In Hesiod's *Works and Days*, Peitho is involved along with the Graces in the making of Pandora since she adorned Pandora with a golden necklace. In ancient Greek culture, golden necklaces were powerful "traditional instruments of erotic enticement." They were viewed as "dangerous and evil as they seduced women into immoral sexual behaviour." Thus, necklaces were used as a symbol of both danger and attraction. Peitho "brings men and women in harmonious delight," but in regard to unlawful relationships, she can produce catastrophic results.[61] While it is possible to make several interesting connections between seduction, the erotic, and architecture, we will discuss seduction as part of the character of architects specifically in relationship to design intent.

It is in the character of architects to be charming, convincing, and persuasive as they are constantly called upon to verbally address clients, zoning boards, and city councils. For architects to build, they must be able to successfully *sell* their ideas to win commissions. This ability to persuade requires a tremendous amount of charisma and involves an understanding of human nature, including what motivates people and how to develop their trust. Charisma is a special charm or appeal that causes people to feel attracted to and excited by someone (often a politician), and it is possible that Peitho possessed this quality. Charisma can additionally be defined as a personal magic of leadership that arouses popular loyalty or enthusiasm for a public figure (a seductiveness or magical appeal).[62] If persuasion means to convince, then seduction can be seen as part of an extreme effort that often incorporates an appeal to the emotions. As we have connected the argument of rhetoric to images, we will, in a similar way, propose that how architects use media can define them as seducers.

Architects have the characteristic power to seduce through verbal presentations, architectural media, and the buildings they make, all extensions of their personal charm. In all these forms, the power of seduction can persuade a distinct position. However, it can also lead architects astray and, if used for deception, it may corrupt. On the one hand, when used responsibly from a position of education and knowledge, the architect's ability to seduce may be used to convince clients to build sensitive environments. On the other hand, the power of seduction could persuade others to extreme and dangerous positions, for instance ones harmful to the environment. While Peitho's ability to seduce was erotic, architects seduce using the power of convincing images.

Artists and architects have as part of their character the ability to define society through their media. There is historical evidence that humans have always attempted to use the built environment to understand the complex mechanizations of their universe. Again, the ancient Egyptian Imhotep can provide an example. He was known as a high priest, astronomer, scribe, physician, and magician, but he also became one of only a few people of non-royal birth to be promoted to godhood (the divine).[63] Like most architects, it may have been Imhotep's ability to predict future construction that earned him this status. He may have been able to read the signs concerning sites and the nature of materials and to then successfully convince those in power to take certain actions. His exceptional talents may have extended to a knowledge of numbers and calculation, areas long understood to have magical origins. The rational beginnings of mathematics— later purported to be the most irrefutable of the arts and sciences—maintained a certain amount of secrecy. Thus, Imhotep may have found them to be powerful instruments of seduction.[64]

Imhotep's talents are reminiscent of the legendary artists and architects of the Renaissance. Their reputations thrived due to their ability to create works of art that were seductive as they achieved a level of naturalness too skilled to be humanly rendered: "In these legends, the image of *Deus Artifex* which culminated in the concrete representation of an artistically active deity or one who collaborates with or aids the artist corresponds to the image of the divine artist."[65] Returning to the notion of *divino artista*, but now from a different direction, the divine artists were defined in terms of (the will of God translated through the artist's brush) their ability to conjure the unknown. This talent imbued them with power that suggested a connection between the artist and the heavens. When artists and architects have *mastery*, divine skills, or seductive control over images, they appear to speak a unique language alien to visually untalented laymen. The Italian author Umberto Eco wrote:

> This also helps us to understand why a person who speaks does not seem to be born with any special ability, but if someone can draw, he already seems "different" from others, because we recognize in him the ability to articulate elements of a code which do not belong to the whole group; and we recognize in him an autonomy in relation to normal systems which we do not recognize in any speaker except a poet.[66]

Figure 4.10 **Statue of Imhotep, Louvre Museum (Paris, France). Source: Louvre Museum, CC0-01.**

Eco was comparing the characteristics of a poet to people with highly developed visual skills. Here the key word is "draw," since architects and artists have seductive visual representation skills that others do not. To some, these talents may appear magical.

In ancient Greek mythology, the Priestess of the Gate at Delphi was able to pronounce words of prophesy, originally through the god Apollo. Speaking in riddles, these words of prophesy, on subjects from politics to human relationships, were interpreted by the Oracle.[67] The Oracle (the shrine) and the temple in the *Sanctuary of Apollo* were constructed on a sacred location where location and words acted in an irrational and inexplicable manner. The location was revered in the Greek world as the center of the earth and the universe and appeared quite magical, offering a view into the power of the supposed irrational.

Chapter 3 discussed traditional magic as a function of *doing*. In this chapter, we are defining magic as meaning the extraordinary power of seduction, the ability to beguile or entice. Magic has been a theme through the history of rhetoric, since those excelling in the techniques of rhetoric were seen to possess powerful skills of persuasion. For example, the Greek philosopher and rhetorician Gorgias was said to have had the great skills of the thaumaturgist, since he was able to mesmerize his audience with compelling oratory:[68] "More than any other text, the Encomium [by Gorgias] invites us to confront the terrifying, exhilarating possibility that persuasion is just power and that no human contact is innocent of its manipulative presence."[69] The *Encomium* suggests a relationship between the deceptions of persuasion and magic, and furthermore, questions the power of images. Robert Wardy writes in *The Birth of Rhetoric* that "the message of Gorgias' Encomium of Helen invokes the persuasive power of vision as well as of language."[70] It was Gorgias who first introduced the convincing qualities of magic in relationship to argument.[71] In *The Encomium of Helen*, he discussed the power of language and implied that words could be seductive and persuasive in a way that transcended reason:

> Sacred incantations sung with words are bearers of pleasures and banishers of pain for, merging with opinion in the soul, the power of the incantation is wont to beguile it and persuade it and alter it by witchcraft. There have been discovered two arts of witchcraft and magic: one consists of errors of soul and the other of deceptions of opinion.[72]

The ephemeral nature of magic means that it relies more on myth and emotions than on science. Magic compels partially because, throughout history, it has produced evident results. The belief in magic may have arisen in part from contact with charismatic leaders who possessed the qualities of a sorcerer. The deceptive manipulation of emotions often involved beguiling or enchantment.

The negative aspects of seduction may be expressed in architecture through illusion. Albert Speer's *Cathedral of Light*, constructed for a Nazi rally at Nuremberg, Germany, provides an example. The design served as seductive Nazi propaganda, and it persuaded many thousands to believe what most today would consider delusional acts. Speer bordered an outdoor stadium with searchlights to construct

Persuading

Figure 4.11
The Cathedral of Light, architect Albert Speer, 1937 (Nuremburg, Germany).
Source: CC-PD-Mark PD US.

a majestic enclosure. The soaring vertical shafts served to heighten the emotions produced by the spectacle of the rally. The architectural theorist Garritt Confurius discussed the negative qualities of seduction when he wrote, "For the most part however, rhetoric is suspected to be an art of delusion, as Kant says 'underhanded art,' a bending of the facts."[73] Confurius continued discussing those falsehoods evident in rhetoric that may be paralleled with the illusion so common in an interpretation of magic: "In architectural theory, rhetoric is continually tainted with connotations of 'mere' rhetoric, of that which persistently upstages the thing itself, of the lie, the inauthentic, the unreal, the dishonest."[74]

In architectural illusion, seduction may not be viewed as deceptive but rather refers to the yet-to-be-constructed building. Illusion could also suggest the ambiguity of uncertainty, where anything is possible. It may be in this undefined period where the image speaks to the architect, that an idea is ultimately revealed. Poetic and seductive drawings are

> . . .traces of the memory and the dreams of the drawer, outbreaks of temperament and wit, provocations of the observer, riddles, vague evocations or gestures of philosophical thesis. . .The transferrals and interpretations which result from them move on all possible levels.[75]

The preliminary renderings for Zaha Hadid's Hong Kong project, *The Peak*, entice the viewer to engage in the promise of a future of flowing forms. The abstract nature of these images compels the viewer to suspend comparison to rational and conventional construction methods and to be seduced by sensuous forms integrated with the landscape. Her renderings are not limited by contemporary building materials but seductively beguile the viewer into believing that a smooth curved line will eventually become a roof. At these early stages in a design process, questions of constructability may be irrelevant. Hadid's images may not be meant to deceive, but instead reflect her personal belief system as she designs. If used to convince a client of design intent, these paintings are just the illusions that can begin conversations. But if she was not thinking of construction while drawing, then Zaha Hadid may have been deceiving herself and others.

Peitho was connected to both persuasion and seduction. As established earlier, part of a definition of seduction includes to lead astray and touches upon an often magical persuasion that may corrupt or, in the very least, may persuade a distinct position. It is in the character of architects to be charming, convincing, and persuasive, in order to engage the imagination of the viewer to propose a future born out of the architect's conviction.

Architect as Developer of Trust

To establish the trust that follows persuasion, architects must develop their position before attempting to convince someone else of their beliefs. The name for the goddess Peitho was a reflection of the ancient Greek verb *peitho*, whose primary meaning was to persuade; however, the word can also be defined as *trust*.[76] Today, trust is viewed as an assured reliance on something, a confidence.[77] This section will discuss the relationship between Peitho and architects' character through the concept of trust in two interconnected ways. First, it will explore how architects learn to trust in their media when developing designs. Second, it will discuss how architects use media to persuade others to trust in their ideas. A firm conviction (or belief system) is necessary for architects to function. Thus, one character trait of architects is the ability to develop trust.

Architects trust in their media when developing their designs. Similar to persuasion, trust concerns confidence, reliance, and implicit faith. To trust in something presents a belief in its value, a belief that it will provide a service or follow through on a task. If architects trust their images, they are then believing those images useful in some way. On a basic level, if architects employ media for design, they have most likely found them useful in the process, although it seems there is more to this. Could there be an explanation of expectations about how and why their sketches, models, and renderings *speak* to them and become persuasive and trusted media for design? It is through looking at these manipulable images that it is possible to view the trust architects put in the media they use to design.

Architects trust in the communication abilities of their images. The products of analog media, its drawings and models, may be deemed credible because they emanate from architects' hands and minds, and therefore reflect their subconscious being. The media help architects to record fleeting thoughts, to evaluate what is seen, or to discover ideas and solutions in the process of designing.[78] The process of making an object represents continual refinement and development which means that architects are at one with the essence of the object. It is through this making that architects can understand what meanings will be conveyed. Since media help architects to visualize, they are indications of the future. Their manipulation can be the first step in the building of architecture (the pre-building) and can give the first impression of a future building. Digital media, especially renderings, may illustrate an accurate (almost photographic) replication of a building as it will appear in the future. This potential truth establishes these renderings as trustworthy and suggests that architects ultimately trust in the persuasive qualities of their media.

Often seen as visual language, preliminary drawings, models, and renderings each embody a manipulative medium, traditionally temporary, that encourages dialogue. For example, architectural sketches are, generally, not precious; they are disposable, incomplete, and require interpretation. Sketches may be seen as dialogue and, as such, they do not need to be precise.[79] In their ambiguity (their quality of being unfinished), they provide sufficient imagery to convey abstract thoughts, and can, therefore, facilitate thinking during the design process. They are playful in their ability to "give and take" because of their incompleteness and affinity for manipulation.[80] It is this incompleteness, the fact that they are outlines or guides, that emphasizes that they function as "preliminary or preparatory to something else," as they refer to a future building.[81] Their importance lies in the process itself. The project as in-process may be compared to a literary *rough draft* that requires continual reiteration and rethinking.[82] These images are the trusted media that assist architects to think through design.

The shared explanatory or representational power of drawing and writing means that they perform similar roles in architecture and literature. It is in the process of putting something onto the page or in words, and sometimes not before that process, that one comes to understand what one thinks.[83]

This relationship between making and understanding also encourages architects to view their designs in a manner that allows evaluation. Media often take on a life of their own and can show unexpected results. Once an image is presented, it can be criticized. It is through its presence that the design becomes clear. As an example, the art historian Ernst Gombrich presents the term *making and matching*. He writes that artists may first put down a line and, in a process of evaluation, alter it in comparison to intention or to the image in their mind's eye.[84] By using media to evaluate, architects can see solutions and subsequently build trust in what they have made.

As discussed earlier, rhetoric is the means of constructing a verbal or written persuasive argument and, comparatively, the media (drawings, models, digital images) that may be used by architects can be employed to promote visual argument. Architects must be completely immersed in the *making* and, thus, the visual *proof* of seeing an image often convinces architects regarding a decision. This aspect of persuasion results in bringing oneself to a state of trust or arriving at an assured belief. Architects come to trust in their media because their experience has shown that drawings, models, and renderings have helped make successful designs. They may become talismans as architects design using tools or media *known to be successful*, that have faithfully represented their inner thoughts, or have proven to provide effective communication.

Architects use media to persuade others to trust their ideas. The Roman philosopher Cicero described the five canons of classical rhetoric that formed the foundation of a persuasive argument. These methods of compiling a speech were deemed necessary for a good presentation.[85] The consideration of *invention*, *arrangement*, *style*, *memory*, and *delivery* can guide our discussion of how architects use media to prepare their visual arguments. When ancient orators employed these five devices of rhetoric, they were reasonably assured of a complete argument, one whose outcome they could trust. Similarly, if architects employ them, they may be able to trust the relative success of their finished buildings.

Cicero, who lived during the first century BCE, was skilled in rhetoric and is renowned as one of Rome's most talented orators and prose stylists. He was certainly knowledgeable concerning ancient Greek philosophy and culture. So it would be logical to assume that he recognized Peitho's position with regard to persuasion. The five canons of rhetoric can be paralleled to how architects trust in their media, and to the consequent development of trustworthy positions.

Invention in rhetoric is the search for persuasive ways to present information and formulate arguments.[86] Compared to architectural media, invention could imply the search for seductive images. These images could be used to persuade when evaluating or transforming arguments. This mode of persuasion may include the search for an appropriate theme during the development of a definitive position:

> Invention is the finding of the subject of the poem. The invention is also equated with the fable or fiction of the poem. . .The "invention" is the fable itself and the theme it carries. It is close to the words "argument" and "device" and should be taken with them. When the fable is stated as a narrative it is the "argument," the plot-line; but argument can also mean the subject, the theme illustrated by the fable. "Device" means plot-line, fable or narrative. "Invention" is the most inclusive term.[87]

For architects, developing a visual counterpart to rhetorical invention may involve finding a concept that is appropriate for the development of an argument. Architects may ask: what is the concept of the project, what guides the design, and what is a convincing design *argument* that makes sense with the constraints of the program, site, and its economic restrictions? Verbal and visual presentations should focus on the best ways to illustrate the future project to exhibit solutions to possible issues and to thus demonstrate trust.

The *arrangement* is the organization of the parts of a speech to ensure that all the means of persuasion are present and properly disposed of.[88] Arrangement concerns a clear and well-developed argument, elocution, or, in the case of architecture, images that are complete and rendered to be understood. Arrangement could suggest the organization or the order of the parts, or the function and relationships that solve the *problem*. For architects, this concept could also concern the completeness of the solution, the resolution of structure, sun angles, and materiality, for example. Arrangement may also extend to the sequence of images in a presentation as it helps convince through logical thinking. As architects must consider the verbal sequence of points in a presentation, they must also organize the visual presentation.

Style in rhetoric is the use of correct, appropriate, and striking language throughout a speech.[89] As it applies to visual presentation, it may involve utilizing poignant, beautiful, and bold images. These images may portray an appropriate architectural *type* or expression, and could act as a mode of representation for a specific architectural intent. Style may depict the *language* or the elements of the visual expression. The appropriateness of style may apply to what is exhibited, and how best to respond to a certain question. Definitions of style in art refer to a constant form that may include constant elements, qualities, or expressions.[90] In painting, style may mean the way an artist chooses a genre for imitation. For architects, this may involve not only the style of the architecture itself but also the use of techniques appropriate to, and consistent with, the concept or theme of the building.

Memory is the use of mnemonics and recall, and requires practice.[91] Memory for architects may evoke architectural precedent, allusions, self-reflectivity, or associations. The images it produces may employ recall or reminiscence. Architectural media epitomize the qualities of memory since everything in the architect's experience, every aspect of his or her entire being, determines the image choices for a presentation. The presentation must also reference the experiences of clients, or its audience generally; if it does not, opportunities for communication are lost, as is trust.

Delivery involves such aspects of the presentation as effective gestures and vocal modulation.[92] For architects, it may comprise color, shadows, texture, or other rendering techniques that make the argument more effective and believable. The effective gestures and vocal modulation of a verbal presentation may be compared to the techniques that give expression to a visual presentation. This may involve taking the time to develop a persuasive rendering. Delivery provokes architects to use all the skills and abilities at their disposal to produce images that accurately and persuasively display the architectural intention.

Trust, then, does not depend entirely on proof or facts, but rather on a belief sometimes not substantiated. Persuasion, as Peitho used it to influence the actions of the gods, is a device that leads to trust, the ultimate outcome of the convincing process. Trust may yield a conclusion, may culminate in a decision founded on belief. It is important for architects to develop a conviction—a belief system or position—because only when this is part of their character can they successfully formulate beliefs, and communicate them to others as they endeavor to establish trust.

Conclusion

This chapter introduced the critical persuasive traits necessary for architects. It compared traditional use of rhetoric to the visual representation employed in communication. Communication can be seen in the way buildings convey meaning to the public, and also in how design media convey knowledge and understanding to architects. Discussing seduction as a beguiling dimension of persuasion emphasized the power architects have to convince through verbal and visual means. The discussion of persuasion, as a character trait, stems from the recognition that architects currently have a tremendous ability to communicate through numerous digital graphic programs. The ability to convince has traditionally been a character trait of architects, as they have always had to persuade themselves, clients, and others during the design and construction processes. New technology has expanded their ability to visually convince with tremendous color, realism, and animation. With this increased ability to influence comes added responsibilities.

Since architects' character traits involve the talents and skills necessary to design and manage the construction of buildings, how media are utilized is central to a discussion of it. Chapter 4, "Persuading," is an extension of Chapter 2, "Imaging," since both demonstrate how images hold great power in the hands of architects. Chapter 2 presented a historical and theoretical approach that focused on the nature of images. As a chiasm, Chapter 4 explored how images can be persuasive and sometimes seductive.

The Greek goddess Peitho personified persuasion and seduction and, through her association with Aphrodite, she was closely tied to beauty. Her presence as a figure in mythology asserts the importance of persuasion in ancient Greek society. With the ubiquitous and pervasive Internet and television media, it is possible to suggest that our society is equally obsessed with aspects of persuasion.[93] Very few people can escape the mass consumption of news, politics, and entertainment that affects our culture. The Greeks believed that there is little objective truth, but that all decisions and beliefs are based on the ability to be convincing. Currently and globally, people may also be engaging the meaning of Peitho. Architects of the past recognized the importance of being respected in society and were also cognizant of the need to convince their clients. The Renaissance architect Filarete goes so far as to suggest that architects sketch in front of their clients as much as to remind them of their skills and talents as to visually support a verbal conversation.[94] Architects' relationships with their clients are critical to a successful building, and building these relationships often requires years of mutual trust.

Persuasion was chosen as the theme of this chapter since it is crucial to architects' design processes. Architects cannot function, and certainly cannot make design decisions, without faith in themselves and their education, experience, skills, and talents.

The media employed for design and also promotional techniques have changed substantially, as evidenced by the video presentations of the architectural firm Bjarke Ingels Group. One brief film, accessible on the Internet,[95] shows Ingels demonstrating the process and intention of the *8 House* in Copenhagen and uses augmented reality. The video casts Ingels in the role of creator as he visually constructs the building within 15 minutes. His charismatic personality dominates as he enthusiastically relates the main design themes of the building, and completely persuades regarding the reasoning and intent that led to its shape. The video employs digitally enhanced images, using the computer to construct

Figure 4.12
Exterior of 8 House, Bjarke Ingels, 2010 (Ørestad, Denmark).
Source: cjreddaway CC-BY-2.0.

diagrams to make it appear that he is forming them with his hands. The presentation techniques used here demonstrate the potential of media as a means of advertising world-wide. It is clear that Ingels understands both the power of the Internet and also the principles of seduction.

Architects and clients must have a reciprocal relationship of trust, and both parties must uphold this trust. Just as clients must accept financial commitments and enter into honest conversations about the expectations for a building, architects have the responsibility to be ethical and honest with their powers of persuasion. Although contractual agreements have changed through history, examples of how architects have sometimes promised more than could be delivered have been revealed in structural failures. The large spanned interior space of the *Hagia Sophia* in Istanbul is a case in point. The dome fell in 563 AD after an earthquake, and it also required repair following collapses in the ninth and fourteenth centuries.[96] A contemporary example is the new town of Tianducheng, China's version of Paris: like many new theme towns, it remains largely unoccupied. Although they may reflect China's modernization, ideas that work well in theme parks designed for entertainment may not translate into viable concepts for contemporary living.[97]

The tasks of convincing a client of specific siting, organization, materials, or processes should be assumed with as much knowledge as possible. Designing for future environmental conditions, by always considering sustainable materials and processes, is a way architects can demonstrate responsibility. Building codes guide minimum standards of construction, and architectural societies stress the importance of honest and ethical behavior. However, there may be a gray area

Persuading

Figure 4.13 Hagia Sophia (Istanbul, Turkey). Source: Marion Schneider and Christoph Aistleitner Self-published work PD-self.

between truth and seduction. Perhaps seduction should not always be viewed negatively. In many cases, seduction techniques, verbal or visual, not only assist in securing a commission but also help establish in the client pride and enthusiasm regarding the prestige and value of their project.

Today, globalization has put into question the powers of seduction. "Starchitects" have been commissioned to design Western-style buildings all over the world, often without consideration for climate or local cultural traditions. The competition to build the tallest skyscraper adds prestige to countries trying to establish reputation and status. These architects are able to persuade future clients, but their spectacular and flashy buildings are often seductive in their own right. Architects must recognize and understand their seductive powers and must be responsible not to present false images or arguments.

Presenting false images or arguments is fundamentally different from forceful convincing. For instance, propaganda is biased communication that promotes a specific view. Although they can be false or exaggerated, one-sided messages are constantly used in mass media advertising. Journalists believe that news stories should be objective, whereas propaganda controls transmissions that assume and manipulate opinions. Although since the 1940s the term *propaganda* has developed negative connotations, it can be used to promote healthy living, for example, with a campaign to floss your teeth. It is the responsibility of architects to promote their opinions about design, especially since their stances are based on facts and

105

Figure 4.14 Propaganda poster "Your Motherland will never forget". Source: CC-PD-MarkPD-Art (PD-old-70) PD 1923.

experience. On the other hand, architects must be judicious regarding how they supply clients with information that informs clear and reasoned decisions.

Have the characteristics of architects changed in regard to persuasion? The ancient Greeks' invention of the goddess Peitho indicates that persuasion was a critical aspect of their society. Rhetoric was important in a democracy that needed an educated population to debate policy issues. It remains critical today. In the past, architecture as a profession needed to present to clients and builders and they are still required to do so today. Similarly, the need to publicize and develop marketing strategies to secure commissions is equally relevant.

Is this characteristic of persuasion and seduction inherent in the nature of architects? Obviously, some people are born with charismatic personalities, and some of these may enjoy the reasoning involved in building and may choose to enter the discipline of architecture. Schools of architecture hone soon-to-be architects' skills in presentation and argument. The public jury, or review system, helps these future architects practice how to verbally justify a design project. The design studio, also, teaches graphic skills preparing students to present their projects in the best possible light.

But in the end, architects must have the conviction of their beliefs so they can advise others, and these convictions must be based on solid research and reasoning. Since these convictions lead to trust, it is important to understand how architects use conviction as a function of trust. This discussion reminds architects that they need to be trusted (by those they work with), be trustworthy (responsible and ethical), and trust in their media (not to ignore its messages). Thus, it is in the character of architects to be persuasive.

As architects recognize their abilities to persuade, they remain inherently builders. Building involves making—assembling productively. Through a consideration of the concept of *fabricating*, we will explore the fact that it is in the nature of architects to make.

Notes

1 Garrit Confurius, "Editorial," *Daidalos* 64 (15 June 1997): 10–11.
2 See Kendra Schank Smith, *Architects' Sketches; Dialogue and Design* (Oxford, UK: Architectural Press, 2008).
3 Amy C. Smith, "Political Personifications in Classical Athenian Art" (Ph.D. thesis, Yale University, 1997), 86.
4 On many Greek friezes and vases, Peitho can be seen attending Eros and Aphrodite.
5 *Oxford English Dictionary*, s.v. "rape."
6 Amy C. Smith, "Athenian Political Art from the Fifth and Fourth Centuries BCE: Images of Political Personifications," in *Dēmos: Classical Athenian Democracy*, ed. C.W. Blackwell (*The Stoa: A Consortium for Electronic Publication in the Humanities* [www.stoa.org], edd. A. Mahoney and R. Scaife), January 18, 2003. Available at: www.stoa.org/projects/demos/article_personifications?page=1&greekEncoding=, accessed September 10, 2017.
7 Smith, "Political Personifications in Classical Athenian Art," 83.
8 *Oxford English Dictionary*, s.v. "persuade."
9 Patricia Bizzell and Bruce Herzberg, eds., *The Rhetorical Tradition* (Boston, MA: St. Martin's Press, 1990), 2.

10   Lee Morrissey, "Toward a Rhetoric of Architecture," Proceedings of the 87th Association Collegiate Schools of Architecture Annual Meeting, Minneapolis, MN (1999): 358.

11   Bizzell and Herzberg, *The Rhetorical Tradition*, 2.

12   Ibid., 1–2.

13   Ibid., 29.

14   Aristotle, *The Art of Rhetoric*, trans. John H. Freese (Cambridge, MA: Harvard University Press, 1926), 17.

15   Vitruvius, *On Architecture*, trans. Frank Granger (Cambridge, MA: Harvard University Press, 1983), 35.

16   Morris Hickey uses the translation "Durability, Convenience, and Beauty." Frank Granger translates the terms as "Strength, Utility, and Grace."

17   The following reflects research assistance from Jessica Stanford, Nicole Rutherford, and Elijah Karlo Sabadjan.

18   *Oxford English Dictionary*, s.v. "logos."

19   See Sextus Empiricus, *Against the Grammarians,* trans. D.L. Blank (Oxford, UK: Oxford University Press, 1998).

20   Antonia Tripolitis, *Religions of the Hellenistic-Roman Age* (Grand Rapids, MI: William B. Eerdmans Publishing, 2002), 378.

21   Aristotle, *The Art of Rhetoric*, 17.

22   Aristotle, *Politics by Aristotle*, trans. Benjamin Jowett (2012), Book 1, Part 2. Available at: http://classics.mit.edu/Aristotle/politics.1.one.html, accessed August 14, 2017.

23   Karsten Harries, "The Ethical Function of Architecture," *Journal of Architectural Education* 29(1) (1975): 14–15.

24   Gregory Caicco, *Architecture, Ethics, and the Personhood of Place* (Hanover, NH: University Press of New England, 2007), 27.

25   William M.A. Grimaldi, "A Note on the Pistis in Aristotle's Rhetoric," *American Journal of Philology* 78 (1972): 58, cited in Mary P. Nichols, "Aristotle's Defense of Rhetoric," *Journal of Politics* 19(3) (1987): 657–677.

26   Juhani Pallasmaa, *The Thinking Hand* (New York: Wiley, 2009), 148.

27   Arthur Erickson, "Untitled," October 2000. Speech presented at McGill University School of Architecture, Montreal, Quebec.

28   Barbara Breitenberger, *Aphrodite and Eros: The Development of Greek Erotic Mythology* (Kindle Edition, Routledge, 2013), 121.

29   *Oxford English Dictionary*, s.v. "metaphor."

30   Linda Hutcheon, *A Theory of Parody* (New York and London: Methuen, 1985), 2.

31   Robin Evans, *Translations from Drawing to Building and Other Essays* (Cambridge, MA: MIT Press, 1997), 153–193.

32   For a theory of signs, see Charles S. Peirce, *Philosophical Writings of Peirce* (New York: Dover, 1955), and Umberto Eco, *A Theory of Semiotics* (Bloomington: Indiana University Press, 1976).

33   Richard Wittman, "Architecture Parlante – An Anti-rhetoric?," *Daidalos* 64 (15 June 1997): 13.

34   Evans, *Translations from Drawing to Building and Other Essays*, 153–193.

35   Eco, *A Theory of Semiotics*, 214; original emphasis.

36   Wolfgang Meisenheimer, "The Functional and the Poetic Drawing," *Daidalos* 25 (15 September 1987): 119; original emphasis.

37   Morrissey, "Toward a Rhetoric of Architecture," 357.

38   Ibid.

39   Ibid., 358.

40   Aristotle, *Poetics*, trans. Malcolm Heath (London: Penguin Classics, 1997), 1459a4.

41   Manfredo Tafuri, *The Sphere and the Labyrinth: Avant-Gardes and Architecture From Piranesi to the 1970s* (Cambridge, MA: MIT Press, 1987), 31–37.

42 Albert C. Smith, *Architectural Model as Machine* (Oxford, UK: Architectural Press, 2004), 100–101.
43 Ibid.
44 R.G.A. Buxton, *Persuasion in Greek Tragedy: A Study of Peitho* (Cambridge, UK: Cambridge University Press, 2010), 32.
45 George Santayana, *The Sense of Beauty, Being the Outline of Aesthetic Theory* (New York: Collier Books, 1961), 23.
46 Plotinus, *On Beauty*, trans. Stephen MacKenna (Boston, MA: Charles T. Branford, 1918), *Ennead* 1.6.
47 Monroe C. Beardsley, *Aesthetics from Classical Greece to the Present* (Tuscaloosa, AL: The University of Alabama Press, 1975), 80–83.
48 Ibid., 93.
49 Ibid., 125.
50 Ibid., 43.
51 "The Dimensions of the Parthenon," www.metrum.org/key/athens/dimensions.htm, accessed June 14, 2016.
52 Beauty and truth have also been connected to function. In the *Xenophon*, Socrates claims "that objects are beautiful if well made to perform their function" (Beardsley, *Aesthetics from Classical Greece to the Present*, 42). This claim supports the idea that what is most beautiful is beneficial, "and in the idea that it is what pleases through hearing and sight; perhaps beauty is 'beneficial pleasure'" (Plato, *Statesman. Philebus. Ion*, trans. Harold North Fowler and W.R.M. Lamb, Loeb Classical Library No. 164 (Cambridge, MA: Harvard University Press, 1925), 303e; cf. Plato, *Lysis. Symposium. Gorgias.*, trans. W.R.M. Lamb, Loeb Classical Library No. 166 (Cambridge, MA: Harvard University Press, 1925), 474d).
53 K.G. Pontus Hulten, *The Machine as Seen at the End of the Mechanical Age* (New York: The Museum of Modern Art, 1964), 9.
54 Ibid.
55 John Ruskin, *The Seven Lamps of Architecture* (New York: Dover Publications, 1989), 34–69.
56 Alberto Pérez-Gómez, *Built Upon Love; Architectural Longing After Ethics and Aesthetics* (Cambridge, MA: MIT Press, 2008), 207.
57 Alberto Pérez-Gómez, "Imagining a Future," *Arkitektur Norway*, June 6, 2014; original emphasis, http://architecturenorway.no/questions/histories/perez-gomez-memory/, accessed June 14, 2016.
58 Kenneth S. Rothwell, Jr., *Politics and Persuasion in Aristophanes' Ecclesiazusae* (Leiden, the Netherlands: E.J. Brill, 1990), 29.
59 *Oxford English Dictionary*, s.v. "seduction."
60 Ibid.
61 Buxton, *Persuasion in Greek Tragedy*, 37.
62 *Oxford English Dictionary*, s.v. "charm."
63 Baldwin E. Smith, *Egyptian Architecture as Cultural Expression* (New York: Appleton-Century Co., 1938), 61.
64 Noah Charney, *The Art Thief* (New York: Washington Square Press, 2007), 306–307.
65 Ernst Kris and Otto Kurz, *Legend, Myth and Magic in the Image of the Artist* (New Haven, CT: Yale University Press, 1979), 58.
66 Eco, *A Theory of Semiotics*, 215.
67 For more information on this subject, see H.W. Parke and D.E.W. Wormell, *Delphic Oracle: The History, Volumes 1 & 2* (New York: Blackwell Publishers, 1956).
68 Bizzell and Herzberg, *The Rhetorical Tradition*, 38.
69 Robert Wardy, *The Birth of Rhetoric* (London: Routledge, 1996), 2.

70 Ibid.

71 Bizzell and Herzberg, *The Rhetorical Tradition*, 38–39.

72 Ibid., 41.

73 Confurius, "Editorial," 10.

74 Ibid., 10–11.

75 Wolfgang Meisenheimer, "The Functional and the Poetic Drawing," *Daidalos* 25 (15 September 1987): 111.

76 The *King James Version New Testament Greek Lexicon* is based on Thayer's *Greek Lexicon of the New Testament* and Smith's *Bible Dictionary*, plus others; it is keyed to the large Kittel's *Theological Dictionary of the New Testament*.

77 *Oxford English Dictionary*, s.v. "trust."

78 "The sketch is ideally suited for capturing the fleetingness of an idea," Werner Oechslin, "The Well-Tempered Sketch," *Daidalos* 5 (15 September 1982): 103.

79 Precision and imprecision can be viewed as a paradoxical statement, but things can be precise at the same time as they are imprecise. The ambiguity of an idea can often be perfectly clear. By the use of the word precise, it is inferred that the images need not be "realistic"; their abstract qualities may reveal more—realism itself being difficult to define.

80 Play as a philosophical concept is described as "give and take," representation, repeatability, a way of gaining knowledge, and the ability to loose oneself in play.

81 *Oxford English Dictionary*, s.v. "sketch." A definition of sketches includes two aspects of the sketch: "to give the essential facts or points of, without going into details. . .as preliminary or preparatory to further development."

82 Judith Robinson-Valery, "The Rough and the Polished," *Yale French Studies* 89 (1996): 59–66.

83 Morrissey, "Toward a Rhetoric of Architecture," 358.

84 Ernst H. Gombrich, *Art and Illusion* (Princeton, NJ: Princeton University Press, 1984), 29.

85 See Elizabeth Rawson, *Cicero: A Portrait* (Ithaca, NY: Cornell University Press, 1983), and H.J. Haskell, *This was Cicero: Modern Politics in a Roman Toga* (New York: Alfred Knopf, 1942).

86 Bizzell and Herzberg, *The Rhetorical Tradition*, 3–7.

87 David Summers, *Michelangelo and the Language of Art* (Princeton, NJ: Princeton University Press, 1981), 103.

88 Bizzell and Herzberg, *The Rhetorical Tradition*, 3–7.

89 Ibid.

90 *Oxford English Dictionary*, s.v. "style."

91 Bizzell and Herzberg, *The Rhetorical Tradition*, 3–7.

92 Ibid.

93 See Richard Kearney, *The Wake of the Imagination; toward a postmodern culture* (London: Routledge, 2003).

94 Filarete, *Treatise on Architecture*, trans. John R. Spencer (New Haven, CT, and London: Yale University Press, 1965), 296–317.

95 Film available at: https://ca.video.search.yahoo.com/yhs/search?fr2=piv-web&p=big+architects&hspart=rogers&hsimp=yhs-rogers_001#id=3&vid=82738b75bc020d2c15e6ad4061f3952f&action=view, accessed September 10, 2017.

96 Marvin Trachtenberg and Isabelle Hyman, *Architecture; from Prehistory to Postmodernity* (New York: Harry N. Abrams, 2002), 171–172.

97 "Familiar Theme: China's Copycat Cities," *Blueprint Magazine*, January 22, 2014, www.designcurial.com/news/familiar-theme-4163306/, accessed June 25, 2016.

Chapter 5

Fabricating

This chapter will discuss how it is part of architects' character to understand, and engage in, fabrication. The exploration will address the myth of the Greek god Hephaestus, who was known for construction and fabrication. This is instructive because, without a solid understanding of fabrication, architects cannot successfully build. Fabricating can be defined as constructing or manufacturing something, especially from prepared components. There is another part of the definition of the word that is troubling since it also means to invent or concoct, typically with deceitful intent—to falsify or fake.[1] Traditionally fabricating and technology have had a close relationship and, at some time periods in history, they have meant the same thing. The story of Hephaestus, as told by ancient Greek authors such as Homer, Hesiod, and Plato, offers a means to understand the importance of fabrication.

Hephaestus was the Greek god of blacksmiths, metallurgy, sculptors, fire, volcanoes, building, and fine arts. He was responsible for crafting some of the most iconic relics of Greek mythology. Born to Zeus and Hera, Hephaestus was deformed and suffered from a club foot.[2] He was initially shunned by his parents and the other gods and, as a result, he was thrown off Mount Olympus. Because of this deformity—some authors write that it was the result of an injury sustained in a fall, while others suggest a birth defect—he was also designated the god of lameness. At the end of the stories from Hesiod and Homer, he was saved by the Sintians and grew up at the base of a volcano on Lemnos, eventually developing a great understanding of the properties of fire, which led to proficiency in metalworking and blacksmithing.[3] Many of the gods sought out Hephaestus to craft iconic armor, machines, and handicrafts for them. Often these instruments and objects were responsible for their great triumphs, as well as for creating disparity amongst them. His skill, displayed in examples of jewelry and metalwork, became so well-known that he regained recognition and the acceptance of the gods, despite his imperfections. Hephaestus also built palaces for the gods celebrating the importance of his role as a contributor to civilization.[4] Building on the idea of civilization as aiding human development, Hephaestus experimented with creating life when he made the first human woman, Pandora, and his self-operating machines called automatons.[5] This chapter will examine various aspects of Hephaestus' story to gain an understanding of architects' characteristic relationship to fabrication.

Aristotle in his groupings of knowledge used the term *praxis* to mean the practical knowledge that emerges from fabricating something. The Enlightenment philosopher Giambattista Vico echoed this belief when he wrote

Figure 5.1 **Hephaestus as depicted in** *Vulcano forjando los rayos de Jupiter*, Peter Paul Rubens, 1636 (Madrid, Spain). Source: Prado Museum, PD-Art (PD-old-100).

verum ipsum factum (one may know that which one has made), and this concept reflects how the act of producing increases the understanding of an object. It may translate for architects to *you trust what you make* (if it is possible to equate knowing with trusting).[6] In *On Architecture*, Vitruvius' discussion of the education of an architect included the following statement:

> So architects who without culture aim at manual skill cannot gain a prestige corresponding to their labors, while those who trust to theory and literature obviously follow a shadow and not reality. But those who have mastered both, like men equipped in full armour, soon acquire influence and attain their purpose.[7]

The important connection between the theory and practice of technology can present an analogy for a pervasive problem created by how people use technology. In ancient Greece, builders were primarily craftsmen. Writing in first-century Rome, Vitruvius' view on this subject was very different from that of the ancient Greeks, since he recognized that the ability to successfully fabricate was only part of being an architect. Vitruvius understood that architects without a solid education cannot hope to develop an architectural theory that is not merely an illusion. His reference to theory and practice may be translated into the *why* and the *how* of fabricating architecture. Through asking *why,* architects can define the reasoning and meaning behind their constructions since answering this question requires design intention. The *how* of architecture may involve the craft and techniques of fabricating a construction. These two related but fundamentally different terms may assist in understanding more about architects' relationship with fabricating and, thus, demonstrate aspects of their character.

Technology is often referred to as double-sided, or as a *double-edged sword*. This emerges from the assumption of its ability to improve people's lives and also because it inherently holds the potential to be destructive. When faced with this dual nature, architects should consider their relationship to technology and their role as either technicians or technologists. A technician is a person who maintains a machine and thus is responsible for ensuring it runs smoothly (the craftsman). In contrast, the technologist is a person who invents the machine, the one who conceives it, understands its meaning, and develops it (the architect as educated craftsman). Although architects must be knowledgeable regarding craft, their primary role is to be technologists. Technology provides the means for architects to fabricate, manufacture, and construct buildings. To understand the differences between what the craftsman and architect are fabricating, it is important to explore how these creations affect society.

The nature of this discussion questions the role of architects as mere craftsmen while at the same time they are the educated conceivers of future buildings. Educated architects, who know construction and materials, can imbue their architecture with meaning and present expressive and inspired buildings. This discussion presents five character traits of architects that include: *architect as craftsman* (technician), *architect as flawed*, *architect as fabricator* (technologist), *architect as inspired inspirer*, and *architect as critical thinker*.

Architect as Craftsman

The person who crafts something is intimately knowledgeable about the construction and workings of that thing. Traditionally architects have needed skills of craftsmanship to fabricate or manufacture buildings.[8] Here the relationship between material, technique, and form merges with the traditional importance throughout history of crafted things being useful or practical.

As mentioned earlier, Hephaestus was the most prominent craftsman in Greek mythology, possessing the skills necessary to fabricate useful things for the gods. The fact that he is known as the god of blacksmiths, sculptors, and metallurgy reflects his breadth of skill. In his workshop, suitably located at the base of a volcano, Hephaestus, along with his twenty bellows, produced much of the equipment and weaponry used by the gods. Specifically, mythology presents Hephaestus as the craftsman of various relics such as Hermes' winged helmet and sandals, the Aegis breastplate, and Achilles' armor and shield that would aid him in the Trojan War.[9] Homer related the process Hephaestus used to make the famous shield, writing that he began with a basic shield and added gold, bronze, and tin, displaying his skill in metalworking with his elaborate decoration of its face:

> The first thing he created was a huge and sturdy shield, all wonderfully crafted. Around its outer edge, he fixed a triple rim, glittering in the light, attaching to it a silver carrying strap. The shield had five layers. On the outer one, with his great skill he fashioned many rich designs.[10]

With his evident skills as a metalworker, Hephaestus can be understood as a craftsman. The word *craftsman* is defined as a worker who is skilled in a particular

Figure 5.2 **Ancient Greek craftsman.** Source: *The Saturday Evening Post*, no known copyright restrictions.

craft.[11] Other definitions include reference to fabricating objects of great beauty through mastery in various fields.[12] Throughout history, *craftsmanship* has been related to activities that require particular skills in making things such as ceramics, furniture, and woven objects. Use of the term *skills* implies that craftsmanship depends upon the process of making as it relates to an object's meaning.[13] Before the Industrial Revolution, craft was achieved through the skill of the hand: "The words 'craft' and 'craftsmanship' not only referred to the quality of the making, but they also assumed the skilled hand was the source of this quality."[14] Thus, the term *craft* suggests that objects can be described by their quality (or their "well-made-ness" as described by the author Howard Risatti) although, today, it is considered that quality objects may be made by hand or by machine.[15]

When discussing the traditional role of craftsman, David Pye in *The Nature and Art of Workmanship* describes the pre-determined activities of workers as the "workmanship of certainty."[16] The use of the term "certainty" implies that this practical knowledge is the remaking of things that have been previously conceived, similar to how a technician works. The Arts and Crafts movement of the early twentieth century revered things made by hand and was against objects made by machines, although William Morris had no objection to machines crafting objects as long as the result was of high quality. He referenced the Middle Ages where craftsmen took pride in their products. Architects will recognize John Ruskin's concern for truth in materials in relationship to craft.[17] He wrote that architectural elements should be well-crafted, that wood should not be painted but instead be left natural, and that structure should express function.

The Bauhaus, a German art school, established in 1919 by Walter Gropius, successfully united fine arts and craft, creating an approach to design.[18] Parallel to the Arts and Crafts movement, the Bauhaus emerged at a time when the aftermath of the Industrial Revolution caused artists to reject less expensive manufactured products. Gropius called for a program of study that brought architecture, sculpture, and painting into a unified creative expression. It reconsidered the divide between the "fine" and the "applied" arts, suggesting some techniques can be taught and others emerge from creative imagination.[19] This plan was in effect to establish a new guild of the craftsman. In this experiment, although students enrolled in workshops such as pottery or carpentry, they did not rely on precedent to learn. Instead, they were expected to collaborate and contribute to creative thinking.[20] The important focus of the Bauhaus was to integrate the skill of craft with inspiration. This notion raises the question that if designers use an abstract process and only draw their designs, there may be a disconnect between them and what they are constructing. The difference between craftsmen and designers may lie in their processes. Craftsmen, traditionally, have constructed one-of-a-kind objects, whereas designers may engage in production and create multiples of their design.

Howard Risatti references David Pye and writes of a more contemporary interpretation of craftsmanship as the "workmanship of risk." He uses the word risk to mean that the outcomes of the process are uncertain.[21] The "workmanship of risk" would be

. . .workmanship using any technique or apparatus, in which the quality of the result is not predetermined, but depends upon the judgment, dexterity, and care which the maker exercises as he works. The essential idea is that the quality of the result is continuously at risk during the process of making.[22]

This risk may be viewed as the creative imagination in the act of design. That is, the creative imagination and the skilled hand are not necessarily separated but, rather, work together to comprise a design plan. Howard Risatti in his book *A Theory of Craft* interprets Aristotle's category of *poiēsis*, to mean knowledge that is involved in the making, producing, or creating something.[23]

Thus craftsmanship should be seen as existing within the realm of *poiēsis* because technical skill and creative imagination come together in craftsmanship to bring the thing into being as a physical-conceptual entity. Craftsmanship, like *poiēsis*, should be understood as a creative act in which actual physical form is brought together with an idea/concept.[24]

Craftsmanship and our ability to fabricate has been directly related to the foundation of architecture. To understand the relationship between craftsmanship and architecture today, it is important first to understand the theoretical beginnings of the role of a craftsman. The first constructed shelters were mostly likely built stressing the importance of craft. The basic necessity for housing is often presented as the first architectural construct. The primitive hut is often used as a starting point in analyzing the evolution of architectural form.[25]

The hut is a simple construction of wooden sticks that are joined to achieve a shelter. The act of building this hut indeed required craft, even at the most basic level, with the simple joinery of wooden supports to the roof structure. The first joints, as Gottfried Semper describes, were done through the knot.[26] Architectural theorist Joseph Rykwert expanded on this analysis by writing that "Semper foreshadows his later reference to the knot as the essential work of art. . .when he considers the term *Naht*: the seam, the joining."[27] Here the simple act of making a knot, which connects elements of the hut together, is *craft* that is beautiful in itself.[28] The achievement of this joint requires craftsmanship and displays an early technological advancement. The craftsmanship of joints is a fundamental concept of architectural expression.

As the craft of joinery was developing through experimentation with building materials, architectural detailing, as a function of craft, added expression to buildings. The work of the Italian architect Carlo Scarpa demonstrated the development of the relationship between craft and architecture. His architecture reveals a close tie to the masons, carpenters, glassmakers, and smiths of Venice, and his buildings speak directly to Venetian craftsmanship.[29] As a result, he displayed craftsmanship in his work, as he presented an architecture that is more than just "rational structure and functional spaces, but rather a work that seeks expression through its making."[30] Here craft is not being used to simply achieve a function, but to serve aesthetically as well. Scarpa's buildings display how he, as an architect concerned with craftsmanship, is not simply focused on fabricating something

Figure 5.3 Detailing in Brion Tomb, Carlo Scarpa, 1978 (Treviso, Italy). Source: PD Italy (20 years after creation).

functional, but rather, as Richard Sennett describes, on "the desire to do a job well for its own sake."[31]

To summarize, at various periods in history, craftsmen, as those responsible for construction, were dependent on common technological knowledge and manifested it in their work. Craftsmen possessed all the knowledge necessary for fabricating a building. Craftsmanship and building maintained a close relationship because skilled craftsmen were essentially the only ones to construct architectural works. This relationship changed, beginning in ancient Rome when architects assumed responsibility for the design of buildings beyond construction techniques.[32] Since the Industrial Revolution, the role of architects as craftsmen has diminished, as technology has been able to provide the necessary craft involved in construction.

Architecture has always had a tenuous relationship with technology, since it provides ease of construction but reduces the importance of craftsmanship. The Greek gods needed Hephaestus because he was a skilled fabricator, but his limited knowledge meant that he was flawed. Many writers such as Vitruvius attempted to rectify this deficiency by recommending that architects are not craftsmen alone, but that they balance theory and practice. It is understood that inspired buildings require this balanced relationship between craftsmanship and knowledge of theory, and many architects are currently designing with the art of fabrication in mind. As architects recognize Hephaestus' flaw, it is important for them to maintain a connection to the character of the craftsman in contemporary practice.

Architect as Flawed

Architects possess many skills and talents, but they are also human and thus have flaws in their character. Hephaestus was a craftsman/technician who constructed palaces for the gods and forged armor and objects from precious metals. However, to Greek society, his flaws meant that he was incomplete. The story of Hephaestus may allude to a greater, more fundamental deficiency in the role of craftsmen. Again, we are reminded of the writings of Roman architect Vitruvius, who stated that complete architects must understand both theory and practice. Hephaestus displayed excellent skills as a craftsman, but he did not possess the education or intellect to be an architect.

Greek mythology presents two different accounts as to how Hephaestus developed his deformities. His imperfections were said to have been either present at birth, or a result of his banishment and subsequent fall to earth.[33] In Hesiod's *To Pythian Apollo*, Hera says:

> But my son Hephaestus whom I bore was weakly among all the blessed gods and shriveled of foot, a shame and a disgrace to me in heaven, whom I myself took in my hands and cast out so that he fell in the great sea.[34]

This implies that Hera, ashamed of her son's deformed foot, was responsible for throwing Hephaestus from Mount Olympus. In another version presented in *The Iliad*, Hephaestus described his rejection by Zeus:

> On a time before this, when I was striving to save you, he caught me by the foot and hurled me from the heavenly threshold; the whole day long I was carried headlong, and at sunset, I fell in Lemnos, and but little life was in me.[35]

Hephaestus then remained on the island of Lemnos and learned the skills of a blacksmith. After years as a smith, his legs were lame but "his neck and chest, however, were strong and muscular."[36]

The ancient Greek gods typically assumed human form and lived in a society similar to human society. Hephaestus exhibited many of the same emotional traits as the human Daedalus, such as love, hate, envy, greed, and the need for revenge. The Greek gods were not omniscient or all-knowing, since they could be tricked. Still, they were invulnerable, as is evidenced by the fact that Hephaestus lived in a volcano and was able to withstand the heat of his forge. They were immortal, and each used their super-human powers to their advantage, to punish or reward, in their particular field of expertise. The possession of superior power, invulnerability, and immortality must have been highly seductive to the ancient Greeks. For instance, the fact that Hephaestus was flawed did not diminish Daedalus' compelling desire to be like him in his hold over technology.

The story of Hephaestus' deformity illustrates ancient Greek society's respect for perfection (especially in their gods), as Hephaestus was an embarrassment to his parents and the other gods. Looking into his role as a craftsman may reveal why he was so disrespected. Ancient Greek craftsmen made extensive use of special effects through mechanical contrivances. The Greek people's amazement at the magic of these special effects may have caused them to overlook the negative connotations of these false impressions, the mistaken perception of reality that they presented.[37] It may be one reason Plato, the classical Greek philosopher, so degraded and devalued craftsmen and artists as technicians. To him, they were mere makers of images, fabricators or manufacturers of shadows and illusions, and purveyors of make-believe, and he placed them and their work in the lowest level of his divided line of knowledge.[38] The art historian Moshe Barasch further explains this situation:

> The low regard in which artists were held in the classical period is amply attested. The sculptor or painter was called a "banausos," that is a mechanic. In a broader context, the term carried the meaning low and vulgar. Burckhardt traced the derivation of this attitude towards the visual artist to the alienation of classical Greek society from any manual work. The sculptor and painter, working with their hands, are merely mechanics. Even among the Gods, Hephaistos, blacksmith and armorer (and thus some divine projection of the artist), is a limping and sooty figure; he plays the cuckold and evokes laughter. As mechanics, artists are excluded from any participation in higher realms of values. To Plato, the poet and the musician are inspired, and inspiration is transmitted even to the bards who only recite the poet's songs, but sculptors and painters are seen as working solely according to the established rules of mechanics.[39]

To further elaborate, we are reminded of Plato's famous Allegory of the Cave and the problems with fabricating the shadows that represented illusions. The prisoners never saw sunlight: they viewed only the flickering shadows of real objects cast upon the cave wall. If the prisoners left the cave and entered into sunlight, they would see the reality of the objects previously perceived only as shadows. Plato, the philosopher, did not trust the craftsmen's ability to make correct interpretations of the "flickering shadows" that influenced the use of technology. He felt that the world perceived by Greek craftsmen was not the real (true) world. In contrast to the fabricated falsehoods of the craftsmen, he believed in a real realm of perfect, unchanging, eternal ideals or forms, which are known only through the intellect. To Plato, craftsmen were capable of fabricating illusions without understanding the meaning of their constructions. Thus, the ability to correctly interpret the relationship between the two realms (the shadowy illusions and the reality of things seen in the light of day) had to be developed through gaining philosophic knowledge of the true, the good, and the beautiful, something that is necessary for developing decisions affecting society.[40]

It is possible that Plato viewed the craftsman's deficiency—his limited ability to interpret—as something that hampered their ability to develop, and their potential for reaching an elevated status in society. To rectify this, Plato proposed rigorous discipline, a high level of education and talent that seemed to be absent from the backgrounds of Daedalus, and also Hephaestus. Hephaestus and Daedalus are often discussed interchangeably by various chroniclers of mythology, although one was a god and the other a human.

The craftsmen architects of various periods in history, such as ancient Greece or the Middle Ages, did not question the dominant style (or paradigm), even though they reached a high level of expertise in their craft. They were not responsible for decisions about how buildings reflected society and culture. Their buildings remained remarkably the same over centuries; the Greek temple form changed slowly, as evidenced by the *Apollo Temple at Bassae* and the *Parthenon*. Another example of religious architecture is the shape of the Cambodian stupa, which also remained the same over many hundreds of years.

As would be expected with vernacular architecture, traditional Japanese houses may provide an example of skilled craftsmen who were not able to define their society's ideals. Here again, the basic building type saw small changes over the centuries but remained significantly the same. The layout and construction techniques used to build Japanese houses were consistent, reflected in such traditional details as wooden lattice façades and the proportion of tatami mats. Although the craftsmen of this period in Japan achieved an extremely high level of skill, their buildings reflected their culture but did not help to define it. They were not able to make significant changes to an existing paradigm.

It is important to recall that the gods threw Hephaestus to earth. We may ask if the act of forcing him out of the heavens was a way for the Greeks to explain how, because he was imperfect, he fit better into the human world. Although Prometheus is credited with giving fire to humans, this story of Hephaestus could also explain how humans acquired technology. It is reported that he forged the chains that bound Prometheus to a rock. Since myths are often analogous, this story could also suggest the benefits and dangers of technology. The era of craft gave way to the era of technology, and current trends suggest that it is the character of architects to be technologists.

Architect as Fabricator

Because architects depend on technology for design and construction, it is in their character to engage its various uses. The story of Hephaestus offers a good analogy to discuss how ancient Greek architects engaged fabrication. Hephaestus was known for building palaces for the gods, using the technology of construction that focused on assembly. As a blacksmith, jeweler, and manufacturer of armor, he employed technology in a traditional fashion to transform natural materials into useful objects. He harnessed the power of fire to light spaces and to provide heat for food preparation, thereby encouraging civilized society.

The meaning of the word *technology* has evolved. In the ancient Greek language, *tekhne* meant art or craft, and the addition of *logos* added the dimension of system or study.[41] This definition of technology is displayed in the myth of Hephaestus. The word technology was not in common use before the seventeenth

Figure 5.4 Traditional Japanese house form. Source: Albert Smith, CC-BY-SA-2.5 Self-published work.

and eighteenth centuries, a time when its meaning was similar to its original Greek, a study of the arts.[42] It was with the advent of the Industrial Revolution that its meaning changed to reference the study of production in the mechanical or industrial arts.

Hephaestus' use of materials and assemblies to fabricate palaces for the gods may present a common analogy for building of the past. Craftsmanship had long been understood as pride in the art of hand-making objects. In regard to historic architecture, craftsmanship involved stacking masonry units or carving trees into beams and columns. The machines employed to construct buildings, such as cranes, forklifts, and fastening machines, are a basic, and traditional, form of technology. Even the materials themselves represent technologies, as they have been developed and crafted. Hephaestus was a blacksmith and he, through the transforming qualities of fire, was able to change ore into steel and to use heat to form these metals into objects such as armor. In relationship to architecture, Robert Meagher finds that "*Technê* is making something into something it is not."[43] Meagher identifies the "essential principles of *technê*: that it is conscious, willful, materially violent, and materially productive."[44] The forging of steel sections is an act of violence using heat to form building components. Today, "'technology' has come to describe the overall system of machines and processes, while 'technique' refers to a specific method or skill."[45] Philosophers define technology as "that constellation of knowledge, processes, skills and products whose aim is to control and transform."[46] This comprehensive description "encompasses both concrete forms (products or artifacts) and abstractions (knowledge, processes, and goals)."[47] Martin Heidegger wrote:

> . . .from the earliest times until Plato the word *technê* is linked with the word episteme. Both words are names for knowing in the widest sense. They mean to be entirely at home with something, to understand or to be an expert in it.[48]

Heidegger is suggesting that *technê* is the name not only for the activities and skills of the craftsman but also for the arts of the mind. Other authors including Marshall McLuhan have seen technology as guiding social change; Jean Baudrillard has compared it to a function of simulacra.[49] However, the term technology has been overused to apply to everything in our lives, describing objects made by living things and also ordered systems.[50] Nevertheless, it is true that contemporary technology and machines are changing the way architects interact with building processes.

Philosophers use the word *machine*, but what do they mean by it? Albert Smith writes: "A machine is generally considered to be something with a practical purpose, a device that substitutes for or extends mankind's own forces. The word itself has the same etymological root as 'might.'"[51] It comes from the Latin *machina* and the Greek words *mechane*, meaning devices or contrivances for doing a thing, and *mechos*, meaning "the means" or "the way by which something is expedited."[52] So, machines work for us and make our lives easier but also hold the potential to be destructive. The *machine* is a metaphor for the systems and

Figure 5.5 The destructiveness of technology as displayed by the "Baker" explosion at Bikini Atoll, 1946. Source: PD US Military.

processes of technology. This is an important concept for architecture since architects may ask: are we just maintaining the status quo or are we being innovative and questioning what our fabricating machines represent?

Recent philosophers have concluded that technology is not neutral. Although it may not determine an outcome, it constitutes the foundation for that outcome.[53] The word *neutral* implies that while people may employ technologies (specifically machines) for good or harm, machines are not intrinsically evil. However, some machines can be used only for destruction, such as bombs or machines that pollute the air, and thus they are not neutral. In a postmodern analysis, Félix Guattari refers to "*machinic* thought" as the flows of ideas about globalization.[54] Guattari suggests that everything is interactive. A sense of networking means that everything is implicated in what he calls complexity and "everything is a machine, in the sense that everything is involved in assemblages that form and unform with this complexity."[55]

With the concept of digital, cybernetics, and cyberspace, architecture has experienced change regarding new ideas enabled by the computer. The shift from a mechanical paradigm to a digital one may be one reason why defining what is true and what is not (fabricating can mean a falsity) has become difficult to do. This shift raises questions about authenticity, reality, and the relationship between the artist and the real object. Misunderstanding the concepts of this current paradigm can compromise the main role of the architectural profession: to translate the meanings of our society into form.

The meaning of the *digital* is aligned with the emergence of interconnections, communication, and interaction and it is still not well understood. According to John Frazer, "Our emerging new worldview is characterized as decentralized, desynchronized, diverse, simultaneous, anarchic, customized."[56] He also writes that there has been a shift from a world of objects to one of relationships, and one from linear relationship to one of complex webs.[57] This complexity can be related to the possibilities of immersivity, virtual reality, interactivity, and tactility—ideas that are linked to the concepts of projection of "mind and hand into screens."[58] This space where minds are connected is cyberspace. It is the space where interactivity happens, as a parallel experience to communication. The existence of this new digital place, seemingly connected directly to the human mind, has expanded the possibility of performing multiple tasks, thus allowing greater diversification. The digital allows or opens space, to a different kind of fabrication. In the absence of prescribed tasks before digital fabrication, the computer assumes an important role in the creative process. Kostas Terzidis explains:

> Computerization is about automation, mechanization, digitization, and conversion. It involves the digitization of entities or processes that are preconceived, predetermined, and well defined. In contrast, computation is about the exploration of the indeterminate, vague, unclear, and often ill-defined processes; because of its exploratory nature, computation aims at emulating or extending the human intellect. It is about rationalization, reasoning, logic, algorithm, induction, extrapolation, exploration, and estimation.[59]

In the construction process, the possibilities of machine automation and 3D printing initiated a system called *file-to-factory* (first explored in architecture by Frank Gehry). A computer-constructed form is transferred immediately to a factory where 3D printers and CNC machines begin manufacturing building components.[60] In this method of production, the craftsman is less involved in fabricating by hand, and there is less human input in construction.

Although Hephaestus was lame, the physical labor required of him in his forge resulted in the development of his muscular neck and chest. The development of his upper body strength can be viewed as an analogy. Possibly Hephaestus was attempting to overcome his deficiencies as an uneducated craftsman by expanding his abilities. This over-compensation may have had as its result that he used his skills with technology to nurture human civilization.

Hephaestus was credited with initiating a system of order because, in the act of civilizing, his ability to fabricate helped move people from cave dwelling into constructed communities. Homer wrote about the ramifications of this civilization:

> Sing clear-voiced Muses, of Hephaestus, famed from inventions. With bright-eyed Athene, he taught men glorious crafts throughout the world— men who before used to dwell in caves in the mountains like wild beasts. But now that they have learned crafts through Hephaestus, the famed worker, easily they live a peaceful life in their own houses the whole year round.[61]

Hephaestus was recognized for defining the cosmos, an orderly harmonious and systematic universe:

> Hephaestus over the craftsman [is] a bringer of peace and a maker of civilization. . .More than a technician, the civilizing craftsman has used these tools for a collective good, that of ending humanity's wandering existence as hunter-gatherers or rootless warriors.[62]

Thus, Hephaestus reflects the ancient Greek craftsmen as technicians and fabricators, but historian Richard Sennett assigns him an even more significant role, considering his responsibility in establishing civilization.

Hephaestus, in making habitations for people, may have used his technology in a manner similar to that discussed by Félix Guattari: the mechanism is at a global scale and is omnipresent. In using technology for civilizing, Hephaestus gave the word new meaning. As the philosopher Jean-François Lyotard believed, "new technologies affect both the production and transmission of knowledge."[63] This notion of knowledge production and dissemination concerns architects who are responsible for the discipline of architecture and for defining what is meaningful in society. Architects' character engages these artifacts of meaning. Marco Frascari wrote in his book *Monsters of Architecture: Anthropomorphism in Architectural Theory* that "The essence of *techne* is by no means technological. *Techne* belongs to the notion of *poiēsis*, which reveals or disclose *aletheia*, the truth."[64]

Architect as Inspired Inspirer

Architects imbue their buildings with meaning in other ways than providing quality craftsmanship. It is in their character to ensure that their buildings are inspirational. It is important to question architects' intentions and to ask if we are fabricating falsities and not revealing the inspiration of our architecture. Greek society created the mythology of the gods as a means to explain a confusing world, and Hephaestus served as a reflection of their view of technology. Again, in his role as a god, it was reported that he fabricated automata (in the form of golden maidens) to assist in his forge. It is well known that in Greek mythology there were similarities and differences between the gods and humans, as in the case of Hephaestus and Daedalus. The significance of Daedalus being human may be closely tied to his ability to create. Daedalus is said to be the inheritor of *metis*, which is the "practical intelligence" and the "wisdom of craftsmanship in the Athenian tradition."[65] His knowledge of craftsmanship makes him "an ancient culture-hero almost of the calibre of Prometheus, for he sought to rival creation itself."[66] Aristotle stated that "incorporeal souls are a primal creation," but Daedalus as a human being was reported to have given life to lifeless machines.[67] These examples emphasize the importance of Daedalus as a human creator, in contrast to a deity like Hephaestus.

Daedalus' abilities to create came with consequences. The design of his wooden cow resulted in a monster that required confinement within the labyrinth, a creation that eventually forced him to flee Crete. Fabricated wings facilitated Icarus' flight but led to his fall and death.[68] Since "myths are the instruments by which we continually struggle to make our experience intelligible to ourselves," the story of the human Daedalus challenging creation may serve as a reminder of the consequences of disobeying the rules set by divinities or, in reality, by nature itself.[69] Since the time of the ancient Greeks, there have been problems with technology creating illusions or "falsifying divine truth."[70] Therefore, Daedalus' stories depict the dangers of over-confidence by humans in the use of technologies.

Humans have always wanted to fly. This desire is demonstrated by myths across different cultures, but its realization is usually confined to divine characters.[71]

Wings with their "power, mobility, and speed" are a symbol of "the unearthly, the superhuman and the divine."[72] The story of Daedalus' flight represents a "new phenomenon" because he fabricated the wings himself.[73] Ovid wrote in *Metamorphoses* that the scene of Daedalus and Icarus flying appeared like the "presence of divinities" to the fishermen or shepherds on the ground.[74] Daedalus' skills allowed him to challenge the laws or limitations imposed on humans by the gods and brought him closer to the realm of the divine.[75]

Daedalus' ability to animate statues through mechanical means (he is credited with carving lifelike sculptures with open eyes and separated legs) demonstrates his ability to *rival* a god.[76] For this reason, some regard him as "the first modern man," who was "exposed to the universal and age-long reprobation of humanity to whom biological inventions are abhorrent."[77] His story anticipates the controversy concerning the creation of artificial humans in modern society, which some consider "tampering with living nature."[78] It is important to explore one of Hephaestus' most critical powers: that ability to create life which was extrapolated by Daedalus into the fabrication of automata. It is similarly in the character of architects to inspire their buildings with *life*.

History provides examples of analogies of God, or a god, to the ultimate architect. In mythology, it was Hephaestus who created the first humans from clay, and he was also said to have made Pandora, as well as the life-size golden maidens that assisted in his forge. He additionally created fire, consequently referred to as the "breath of Hephaestus." It is only logical, given all these acts, that Hephaestus be considered the ultimate creator, the inspirer of life.

The word *inspire* means to cause something to happen or to be created. Its definition also comprises causing a feeling or emotion. The word *spirit* emerges from the Latin *spiritus* or breath, literally meaning breath of life, in particular, that bestowed by a deity. When a person receives inspiration, it means to breathe in the spirit; thus, to be inspired can mean to be guided or directed by a divine influence.[79] The fabrication of automata was an attempt to produce artificial life. The word *automata*, the plural of *automaton*, is from the Greek *automatos* and means self-acting.[80] When a thing is animated, it is endowed with breath or a soul. In the case of humans, this means to bring to life. To automate in the case of automata means to endow with the ability to act in a fashion that is inspired. To be brought to life as a human, and to be automated as a work of architecture, are two different things. However, making a comparison between them may help explain the importance of making inspired architecture.

Throughout history, automata have fascinated philosophers and architects in the search for divinity. Automata and robots have traditionally been fashioned after the human body, demonstrating human characteristics and performing human activities. The seventeenth-century philosopher Descartes, in his search for a rational life, was reported to have built the automaton Francine. She demonstrated the division between a mechanical body and a human spirit. While the human body could be precisely measured, the spirit in its abstraction is difficult to quantify.

In 1818, Mary Shelley's story *Frankenstein; or The Modern Prometheus* introduced a rational scientist discovering the secret of bestowing life. The automaton, closely resembling a man, revealed itself to be a monster that destroyed everyone

Figure 5.6 **Very humanlike doll, Centre International de la Mécanique d'Art, late nineteenth century (Sainte-Croix, Switzerland).** Source: Centre International de la Mécanique d'Art, CC BY-SA.

Figure 5.7 **Earliest illustration of Frankenstein's Monster, frontispiece of first edition of Mary Shelley's** *Frankenstein*, **1831.** Source: CC-PD-MarkPD OldPD-Art (PD-old default) PD-Art (PD-old).

dear to him. It was the absence of a complete soul in Dr Frankenstein's creation that was responsible for its transformation into a monster.[81] The story is an indictment of the failure of science to completely define the full measure of mankind. Other literary works, such as the play *Rossum's Universal Robots* by Karel Čapek, address the dehumanization of mankind in a technological civilization.

The quest to understand artificial life is a recurring theme in films, such as Steven Spielberg's *A.I.*, a contemporary Pinocchio story in which a robot aspires to become a human being. The representation of machines as people has always exerted fascination not only as a *marvel* but also because the existence of automata poses an important question about the differences between humans and human-appearing machines. It was considered sacrilegious that these were humans in physical form only, created by humans but without complete souls.[82]

While architecture obviously does not possess bodily life, it can reflect the spiritual life of humans. It should demonstrate an understanding of a culture's place in the world, and inform society about the current condition of the human spirit.

Buildings are constructed to accommodate people, and people have traditionally been used as a measure for buildings. The Classical body of humanism reflected human geometry, for example Leonardo da Vinci's Vitruvian Man. Michelangelo's buildings considered the body in motion but did not copy the human body's form.[83] Architects of the Romantic period viewed buildings as reflecting human emotions and sensations.[84] Architects have long represented human qualities in their buildings. In a conversation with Louis Kahn, John W. Cook and Heinrich Klotz question whether he had implied that a building has a mind. Kahn answered, "the building has not mind, but it has the quality to respond to the mind."[85] Similarly, W.R. Lethaby writes that "architecture, then, interpenetrates building, not for satisfaction of the simple needs of the body, but the complex ones of the intellect."[86] Architecture can thus be perceived as a form of mechanism that animates people's thinking and brings them pleasure, creating a reality that connects the senses with the physical world.[87] Marco Frascari described this concept when he stated, "If we consider architecture to be a machine that is analogous to the human mind, then buildings exemplify and suggest rather than determine or impose."[88] Buildings as inanimate objects can also be understood as being *inspired*, containing life, or being *animate* as they enrich humans' experience of architecture.

Toward the end of the Modernist period, two buildings designed by the French architect Le Corbusier, *Notre Dame du Haut*, in Ronchamp and the *La Tourette* monastery, stand out as expressing the spiritual in architecture. The exceptional treatment of light and space in these religious buildings provides animating features. As chronicled in the *Mécanique Spirituelle* by Richard Moore, Le Corbusier in his later years began to embrace spirituality in his life and also his buildings.[89] Moore reveals how Le Corbusier shifted his attention toward symbolism in his sketches and graphic work, as he emphasized light. These two buildings demonstrate how he utilized dramatic lighting effects and undulating forms to give his architecture *spirit*. Angled skylights focus and reflect light that is often modulated with color. The slit windows separating the walls from the roof accentuate an inside/outside environment. The textured concrete formwork on the walls is

Figure 5.8
Convent Sainte-Marie de La Tourette, architect Le Corbusier, 1959 (L'arbresle, France). Source: CC-BY-SA-3.0.

contrasted by smooth floor surfaces. Walls that slant and flow allude to caves or a womb, and provide a narrative of emotions and meaning to inspire inhabitants.

If architecture is to be more than simply shelter from the elements, it must be infused and inspired with meaning. Ancient Greek society understood that architecture should demonstrate an understanding of the cosmos, and inform its inhabitants about the current condition of the human spirit. Craftsman (with the responsibility to build) may have been unable to inspire their fabrications. Thus, the character of Daedalus was flawed, just as Hephaestus was imperfect.

Being inspired, or being the inspirer, involves not only being animated but also being elevated to the realm of the soul. The search for the soul through representation compels the human mind to engage the spiritual, although not necessarily the religious. Throughout history, architecture has served not only to provide for our physical comfort and safety but also to fulfill our spiritual needs. Our current and future architecture should reflect this goal. It has been demonstrated that it is in the character of architects to be inspired and to inspire what is fabricated. This ability to inspire requires the talents of critical thinking.

Architect as Critical Thinker

The ability to infuse architecture with spirit requires architects to be educated, and thus able to be critical of what they construct. Hephaestus was credited with teaching his skills to mortal artists. It is generally accepted in Greek mythology that his wise character was similar to that of Athena, the goddess of wisdom. As a craftsman, he was not necessarily learned, but his connection to wisdom most likely was a result of his experience (know-how and familiarity) with crafting both objects and buildings. To succeed in contemporary practice, architects have the responsibility to be educated in a wide variety of disciplines. This education can help them to gain knowledge and to avoid being deceived by illusions that obscure the higher realm of truth. Knowledge provides a foundation for them to become critical thinkers who can analyze, reflect, and foster innovative solutions to complex design problems. The critical-thinking aspect of the character of architects is what allows them to utilize fabrication as a means to achieve their design intention.

Just as technology can be misused, Hephaestus' crafting skills did not always lead to positive results. He was ordered by Zeus to sculpt Pandora out of clay to take revenge on Prometheus and mankind.[90] Delivered to Prometheus' brother Epimetheus, Pandora was cunning and deceitful.[91] After Epimetheus had accepted the gift from Hephaestus, he recalled that Prometheus had warned him not to accept anything from Zeus. But it was too late. Pandora opened her jar of evils, some of which were muted by Zeus, to bring diseases, plagues, and misery upon mankind.[92] Human beings suffered in "hostile silence" and were helpless because they had not foreseen the arrival of the muted evils.[93] This myth may serve as an analogy for the misleading illusions that can be created through misuse of technology. Without the education and ability necessary to assess the use of technology and fabrication in the design process, architects may be susceptible to downfalls.

As discussed in Chapter 3, architects have throughout history pursued various aspects and types of education. Again, Greek architects were master builders who controlled construction but did not participate in design or the conception of new architectural paradigms.[94] Vitruvius in his *On Architecture* advocated for Roman architects to be educated craftsmen trained in both theory and practice, and to be proficient in various fields of knowledge.[95] The Renaissance architect Leon Battista Alberti reinforced the idea of the educated craftsman by suggesting that architects are craftsmen who must be of the "highest learning," in other words, an educated person.[96]

The requirement for education that results in knowledge has remained essential to the profession of architecture. It is necessitated by their primary responsibility of translating meanings of society into buildings, as well as by the need to make thoughtful decisions. A broad education comprising such different disciplines as philosophy, history, and social science allows architects to understand all the relevant influences involved in a design. Only with this knowledge can architects synthesize all factors into a meaningful design. Education forms the foundation of critical thinking, something essential to the act of creating as it involves understanding and questioning previous tenets. Critical thinking requires reasoning and the ability to re-assess, and so architects' education must help them acquire sound judgment. They must also remain mindful that Hephaestus could be tricked; if architects possess the ability to question the meaning and implications behind their creations, they can avoid dangerous and misleading illusions as they fabricate.

Figure 5.9 **Pandora and Pandora's Box.** Source: Private Collection of John William Waterhouse, PD-Art (PD-old-auto).

The ability to critically reflect on the use of technology is especially important today. As mentioned earlier, advancements in fabrication are changing the process of conceptualization to production. Authors of computational design, Dan Willis and Todd Woodward have established that much of the technological developments in today's architectural practice originated in the engineering industry, where functionality and economic feasibility are often more important than meaning or symbolic content.[97] Over-reliance on complex computational techniques to guide decision making distances the designer from an "immediate understanding of the consequences of their actions."[98] Because of the computer's ability to perform complex calculations beyond human capacity, computation has the potential to usurp the designer's role in exploring the undefined in the design process. For instance, parametric modeling is one area of technological development that is currently influencing architectural practice. It involves the input of "mathematical descriptions of certain geometric relationships" to generate design output.[99] At the start of the design process, parameters of the design are defined, as opposed to specific, fixed shapes developed through sketching. When different values are assigned to the parameters, a broad range of design opportunities can be generated and explored, an option that is not possible for the human mind within the same time frame.[100]

The systematic approach of parametric design ensures efficiency and is theoretically capable of computing an infinite number of design options.[101] However, its "unambiguous" modeling cannot address those "qualitative and unmeasurable qualities" such as materiality, context, and spatial qualities that are intrinsic to architectural design.[102] These form a complex web of factors that can be critically analyzed by the human intellect. The intuitive decisions made by the architect that arise from these qualities are irreplaceable, and should not be compromised with the use of technology during the design process. This logical, systematic framework for generating options may also take away from those "serendipitous occurrences," evidenced in variations in local craftsmanship, that can introduce layers of richness into a design.[103]

Architects may question how new developments in fabrication are affecting the image of contemporary architecture. One of these developments is mass customization, which enables the "mass production of individually-customized goods and services" with "increase in variety" but without "increase in costs."[104] Theoretically, it promises the production of better designs with unique parts and components at affordable market prices, benefiting more end-users.[105] However, the implications of mass customization on architecture require critical assessment. By making difficult and costly details more accessible, mass customization may devalue the status of architectural details.[106] Marco Frascari described details "as the minimal units of signification in the architectural production of meanings."[107] If details are primarily driven by ease of assembly and economic feasibility, rather than by their narrative or expression, then the meaning signified by these units becomes questionable, or worse, no longer existent.[108]

The use of technology without critical thought and consideration can potentially create illusions that prevent designers from understanding the real implications of their design. Architects should not only know how to fabricate using technology but also possess the theoretical background that enables them to critically assess what they are creating. The capabilities of technology should be used to enhance the design intent, rather than hinder the decision-making process. In the end, architects as critical thinkers are ultimately responsible for determining what is to be achieved with the use of technology. Furthermore, architects are responsible for preventing their architecture from becoming mere formal, functional, or economically driven objects, without a cultural or spiritual role. Architects must be mindful of the fact that, as technologists and not solely as technicians, they must be reflective and critical thinkers who are not fooled by illusions.

Conclusion

Using the myth of the Greek god Hephaestus, this chapter illustrated various aspects of the evolving relationship between architects and their technology. As the god of craftsmanship, fire, building, and fine arts, Hephaestus' role was analogous to that of architects who not only are proficient in fabricating but also pursue expressive qualities through the art of construction. The stories of Hephaestus identify the dualities evident in his character, specifically that he had the skills of craftsmanship, but also carried the burdens of his deformities. The dualities of Hephaestus' character can be illustrated through several examples.

Hephaestus produced useful objects that were viewed to be beneficial, as well as producing works of great malevolence. He was said to have presented his mother, Hera, with a golden throne as an expression of gratitude towards the offer to allow him back onto Olympus. However, once seated, the throne trapped her and subsequently she was required to negotiate her release. This story of revenge reveals the negative, or unattractive, aspects of Hephaestus' personality. Although he utilized technology to transform objects around him that improved conditions for humankind, he was in some ways vindictive. His story should stand as a warning to architects as they employ technology to construct buildings, transforming materials into inhabitable spaces.

Hephaestus was a talented technician, but his lack of education meant that he never quite received respect from the other gods. For this reason, he never reached the exulted state of technologist/inventor as Hermes did. He certainly had skills to fabricate (practice), but because he was uneducated, he was not able to engage theory, unlike architects. His imperfections and deformities indicated his lack of education, and it is a similar lack that separates the craftsman from the architect. Hephaestus worked primarily alone in his forge but was nevertheless credited with establishing civilization, since it was he who built the first dwellings. Although he crafted Pandora and automatons, he had a limited ability to foresee the ramifications of his actions. The automata were animated, but they were limited in their usefulness since they only served as attendants in his forge. They had *life* but did not possess independent thinking.

Hephaestus' creation of Pandora demonstrates the falsities that can be created with technology, and thus the importance of education and critical thinking in overcoming potential illusions. The duality of Hephaestus' character exemplifies

Figure 5.10 Hephaestus and automata. Source: Wenzel Hollar, CC-PD-Mark-old-100-1923PD-Art (PD-old-auto-1923).

the nature of technology as a double-edged sword that can both improve lives and cause destruction. Viewing Hephaestus as an analogy, it is possible to understand the influences of technology on fabrication, which recognizes the importance of education as a driver for inspired work.

The use of technology to create inspiring architecture brings us to a discussion of tectonics in architecture. The term *tectonic* originates from the Greek word *tekton,* meaning builder or carpenter. The term led to the word *architeckton* or master builder, and the definition of *tekton* eventually broadened to encompass aesthetic qualities.[109] Tectonics in its definition pertains to the science of construction.[110] Architectural theorist Kenneth Frampton stated that *tectonics* has a poetic dimension which reveals the "spiritual value" of built objects.[111] In a further definition, Robert Maulden writes that "tectonics is primarily concerned with the apparent self-consciousness of a building with respect to its construction."[112] Evidently, as architecture is an art of craft and construction, tectonics constitutes a critical role in defining not only the appearance—that is, the physical form—but also the "metaphysical presence" of the creation as manifest in the construction details.[113] Technological advancements such as parametric modeling give rise to innovative opportunities which may lead to new "systems of signification" that reflect the complexity of the current built environment and contemporary practice.[114]

To engage tectonics in their designs, architects need full understanding of the technologies that enable construction, and of the materials and techniques involved. At the same time, architects must be continually conscious of the expressive power of their constructions. Architect Patrick Schumacher defines tectonics as "the architectural selection and utilization of technically motivated, engineered forms and details for the sake of an articulation that aims at legibility."[115] Tectonics, as Schumacher stated, is the result of the integration of technology with "architectural articulation" to fulfill the "social function" of architecture. It is important to note that technology remains subordinated to the overall intention of the work since tectonic expression is not an end in itself, but is driven by conscious decisions to reconcile technical requirements with the architectural narrative.[116] Having the character to engage critically in fabrication ensures that the use of technology is always driven and governed by architectural intentions.

Being able to employ technology for fabrication requires both theory and practice. As discussed previously, Vitruvius stated that architects without proper understanding of craft and construction are incomplete. At the same time, craftsmen without education and knowledge are prone to developing architectural theories that are mere illusions distant from reality. Individuals who are immersed in the newest technologies without questioning their true implications may find themselves merely following trends. Architects must have it in their character to maintain a balance between theory and practice, thereby elevating them from craftsmen to architects who create with intention and conscious decisiveness.

The need to understand and engage with technology is especially important to contemporary practice as technological advancements are greatly influencing the relationship between architects and their designs. Technology now has an increased involvement with the design and thinking process. However, architects should be mindful of the deceptive aspects of technology that may impact the design. Many 3D software programs present the ability to model a virtual simulation of the designer's idea. However, the usage of these technologies should not limit the designer's ability to understand the reality behind what they are modeling. The use of technology should never be a substitute for the thoughtful consideration of forms and the spaces modeled and their relationship with the physical world.

Building Information Modeling (BIM) is currently transforming how architects are involved in the construction processes. Theorist Branko Kolarevic writes that architects today are again assuming the role of the master builder and, with the capability of new technologies, they can now become "information master builders."[117] In the past, there was a separation between design and construction, which mandated the production of drawings to bridge the gap. Architects were removed from the construction process, counter to the traditional role of the master builder assumed by architects in the Middle Ages.[118] With the advancement of BIM, architects can gain "the ability to digitally generate and analyze the information, and then use it directly to manufacture and construct buildings."[119] The re-integration of design with construction, again, emphasizes the importance of maintaining a balance between theory and practice; both are essential in the fostering of architecture that is not only technically feasible but also inspiring.

Hephaestus' creation of the first buildings, and thus of civilization, demonstrates his leadership status. His construction of communities improved the lives of both gods and humans. This is analogous to architects' involvement with urban design and their ability to essentially create order. Hephaestus' usage of his

Fabricating

automata to carry out various functions suggests the architect's position as a leader who can coordinate the numerous trades involved in building. It is clear that Hephaestus was indeed a leader and someone who would be able to orchestrate the various forces involved in a large-scale building project. In the end, architects are also leaders because of their role in defining the future of their society through their buildings. An understanding of both practice and theory is required to be able to explore new areas of design without being subjugated to the illusions of technology. It is only with the conscious use of technology and an understanding of its implications that architects can effectively plan for the future.

Technology, as a system of processes, has influenced the way architects fabricate, from assembly and craft to the digital systems and processes currently utilized in design and construction. This chapter has introduced the ideas of craft and technology, presented its limitations, and then proceeded to explain how these limitations can be confronted with education, resulting in an architecture that is inspired. As the final episode of this book, the chapter examined the tools and strategies which help architects to transform their architectural definitions and images into physical reality, and at the same time highlighted the disparity that exists between designing and fabricating. Furthermore, it emphasized fabricating as a process, making it clear that most buildings cannot be resolved with mere production. The analogy of the Greek gods emphasized the traditional view of the gods as those who bestow gifts on humankind. Hephaestus gave the gift of craft and Athena gave the gift of knowledge. Architects must have the ability to balance these two gifts. The chapter underlined the importance of the balance between theory and practice, both of which are critical not just to the creation of buildings,

Figure 5.11 **Intricacies of the roof structure of Terminal 3, Shenzhen Bao'an International Airport, made possible by parametric design, architects Massimiliano and Doriana Fuksas, 2013** (Shenzhen, China). Source: **CC-By-SA 3.0.**

but to an overall understanding of the field of architecture. Hephaestus and Daedalus help architects to recognize what the gods know, and to understand what they do not, an important ability since architects, as they create environments, are continually attempting to rise to the level of the divine.

We have discussed the character traits essential for architects to possess so that they may successfully engage with technology as they fabricate their designs. These, in contrast to those of craftsmen (skills, concern for a quality product, sensitive use of materials, and experience in construction), must include intention aligned with foresight, an understanding of the innovative aspects of design, the possession of skills to coordinate complex processes, and the ability to be a leader and critical thinker. We have also highlighted the challenges that confront users of technology in contemporary practice. Having the characteristics presented here are conducive to developing good judgment, and the critical thinking essential for leadership. These latter topics will become the focus of the Conclusion of this book.

Notes

1   *Oxford English Dictionary*, s.v. "fabrication."
2   In *The Iliad*, Homer presents Hephaestus as being born with a deformity; his mother, upon seeing his deformed foot, throws her son off of Mount Olympus. Hesiod's version presents his deformity as a result of Hephaestus siding with his mother during an argument, with the result that Zeus throws Hephaestus off of Mount Olympus in rage.
3   Homer, *The Iliad of Homer*, trans. A.T. Murray (Cambridge, MA: Harvard University Press; London: William Heinemann, Ltd., 1924), I.590–594.
4   Ibid.
5   Ibid.
6   Giambattista Vico, *The New Science of Giambattista Vico*, trans. T. Bergin and M.H. Fisch (Ithaca, NY: Cornell University Press, 1968). *Factum* is the artifact and *verum* the truth. Others may translate this saying as there is truth in the constructed artifact.
7   Vitruvius, *On Architecture*, trans. Frank Granger (Cambridge, MA: Harvard University Press, 1931), Book I, Chapter 1.
8   We have considered using gender-neutral language and use of the term *craftsperson*, but since the traditional term is craftsman, we find it difficult to replace it without losing meaning.
9   Homer, *The Iliad*, Book 18, lines 478–608.
10   See Homer, *The Iliad*.
11   *Oxford English Dictionary*, s.v. "craftsman" and "craftsmanship."
12   *Oxford English Dictionary*, s.v. "craft."
13   Howard Risatti, *A Theory of Craft: Function and Aesthetic Expression* (Chapel Hill, NC: University of North Carolina Press, 2007), 14.
14   Ibid.
15   Ibid.
16   David Pye, *The Nature and Art of Workmanship*, eds. James Pye and Elizabeth Balaam (Bethel, CT: Cambium Press, 1995), 17–29.
17   John Ruskin, *The Seven Lamps of Architecture* (New York: Farrar, Straus and Giroux, 1988), 39. Ruskin writes about architectural deceits under three topics: the suggestion of a mode of structure or support, other than the true one; the painting of surfaces to

represent some other material than that of which they actually consist, or the deceptive representation of sculptured ornament upon them; and the use of cast or machine-made ornaments of any kind.

18 See Herbert Bayer, Ise Gropius, and Walter Gropius, eds., *Bauhaus 1919–1928* (Boston, MA: Charles T. Branford Company, 1959); Barry Bergdoll and Leah Dickerman, *Bauhaus: Workshops for Modernity* (New York: The Museum of Modern Art, 2009); and Kathleen James-Chakraborty, *Bauhaus Culture* (London: University of Minnesota Press, 2006).

19 Frank Whitford, *The Bauhaus: Masters & Students by Themselves* (London: Conran Octopus, 1992), 21.

20 See Bayer, Gropius, and Gropius, *Bauhaus 1919–1928*.

21 Pye, *The Nature and Art of Workmanship*, 17–20.

22 Risatti, *A Theory of Craft*, 162–165.

23 Ibid., 167–169.

24 Ibid., 168.

25 See Gottfried Semper and Harry Francis Mallgrave, *The Four Elements of Architecture: And Other Writings* (Cambridge, UK: Cambridge University Press, 1989).

26 Ibid.

27 Joseph Rykwert, "Preface to London Lecture by Gottfried Semper," *RES: Anthropology and Aesthetics*, 6(1983): 125.

28 Also see Marco Frascari, *Monsters of Architecture: Anthropomorphism in Architectural Theory* (Savage, MD: Rowman and Littlefield, 1991), 117–119.

29 Marco Frascari, "The Tell-the-Tale Detail," in *Theorizing a New Agenda for Architecture: An anthology of architectural theory*, ed. Kate Nesbitt (New York: Princeton Architectural Press, 1996), 506.

30 Ibid., 502.

31 Ralf Jeremias, "The Craftsman – By Richard Sennett," *Working USA* 13(1) (2010): 9.

32 Ibid.

33 Homer, *The Odyssey*, Books 1–12, ed. George E. Dimock, trans. A.T. Murray, Loeb Classical Library No. 104 (Cambridge, MA: Harvard University Press), 8.308; Homer, *The Iliad*, 18.397.

34 Hesiod, *The Homeric Hymns and Homerica*, trans. Hugh G. Evelyn-White, Loeb Classic Library Edition (London: William Heineman, 1926), Book III, *To Pythian Apollo*, line 315.

35 T.L. Agar, "Hesiod, the Homeric Hymns and Homerica," Loeb Classical Library (Cambridge, MA: Harvard University Press), *The Classical Review*, 30(01) (1916): 316–321.

36 Homer, *The Iliad*, Book 18, lines 136ff.

37 C.T. Onions., ed., *The Oxford Dictionary of English Etymology* (London: Oxford University Press, 1966), 462.

38 Plato, *Plato: Republic, Volume II*, Books 6–10, trans. Christopher Emlyn-Jones and William Preddy, Loeb Classical Library (Cambridge, MA: Harvard University Press, 1913), 509 to the end of Book VI; the famous example of the couch in Book X should also be considered. Plato argues that there is only one form or idea of a couch. The craftsman initiates this idea making the couch of specific material while the painter produces only the optical appearances of the couch from a certain angle and is twice removed.

39 Moshe Barasch, *Theories of Art, from Plato to Winckelmann* (New York: New York University Press, 1985), 23.

40 Plato, *The Republic*, Book X, 596a–598b.

41 Andrew Murphie and John Potts, *Culture and Technology* (Basingstoke, UK, and New York: Palgrave Macmillan, 2003), 3.

42 Ibid.

43 Robert Meagher, "Technê," *Perspecta* 24 (1988): 159

44 Ibid., 160.

45 Murphie and Potts, *Culture and Technology*, 4.

46 Lorenzo C. Simpson, *Technology and the Conversations of Modernity* (New York: Routledge, 1995), 16.

47 Murphie and Potts, *Culture and Technology*, 4.

48 Albert C. Smith, *Architectural Model as Machine* (Oxford, UK: Architectural Press, 2004), 122.

49 See Jean Baudrillard, *Simulations* (New York: Semiotext(e), 1983), and Marshall McLuhan, *Understanding Media* (London: Abacus, 1974).

50 Arnold Pacey, *The Culture of Technology* (London: Basil Blackwell, 1983), 6.

51 Smith, *Architectural Model as Machine*, 63.

52 *Webster's Third International Dictionary*, s.v. "machine."

53 Murphie and Potts, *Culture and Technology*, 23.

54 Ibid., 30–35.

55 Ibid., 196.

56 John Frazer, "The Architectural Relevance of Cyberspace," in *The Digital Turn in Architecture 1992–2012*, ed. Mario Carpo (New York: John Wiley and Sons Ltd., 1995), 48–56.

57 Ibid.

58 Derrick De Kerckhove, *The Architecture of Intelligence* (Basel, Switzerland: Birkhauser, 2001), 38.

59 Kostas Terzidis, *Expressive Form; A Conceptual Approach to Computational Design* (New York: Spon Press, 2003), 69.

60 CNC (Computer Numerical Control) is the computer automation of machine tools used to fabricate three-dimensional objects.

61 Hesiod, *Hesiod, the Homeric Hymns and Homerica*, trans. H.G. Evelyn-White, Loeb Classical Library (Cambridge, MA: Harvard University Press, 1945), Book XX, To Hephaestus, line 5.

62 Ibid.

63 Murphie and Potts, *Culture and Technology*, 207.

64 Frascari, *Monsters of Architecture*, 117.

65 Alberto Pérez-Gómez, "Myth of Daedalus," *AA Files* 10 (1985): 51.

66 Michael Grant, *Myth of the Greeks and Romans* (London: The Orion Publishing Group, 2011), Chapter 1.

67 Philip Ball, *Unnatural: The Heretical Idea of Making People* (London: The Bodley Head, 2011), 33.

68 Grant, *Myth of the Greeks and Romans*, Chapter 1.

69 Mark Schorer, "The Necessity of Myth," *Daedalus* 88(2) (1959): 360; Tony Ullyatt, "'Impelled by Circumstance': Reflections on Some Connotative Meanings of the Myth of Daedalus and Icarus," *Myth and Symbol* 6(1) (2010): 39.

70 Pérez-Gómez, "Myth of Daedalus," 52.

71 Arthur Milton Young, *Legend Builders of the West* (Pittsburgh, PA: University of Pittsburgh Press, 1958), 141.

72 Ullyatt, "Impelled by Circumstance," 35.

73 Young, *Legend Builders of the West*, 143.

74 Ibid.

75 Ullyatt, "Impelled by Circumstance," 38.

76 Grant, *Myth of the Greeks and Romans*, Chapter 1; Pérez-Gómez, "Myth of Daedalus," 52.

77 Ball, *Unnatural*, 36.

78 Ibid.

79 *Oxford English Dictionary*, s.v. "spirit."

80 The history of automata contains stories of the creation of human-like androids and animals. The first complex machines created by humans were reported to be automata (S.A. Bedini, "The Role of Automata in the History of Technology," in *Technology and Culture*, 5 (1964), 32). For example, King-Shu of China (500 BC) made a flying bird and a wooden horse that were mechanized through the use of springs. Arabs transmitted the tradition from antiquity to the Middle Ages showing automata as marvels at court and medieval fairs. Some of the most famous automata were those created by Jacques Vaucanson in France and Pierre Jacquet-Droz in Switzerland. Vaucanson's mechanical duck was presented in 1738 to the Academie Royale des Science, along with a mechanical flutist and drummer. In 1770, Jacques-Droz presented an automaton of a boy who, it was claimed, could write (K.G. Pontus Hulten, *The Machine as seen at the End of the Mechanical Age* (New York: The Museum of Modern Art, 1968), 21, 10).

81 Mary Shelley, *Frankenstein; or The Modern Prometheus* (New York: Bantam Classics, 1984).

82 Albert C. Smith and Kendra Schank Smith, "Architecture as Inspired Machine," *The Built Environment* 31(1) (2005): 79–88.

83 James S. Ackerman, *The Architecture of Michelangelo* (Chicago, IL: University of Chicago Press, 1961), 41.

84 Marvin Trachtenberg and Isabelle Hyman, *Architecture From Prehistory to Post-Modernism* (Englewood Cliffs, NJ: Prentice-Hall, Inc, 1986), 399.

85 Jules David Prown and Karen E. Denavit, *Louis I. Kahn in Conversation: Interviews with John W. Cook and Heinrich Klotz, 1969–70* (New Haven, CT: Yale University Press, 1973), 206.

86 W.R. Lethaby, *Architecture, Mysticism and Myth* (Mineola, NY: Dover Publications, 2004), 1.

87 Frascari, *Monsters of Architecture*, 36.

88 Ibid.

89 See Richard A. Moore, "Le Corbusier and the Mecanique Spirituelle: an Investigation into Le Corbusier's Architectural Symbolism and its Background in Beaux-Arts Dessin" (Ph.D. thesis, University of Maryland, 1979). University Microfilms International.

90 Hesiod, *Hesiod, the Homeric Hymns and Homerica*, trans. H.G. Evelyn-White, Loeb Classical Library (Cambridge, MA: Harvard University Press, 1915), *Works and Days*, 70–90.

91 Ibid., 75–80.

92 Ibid., 80–95.

93 Katherine Olstein, "Pandora and Dike in Hesiod's *Works and Days*," *Emerita* 48 (1980): 302.

94 J.J. Coulton, *Ancient Greek Architects at Work: Problems of Structure and Design* (Ithaca, NY: Cornell University Press, 1977), 16–21.

95 See Vitruvius, *On Architecture*.

96 Leon Battista Alberti, *On the Art of Building in Ten Books*, trans. Joseph Rykwert, Neil Leach, and Robert Tavernor (Cambridge, MA: MIT Press, 1988), 315.

97 Dan Willis and Todd Woodward, "Diminishing Difficulty: Mass Customization and the Digital Production of Architecture," in *Fabricating Architecture: Selected Readings in Digital Design and Manufacturing*, ed. Robert Corser (New York: Princeton Architectural Press, 2010), 188.

98 Ibid., 190.

99 Ibid., 187.

100 Branko Kolarevic, "Digital Morphogenesis," in *Architecture in the Digital Age: Design and Manufacturing*, ed. Branko Kolarevic (New York: Spon Press, 2003), 17.

101 Ibid., 18.

102 Willis and Woodward, "Diminishing Difficulty," 188.

103 Ibid., 183.

104 Kolarevic, "Digital Morphogenesis," 52.

105 Ibid.

106 Willis and Woodward, "Diminishing Difficulty," 198.

107 Frascari, "The Tell-the-Tale Detail," 500.

108 Willis and Woodward, "Diminishing Difficulty," 207.

109 Kenneth Frampton, *Studies in Tectonic Culture: The Poetics of Construction and Twentieth Century Architecture*, ed. John Cava (Boston, MA: MIT Press, 1995), 3–4.

110 *Oxford English Dictionary*, s.v. "tectonic."

111 Kenneth Frampton, "Rappel a L'Ordre: The Case for the Tectonic," in *Labour, Work, and Architecture: Collected Essays on Architecture and Design* (London: Phaidon Press, 2002), 95.

112 Robert Maulden, "Tectonics in Architecture: From the Physical to the Meta-Physical" (M.Arch. thesis, Massachusetts Institute of Technology, 1986), 11.

113 Ibid.

114 See Patrik Schumacher, "Tectonics – The Differentiation and Collaboration of Architecture and Engineering," in *Stefan Polónyi: Bearing Lines, Bearing Surfaces*, eds. Ursula Kleefisch-Jobst, Peter Köddermann, Katrin Lichtenstein, and Wolfgang Sonne (Stuttgart, Germany: Edition Axel Menges, 2012).

115 Patrik Schumacher, "Tectonic Articulation – Making Engineering Logics Speak," *Architectural Design* 4 (2014): 44–51.

116 Ibid.

117 Kolerevic, "Information Master Builders," 57–59.

118 Ibid.

119 Ibid., 59.

Conclusion

This book has explored twenty-five essential characteristics that have traditionally been fundamental to the identity of architects. It looked to Greek mythology to find a foundation or origin for these traits that have relevance for contemporary architectural practice. However, undoubtedly, there are further traits, not discussed here, which are important to establishing the nature of architects. A few of these are the subjects of this conclusion, and these are the overarching topics that tie the characteristics together as a whole. These topics also could be viewed as foundational for a clarification of the traits.

It is important to return to a discussion of archetypes. They not only are useful for identifying recurring themes in architecture, but also illustrate that the concerns of inhabitants of architecture are similar through history. A discussion of the rational process of critical thinking is a precursor to a discussion of judgment because architects must make wise choices throughout the design and construction of a building. It is important that they make wise decisions since they have a leadership role in defining societies' cosmos. Finally, this chapter will conclude with a discussion of the importance of architects' character to the design process.

Building the Architect's Character: Explorations in Traits began by presenting traits that are innate to architects. The first chapter, "Defining," introduced Daedalus and definition, which set the foundation of the entire book, discussing how architects need to clearly define, to understand and create an architectural measure that a building's inhabitants can engage with, to understand manner and select an appropriate mode to design within, to develop the ability to play with ideas, and to be able to set boundaries. As part of this foundation, Chapter 2, "Imaging," dealt with images and creativity that have traditionally been the purview of artists and architects. The use of the ancient Greek myth of the Muses assisted in recognizing how architects have always employed images for imagination, communication, and presentation. This understanding is important since it should be in the character of architects to demonstrate skills in the use of imagination and creativity. This chapter explored the characteristics of an architect to be inspired, an imitator, and an imaginer or one that creates images, to use *mneme* or memory, and to assume the role of a prophet.

The first two chapters presented a theoretical exploration and concentrated on architectural thinking, while the final two chapters engaged ideas about fabricating the artifacts of architecture. Chapter 3, "Transforming, Transitioning, Translating," presented an evolution from theory to the actions and skills manifest in the production of architecture. Using the myth of Hermes, it investigated the characteristics of an architect as *messenger*, *traveler*, *thief*, *magician*, and *inventor*. Chapter 4, "Persuading," turned to the Greek myth of Peitho, chosen because it offered insight into the characteristics of architects as they persuade both verbally and through their designs. This chapter discussed architects' character as a *rhetorician*, *persuader*, *seeker of beauty and truth*, *seducer*, and *developer of trust*. The final chapter, "Fabricating," used the myth of the Greek god Hephaestus, who fabricated objects and dwellings for the gods, to discuss how it must be in architects' character to understand and engage technology. The characteristics discussed included the architect as a *craftsman*, as *flawed*, as a *fabricator*, and as someone who produces *inspired* work and thinks *critically*. Comparison to the gods illustrated the many traits necessary for success as an architect.

The book has employed various Greek myths to demonstrate the character of architects. Greek mythology not only reflected the local culture of ancient Greece but was also influenced by the Egyptians, Minoans, and other Mediterranean cultures. Because ancient Greek culture has impacted contemporary culture, it may be viewed as foundational to current thinking. Thus, myths provide insight into the typical character of architects today as they represent universal patterns in human nature. Their stories offer a representation of the common and recurring characteristics not only of a specific human culture but of the entire human race.

The responsibility of ancient Greek architects in defining their society was somewhat different than that expected of today's architects. It was valuable to revisit Greek mythology to compare the characteristic traits that were less important for architects during that time but that are currently more relevant. As discussed earlier, although ancient Greek architects had some responsibility for design, they held considerably less influence over defining a building's meaning than contemporary architects do. The expanded influence of contemporary architects reflects their influence as they define society through building a culture's cosmos. For the ancient Greeks, the responsibilities connected with such characteristics existed but were handled by other members of society.

Returning to archetypes reinforces a relationship between the myths of the Greeks and current architectural practice. The concept of archetype can be found in a range of subject areas including behavior, modern psychological theory, and literary analysis. An archetype can be defined as a statement, a pattern of behavior, or a prototype which other statements, patterns of behavior, and objects copy or emulate. It can refer to pure forms which embody the fundamental characteristics of a thing. An archetype can be viewed as a collectively inherited unconscious idea, a pattern of thought, or an image that is universally present in individual psyches. In literature, painting, or mythology, it can be a constantly recurring symbol or motif.[1]

Sir James George Frazer's book *The Golden Bough: A Study in Magic and Religion* discusses how archetypes may occur in seemingly unrelated cases in classic storytelling or media where examples of characters or ideas sharing similar traits can be found. Frazer attempts to define the archetypical elements of religious belief and scientific thought: he discusses fertility rites, human sacrifice, the dying god, the scapegoat, and many other symbols and practices whose influence has extended into twenty-first-century culture.[2] Another example of archetype may be found in Joseph Campbell's study of comparative mythology *The Hero with a Thousand Faces*. In it, Campbell explains his theory of the journey of the archetypal hero as found in world mythologies. He proposes that major myths world-wide that have survived for thousands of years share a fundamental structure. Campbell calls these "monomyths." He summarized the monomyth in the Introduction to *The Hero with a Thousand Faces*:

> A hero ventures forth from the world of common day into a region of supernatural wonder: fabulous forces are there encountered, and a decisive victory is won: the hero comes back from this mysterious adventure with the power to bestow boons on his fellow man.[3]

The concept of psychological archetypes was central to the work of Carl Jung. He believed archetypes are innate, universal prototypes for ideas and may be used to interpret observations. Jung noted that symbols from different cultures are often very similar because they have emerged from archetypes shared by the whole human race. He thought that our primitive past was the basis of the human psyche, directing and influencing present behavior. He influenced the work of many psychoanalysts and psychiatrists such as Jacques Lacan, Wilfred Bion, and Robert Langs. In Part One of *Man and his Symbols*, Jung stated:

> My views about the "archaic remnants," which I call "archetypes" or "primordial images," have constantly been criticized by people who lack a sufficient knowledge of the psychology of dreams and mythology. The term "archetype" is often misunderstood as meaning certain definite mythological images or motifs. But these are nothing more than conscious representations, it would be absurd to assume that such variable representations could be inherited. The archetype is a tendency to form such representations of a motif—representations that can vary a great deal in detail without losing their basic pattern.[4]

To understand the importance of archetype in architecture, it may be instructive to look to the work of English architect and theorist W.R. Lethaby. In the preface to his book *Architecture, Mysticism and Myth*, Lethaby states that he plans "to set out, from an architect's point of view, the basis of certain ideas common in the architecture of many lands and religions, the purposes behind structure and form which may be called the esoteric principles of architecture."[5] In the book, he refers to the mythology, philology, ethnology, anthropology, archaeology, iconography, semiotics, and art history of many ancient cultures.

Contemporary culture exhibits a range of archetypes in films and literature. Possibly the best known of these is the *hero* archetype, one outstanding example being Luke Skywalker in the *Star Wars* movies. The wizard Gandalf from *The Lord of the Rings* offers an example of the mentor archetype. A villain type can be seen in the likes of *Silence of the Lamb*'s Dr Hannibal Lecter, *Psycho*'s Norman

Figure C.1 The Hal 9000 computer from *2001: A Space Odyssey*, directed by Stanley Kubrick, 1968.
Source: CC-BY-SA-4.0.

Bates, or even the deranged computer HAL 9000 in *2001: A Space Odyssey*. The characteristics of architects may be archetypical also, in that traits common to our designing ancestors may continue to some extent into our contemporary society. The fact remains that architects of any generation must be able to think critically, judge and decide, and lead and influence, must have talent, and of course must be able to design buildings.

Critical Thinking

This book has explored topics such as questioning, reasoning, and analysis that can be considered components of *critical thinking*. Skills in critical thinking were important to architects of the past and are continually relevant. The character traits that make architects successful at critical thinking can help them to avoid making poor decisions throughout the design process. It is not necessary to iterate all the literature on the subject, nor to thoroughly explain the research into various methods specific to an established theory of critical thinking. Since the subject of this book is not the design process, but rather the character traits of architects, critical thinking may support our concluding thoughts. Critical thinking may be similar to that employed during the architectural design process. However, it should be questioned when it becomes too formal or restrictive. Architects' design processes are never universal, and are, rather, individual, but all architects understand and utilize the overarching concepts. Thus, there is value in the broad-based ideas of critical thinking.

Critical thinking is a common thread through architects' character traits, and this book has touched on this mode of thinking. Recently, various disciplines have included critical thinking theories in their curriculum in the form of entrepreneurial and creative studies. This form of education has often been referred to as *design thinking* and has been introduced in some business schools to encourage innovation.[6] Critical thinking as a field of study has included systematic approaches to analysis, questioning, criticism, and logical decision making. It may be useful to outline briefly what critical thinking involves.

Critical thinking was founded on the teaching practice of Socrates. He understood that passionate and emotional rhetoric could be lacking in logical and objective thinking. His method emphasized the value of posing meaningful questions before accepting any idea as a belief. As expounded by Plato, it required thinking systematically, thinking that is comprehensive, is well-reasoned, and can withstand rigorous questioning. Thomas Aquinas and, later, such philosophers as Descartes, Hobbes, Locke, and Kant wrote (to varying degrees) about the search for deeper thinking and noted that it involved use of analysis, questioning, and critique. In a similar vein, William Graham Sumner was critical of educational systems that supported conventional thinking. Aside from educational systems, it is easy to understand how peoples' minds can be deceived and how they can accept stereotypes and rationalize false information. Many theories of critical thinking emphasize the importance of systematic thinking that can be analyzed for its "clarity, accuracy, relevance, depth, breadth and logicalness."[7]

Architects have characteristics that assist them to think systematically; it is for this reason that they are talented in design. A comparison between design thinking and critical thinking may reveal how architects make decisions. Critical thinking has five common components. First, it is important to identify the problem. This requires analysis to break the problem down into separate pieces for study or inspection. For architects, this may include questions that come up during the design process. These questions might include: what type of building will I design, where will it be located, who will be its inhabitants, and what is my budget? The subsequent course of action is to gather information, to learn as much as possible and consider possible solutions. The information obtained about a problem and how it was solved in the past can be useful in pointing to possible future solutions. Of course, architects would call these examples precedents. For architects, gathering information might include such things as taking soil samples, referring to local building codes, and speaking with future users of a building. This synthesis of the information requires assembling it to establish a new understanding. The third step is to evaluate the evidence to see what it means. This might require a certain amount of questioning or interpreting of the information at hand. It would be wise for architects to develop this habit to avoid making costly or dangerous decisions based on erroneous information. The fourth step involves considering various solutions to the problem. This step can be related to the idea of problem-solving, a term used in many disciplines, sometimes with different perspectives. Typically, at this stage, architects would look at a series of different but logical possible solutions. They could create a series of sketches or study models to more clearly see which possible solution is best to address the issues. Since it is impossible to know everything, architects would most likely use *abductive* reasoning to decide on the most appropriate solution. Abductive reasoning is a term that originates with the philosopher and semiotician Charles Sanders Peirce.[8] Recognizing that there are things we will never know completely, Peirce viewed abduction as a form of logic where humans can utilize data and establish a hypothesis that attempts to explain the importance of evidence. Abduction can be interpreted as educated guessing.[9] Once you know as much relevant information as possible, you need to draw conclusions based on your interpretation of the facts, and on what is reasonable to assume. This involves the ability to make well-thought-out decisions based on information gained from the earlier steps. To be successful at this stage requires sound judgment and the ability to implement the chosen solution. For architects, good judgment is a challenging concept and one that requires character.

Judgment and Decision Making

When architects design, they are making a *mark*. For example, they mark out where a wall should be placed or a ceiling located. By using sound judgment, architects can choose the best solution from many possibilities. To judge is to form an opinion about something through careful weighing of evidence and the testing of a premise.[10] Judgment concerns making balanced or just decisions.

Similar to judges, architects are required to make wise and responsible choices. It is a character trait of architects to be first critical, and then decisive.

The first chapter, when discussing definition, alluded to how boundaries act to establish parameters for judgment. Choosing, by definition, is the mental process of judging the merits of various options and selecting one or more of them. This is what architects do when they design.[11] Architects are continually required to make important decisions that directly affect the way people will live, and the many decisions made throughout the design process must support this responsibility. Essential to the discussions of *imaging* and *persuading* is an awareness that making choices is necessary to understand what is being explored and its intended meaning. Chapter 5 also included an underlying subtext that questioned the critical use of technology in *fabricating*. Making good decisions requires confidence, clear thinking, and reasoning. In fact, architects' abilities to use good judgment in making decisions engages, and is supported by, an amalgamation of all the character traits we have discussed and is one of the most important skills an architect can possess.

In our discussion of character and good judgment, it was necessary to introduce the concept of ethics. Our concern is primarily with ethics as it pertains to character, and how character, in turn, affects good judgment. Again, ethics are described as "the moral principles by which a person is guided."[12] However, today making ethical judgments in the design process may be more difficult. Good judgment and the ability to be critical may rely on the character of architects to interpret, especially when the rules of the profession are constantly changing and architects are being called upon to make decisions when solutions are less clear. The use of new technologies, materials, and processes and trends toward globalization and specialization may be influencing architects' ethics and critical judgment.

One reason to hire architects is that they possess the good judgment required for the many choices involved in creating a building. Today, architects are faced with far greater choices than in the past. With the end of Modernism came the possibility of many new and unusual ways to think about and build architecture. New forms of architecture began to redefine the profession of architecture even as it shaped society. Buildings become part of an exchange of diverging views about what architecture, as well as society, is. In other words, architects were given more responsibility to use their judgment to design buildings, remembering that they have a leadership role as they are responsible for protecting humans and designing good spaces for them to live, work, and enjoy. As such the profession of architecture has assumed an increasingly greater responsibility for protecting the health, safety, and welfare of the public.[13] The profession has responded to these issues with expanded requirements for the registration and licensure of architects. The expanded requirements have made it clear that a professional attitude is essential when listening to clients, programming required spaces, ensuring that projects are finished on time, observing confidentiality, giving objective advice, fully informing everyone, making a complete set of drawings, utilizing new information systems, and implementing all the other ethical practices that are expected of architects today.

In a consumerist, media-rich world where money and power can confuse citizens regarding ethical behavior, it remains architects' duty to judge clearly and decisively on what is right—and this takes character. Good judgment keeps the profession relevant. Architects should ask how to remain relevant in a new era of changes that include globalization and specialization. As has been established, ethical behavior and good judgment are relative. Architects should be able to adequately criticize and interpret the environment and be judicious regarding their manipulation of it. Criticism and interpretations should be based on ethical judgment.

Leadership and Influence

Architects should be leaders and, as was discussed earlier, as such they influence the environment. When others view an architect as a leader, it may mean that they see him or her as someone with commanding authority or influence. Leaders have certain powers, among them the ability to influence others and to influence society. Certainly, architects traditionally have maintained authority over other workers on a site. They have the ability, in varying degrees, to influence the lives of inhabitants through building designs. It is this aspect of leadership through influence and its connection to the character of the architect that will be discussed in this section.

Once again, an excellent example of an architect as an influential leader comes from ancient Egypt. Serving as an example for future architects was Zoser's High Priest, Imhotep, the first recorded architect and the designer of the *Pyramid of Djoser*. In many ways, Imhotep set the standards for all Egyptian architects. He attained the position of chief architect, ascending to the peak of the governing hierarchy. Imhotep was highly influential in his roles of scribe, astronomer, magician, and healer.[14] Interestingly, it was as a healer, not as an architect, that he was later deified. Known for his great wisdom, architecture was merely one of the many fields of learning he commanded.[15]

Imhotep's broad background was not far removed from the education recommended centuries later by the Roman architect Vitruvius. To reiterate, the influence of ancient Greek architects on their society was considerably less than that of Imhotep or the ancient Romans. Architects in ancient Greece were not considered to be members of the highest class and, certainly, were not in the same class as the philosophers. The historian J.A. Bundgaard advances the theory that Greek architects did not, strictly speaking, design buildings. This may explain why not a single Greek architectural drawing survives from this time. According to Bundgaard, both the form and the construction of Greek temples were traditionally pre-determined sufficiently for the architect only to need to settle specific construction issues on the site.[16] It appears that many important design decisions made were not made by Greek architects.

There was not much praise for architects in ancient Greece. Even though they rose above the level of common craftsmen, none ever attained the influence or high position of the Egyptian priest/architect Imhotep. The mysterious and divine roles maintained by Egyptian architects bonded the Egyptian state architects to a ruling class; this relationship was not evident in the straightforward world of Greece. It was perhaps because buildings had mixed and confused authorship that those who practiced architecture were not prone to be lionized by the public.

Vitruvius points out that Roman architects had a different relationship to their society than did those of ancient Greece. Though still influenced by tradition, Roman architects were allowed a greater freedom in developing their designs. This new freedom required an expanded liberal education, something that was necessary in order to overcome difficulties that arose when interpreting designs. This greater ability to interpret also allowed Roman architects, through their buildings, to have an increased influence on establishing broad definitions of the Roman cosmos. This may be the reason why Roman architects maintained a higher social standing than that of their Greek counterparts.

Vitruvius believed that the training of the ideal architect depended on upon many disciplines and arts. Like the Greeks of the Golden Age, he recommended a balanced middle course for the architect, with some exceptions. Vitruvius wrote that an architect should be a person of letters, a skillful draftsman, a mathematician, familiar with historical studies, a diligent student of philosophy, acquainted with music, not ignorant of medicine, learned in the responses of jurisconsult, and familiar with astronomy and astronomical calculations.[17] He described the necessity for an architect to combine the knowledge gained from a broad education with craft. This education was necessary to become a leader in society. In fact, this education allowed Vitruvius not only to write his famous book, written to influence Caesar Augustus, but also to understand what was lacking in Greek architects.

The Renaissance architect Leon Battista Alberti offers a good example. Alberti, like Vitruvius, believed that architects should be more than mere craftsmen. He writes:

> Him, I consider the architect, who by sure and wonderful reason and method, knows both how to devise through his own mind and energy, and to realize by construction, whatever can be most fitted out for the noble needs of man, by the movement of weights and the joining and massing of bodies. To do this, he must have an understanding and knowledge of all the highest and most noble disciplines.[18]

The requirement for a broad-based education for architects remains relevant today. In many ways, such an education could well be an architect's most important characteristic. We can point out individuals who influenced architecture without possessing any manual craft skills. For instance, Abbot Suger (1081–1151) influenced the creation of Gothic architecture. As a child, he showed a high level of intelligence and was brought to the nearby Abbey of Saint-Denis to receive an education from the monks. Suger chose to remain at the Abbey, eventually becoming abbot of St. Denis and right-hand man of both Louis VI and Louis VII.[19] Anne Rockwell believes that it was his responsibility for rebuilding of the choir of St. Denis (1135–1144) that crystallized in a single moment the elements which designate Gothic architecture:

It is believed that he was the inspiration behind many of the architectural innovations employed in the project, which includes an original use of the pointed (rather than round) arch and the ribbed vault and extensive use of stained glass, including a rose window in the facade.[20]

It is important to remember that Suger was an architectural client and not a builder; he did not, in fact, have any responsibility, even as an amateur, for any of the actual construction work. It should also be noted that the names of the actual craftsmen of the church were never mentioned in Suger's writings. Could this have been because the builders of the cathedral were considered merely craftsmen whereas Suger influenced the creation of a new type of cathedral and was its real architect? While this example may be an extreme case, certainly contemporary clients (as well as Renaissance patrons) such as the Guggenheims or developers such as Gerald Hines have influenced the outcome of the buildings they commission. This book has argued that architects need to understand craft, but the question must also be posed: in current practice, how much must they know? In our present culture of specialization, architects are forced to consider what it means to control *every* detail, as opposed to guiding the project. Many in the architecture, engineering, and construction industries (especially with the use of *Building Information Modeling*) question who should be guiding the design and construction of buildings. Obviously, the team of specialists works in a consortium, but does this mean the process is rudderless? A true definition of leadership may not necessarily mean telling others what to do, but may be understood as encouraging others to accomplish the best possible. This would render the question of leadership in design and construction even more crucial. Architects must be continually conscious of their role as leaders and must comprehend their related responsibility to the environment. Fortunately, leadership roles come naturally to architects.

Talent

Natural ability, often labeled talent, may be considered one of the architect's characteristics; however, this interpretation may be somewhat superficial. Talent refers to a special ability that allows someone to do something well, to the unique abilities possessed by a person or group of individuals with a particular inclination or disposition.[21] However, the etymology of the word *talent* reveals a completely different meaning. It originated from the ancient Greek *talanton*, and the Latin *talentum*, meaning scale, balance, sum. A talent was one of several ancient units of mass, a commercial weight, as well as corresponding units of value equivalent to these masses of a precious metal.[22] Today, when we apply the term talent to someone's personality, we may mean something close to charisma. While charisma was initially discussed in regard to its connection to a magician's seduction, it can also clarify a notion of talent. The word charisma comes from the Greek *khárisma*, which means a favor freely given or gift of grace.[23] The term and its plural *charismata* derive from *charis*, meaning "grace." The term originally comprised a meaning that is similar to our understanding of the word today:

Figure C.2 **Interior vaulting conditions of the Basilica of St. Denis, eleventh century (St. Denis, France).**
Source: CC-BY-SA-3.0.

Conclusion

someone with a charismatic personality is "filled with attractiveness or charm," "kindness," or "to be favored or blessed."[24] In ancient Greek, these terms when applied to the gods did not have the same connotations they have in modern religious usage.[25] Ancient Greeks ascribed the charisma of personality to their gods. For example, the Greeks attributed charm, beauty, nature, human creativity, and fertility to goddesses they called the Charities. Today we still consider the talented as those marked with an innate ability, those who are blessed or are uniquely attractive. Our culture certainly continues to celebrate the talented such as great musicians, writers, and artists with fame and awards. Such talented individuals are considered unique for they are naturally endowed with capabilities of superior quality. The talented are specifically referred to as *gifted*, a term that expresses their ability to surpass the typical. It has long been considered that this *gift* of talent comes from the gods. The talent of architects manifests itself in manipulation of the environment, and the understanding and production of images come easily to them. Most architects enjoy working with various constituents to design habitation for people, and most would report that it brings them satisfaction to witness a building realized.

Design

This book began by recognizing that the character of architects has an important impact on the design of buildings. Since design is the primary role of architects, it is critical to conclude by returning to the act of design in architecture. Design has been a subtext through each of the chapters as they explored the character traits of architects in relationship to what they do—thus the action terms: *defining*, *imaging*, *transforming/transitioning/translating*, *persuading*, and *fabricating*.

Design, often misinterpreted as the aesthetic component of a building is, as Alberti wrote, the bringing together of all a building's parts. It then can encompass all the actions necessary to ensure a complete building, including the solidity that causes it to stand, the function of the program, and the meaning so critical to its beauty. Expanding this definition, design also entails the way construction documentation is organized, the details that reflect the whole, and the management of the construction. It may even extend to the project manager's organization of the site during construction. Each of these actions affects the outcome of the building.

It seems appropriate at this point to return to Vitruvius. Although he was a Roman writing in the first century CE, Vitruvius was well versed in Greek architecture, philosophy, and mythology. His treatise is the oldest surviving document that thoroughly explains ancient construction processes and the role of architects in construction. He addressed his treatise to his contemporary Caesar Augustus, writing that it represented the state of the profession of architecture. He also had the ability to *define*, to influence, and to persuade Caesar regarding his views on architecture:

I set about the composition of this work for you. For I perceived that you built, and are now building on a large scale. . .I have furnished a detailed treatise

154

so that, by reference to it, you might inform yourself about the works already complete or about to be entered upon.[26]

Many have interpreted this statement to mean that Vitruvius was referring to the examination of precedents, along with architects' current professional practice in Rome.

This book explored twenty-five traits distinctive of architects, all of which assisted architects to be better practitioners. Vitruvius wrote in his first chapter, "The Training of Architects," about the education and skills that an architect must possess and that, therefore, may be considered architects' traits. A reason every architecture student reads Vitruvius is that much of what he wrote can be compared with the current discipline of architecture. Although many ancient practices of design and construction are still valid today, there are also differences in how they can be applied in contemporary architecture.

Vitruvius wrote that "an architect must be a man of letters that he may keep a record of useful precedents."[27] In writing this, he was advocating for architects to be *travelers* and *thieves* in their pursuit of good architecture. His use of the term "man of letters," indicates his belief that architects should be educated and cultured; he also wrote they should be "lofty thinker[s] and eloquent speaker[s]."[28] An application of these ideals to contemporary practice means that architects must have the character trait of being *critical thinkers*, and also must be able to act responsibly, as Peitho, to *persuade* others regarding their beliefs. Vitruvius wrote that architects should be "acquainted with music."[29] In contemporary practice, this could be compared to the design of appropriate acoustics in buildings. But it could also refer to a general education in the arts and culture, things that the Muses remind us are necessary to the character of architects.

The treatise *On Architecture* contains several references to mathematics, arithmetic, geometry, and proportion. Vitruvius wrote, "Mathematics again furnishes many resources to architecture. It teaches the use of rule and compass and facilitates the laying out of buildings on their sites by the use of set-squares, levels, and alignments."[30] These statements, of course, relate to the traditional tools used for design and construction, but in a larger sense, they can be equated with the principles inherent in these tools. Although today's tools are primarily digitally driven, their value is still relevant given the fact that architects continually use media for design and presentation. Related to a definition of *truth* and *beauty*, architects are still concerned, as were the Muses, with proportion, specifically as they *fabricate*. The ancient Greeks certainly saw *beauty* in proportion and felt a need to make their buildings *inspired*. There may be some truth to the claim that the paradigm of acceptable architectural style was limited but, nevertheless, the Greeks had very sophisticated beliefs regarding a *definition* of *beauty*. This definition was manifest in the proportions and refinement of architectural elements that can be viewed in temples such as the *Parthenon*. The Greek temples represented strong connections to the gods as well as an understanding of the cosmos. Other societies have achieved equally sophisticated refinement in their religious buildings, buildings that provide ritual procession, sacred space, and expressive forms. Examples that beautifully demonstrate this include historical

Conclusion

temples of Southeast Asia, such as *Angkor Wat* in Cambodia and the *Shwedagon Pagoda* in Rangoon, Myanmar.

Vitruvius' *On Architecture* presents much discussion on construction methods of his time and, thus, we may think that the architects of first-century Rome did not consider theory. However, Vitruvius referred to *measuring* and cost estimating in construction management when he stated, "By Arithmetic, the cost of building is summed up; the methods of measuration are indicated; while the difficult problems of symmetry are solved by geometrical rules and methods."[31] Vitruvius did express a theory concerning order, proportion, and symmetry as they relate to good design. These aspects of organization and beauty recur through history, and were especially prevalent during the Renaissance and again during the Modernist period. Le Corbusier developed the Modular and also continually used regulating lines for proportion. Architects in the twenty-first century may have a larger palette of materials available to them, but they are still concerned with many of the same things as their predecessors. Creating *inspired* buildings is one of their concerns.

In expressing his belief that architects "must know the art of medicine in its relation to the regions of the earth (which the Greeks call *climata*); and to the characters of the atmosphere, of localities (wholesome or pestilential), of water supply," Vitruvius was addressing various contemporary architectural issues that are associated with architects' character traits.[32] This passage, as applied to contemporary practice, could be seen to include physiology, *measuring*, and scale, since human physiology provides the basis for *measure* and scale. Hermes was the god of medicine and the relationship of the body to proportion is evident.

The health of the earth is vital to building. For example, it is critical that builders know if a potential location is a brownfield site, since the presence of one could affect people's health. Architects in the twenty-first century must consider sustainable design to protect the environment, and also must use healthy sites for construction. Vitruvius' reference to astronomy—"familiar with astronomy and astronomical calculations"—also suggests order and measure, and of course obviously alludes to physics.[33] When Vitruvius mentioned optics, lighting, cardinal directions, and sun orientation, he did so in reference to how the sun acts in a building. However, the same considerations could be applied to the meaning of the cosmos and the heavens, such as understanding the order of the universe. Contemporary architects certainly care about the meaning that their architecture conveys to inhabitants since their beliefs are reflective of their culture.

Vitruvius mentioned the value of *imaging*, *persuading*, and *fabricating*—all important character traits of architects. He wrote that architects must be skilled draughtsman and use "coloured drawing to represent the effect desired."[34] He recognized the importance of *imaging* to representation in architecture: it involves being a *messenger*, *persuader*, and *seeker of beauty and truth*. Alluding to the skills of a craftsman (Hephaestus), Vitruvius wrote that an architect should have knowledge of the trades, "to judge if things are done well."[35] It is clear that architects must possess knowledge of how buildings are *fabricated*. Vitruvius' words could also be interpreted as an acknowledgment of architects' central role

Conclusion

in the process. This remains true in contemporary practice, since architects still direct the work, just as did Apollo, who led the Muses.

Vitruvius, when conveying the professional aspects of practice in Rome, discussed the ethical and contractual responsibilities of architects. These certainly relate to the character traits architects must have. He wrote that architects must be diligent students of philosophy and clarifies this condition by adding:

> Philosophy, however, makes the architect high-minded, so that he should not be arrogant but rather urbane, fair-minded, loyal, and what is most important, without avarice; for no work can be truly done without good faith and clean hands.[36]

Here Vitruvius was advocating for architects to be cultured ("urbane"). The knowledge of philosophy, which requires *critical thinking* and *education*, prepares architects to understand their work in relationship to cultural thought. Architectural education today is based on an awareness of the need for students to receive some general education and also to have broad experience, both valuable conditions for their development of reasoning and critical thinking. An essential point in Vitruvius' work is the suggestion that architects must be ethical in their practice and maintain good faith. By saying architects should have "clean hands," Vitruvius means that they should be honest. One of the underlying themes in his work is that of altruism. This reference reminds us that the gods Hephaestus and Hermes were generous to humans. Their altruism set an example that contemporary architects can follow.

Vitruvius advised architects of first-century Rome to demonstrate ethical behavior: "Let him not be greedy nor have his mind busied with acquiring gifts, but let him with seriousness guard his dignity by keeping a good name."[37] Surprisingly, he also discussed legal issues, writing that architects should be learned in the responses of jurisconsults (lawyers):

> He must be familiar with the rights of easements. . .so that, before building is begun, precautions may be taken, lest on completion of the works the proprietors should be involved in disputes. . .again, in writing the specifications, careful regard is to be paid both to the employer and to the contractor.[38]

These are obvious references to contracts and to responsible professional practice, both of which reflect the *boundaries* and limits architects must work within.

As has been discussed throughout this book, there are many character traits that architects must have, or acquire, to be successful in their discipline. Vitruvius was reviewed because he knew and respected the ancient Greeks and their myths and used them to understand Roman architectural practice. The examples demonstrate clearly that Vitruvius was interested in the traits that define architects, traits that can be related to *defining*, *imaging*, *transforming/transferring/translating*, *persuading*, and *fabricating*.

Having come full circle, this book has asked if the character traits of architects that were recognized in antiquity are still relevant today. It has answered that many

157

traits requisite in ancient times are still critical to architectural practice today. Although the nature of practice on the site, and of contract documents, has changed, and although the computer is strictly a modern innovation, archetypal characteristics that are crucial for an architect remain the same today as they were long ago.

Notes

1 *Oxford English Dictionary*, s.v. "archetype."
2 Sir James George Frazer, *The Golden Bough: A Study in Magic and Religion* (New York: Collier Books, Macmillan Publishing Company, 1922). The theme runs throughout the book.
3 Joseph Campbell, *The Hero with a Thousand Faces* (Princeton, NJ: Princeton University Press, 1968), 23.
4 Carl G. Jung, *Man, And His Symbols* (New York: Dell Publishing, 1964), 58.
5 W.R. Lethaby, *Architecture, Mysticism and Myth* (New York: Dover Publications, 2004), vii.
6 There are a variety of excellent books on this subject. For further reading: Francis Watanabe Dauer, *Critical Thinking: An Introduction to Reasoning* (New York: Barnes and Noble, 1996); Alec Fisher and Michael Scriven, *Critical Thinking: Its Definition and Assessment* (Norwich, UK: University of East Anglia, Center for Research in Critical Thinking, 1997); Brooke Noel Moore and Richard Parker, *Critical Thinking* (New York: McGraw-Hill, 2012); and Carl Sagan, *The Demon-Haunted World: Science As a Candle in the Dark* (New York: Ballantine Books, 1995).
7 Richard Paul, Linda Elder, and Ted Bartell, *California Teacher Preparation for Instruction in Critical Thinking: Research Findings and Policy Recommendations: State of California, California Commission on Teaching Credentialing* (Sacramento, CA: California Commission on Teaching Credentialing, 1997).
8 Justus Buchler, *Philosophical Writings of Peirce* (New York: Dover Publications, 1955), 98–119.
9 Ibid.
10 *Oxford English Dictionary*, s.v. "judging."
11 *Oxford English Dictionary*, s.v. "choose."
12 *Oxford English Dictionary*, s.v. "ethics."
13 "American Institute of Architects," www.aia.org, accessed August 14, 2017.
14 E. Baldwin Smith, *Egyptian Architecture as Cultural Expression* (New York: D. Appleton-Century Co., 1938), 61.
15 Spiro Kostof, *The Architect: Chapters in the History of the Profession* (New York: Oxford University Press, 1977), 3.
16 J.A. Bundgaard, *Mnesicles a Greek Architect at Work* (Copenhagen, Denmark: Scandinavian University Press, 1957).
17 Vitruvius, *On Architecture*, trans. Frank Granger (Cambridge, MA: Harvard University Press, 19313), Book 1, Part 3.
18 Leon Battista Alberti, *On the Art of Building in Ten Books,* trans. Joseph Rykwert, Neil Leach, and Robert Tavernor (Cambridge, MA: MIT Press, 1988), 3.
19 Helen Gardner, *Art Through the Ages* (New York: Harcourt Brace Jovanovich, 1980), 318.
20 Abbot Suger, *Encyclopedia Britannica* (Chicago, IL: Encyclopedia Britannica Inc., 1985), 357. The reader can also refer to Otto von Simson, *The Gothic Cathedral* (Princeton, NJ: Princeton University Press, 1962), 61–90.

21 *Oxford English Dictionary*, s.v. "talent."
22 Ibid.
23 *Online Etymology Dictionary*, s.v. "charisma."
24 Robert Beekes, *Etymological Dictionary of Greek* (Leiden, the Netherlands: Brill, 2010), 1607; and Michael N. Ebertz, "Charisma," in *Religion Past & Present,* ed. Hans Dieter Betz, et al. (Leiden, the Netherlands: Brill, 2007), 493.
25 Ebertz, "Charisma," 493.
26 Vitruvius, *On Architecture*, Book I, Preface, 3.
27 Ibid., Book I.c.I.3.
28 Ibid., Book I.c.I.18.
29 Ibid., Book I.c.I.3.
30 Ibid., Book I.c.I.4.
31 Ibid.; Vitruvius' meaning of symmetry is similar to proportion or design.
32 Ibid., Book I.c.I.8.
33 Ibid., Book I.c.I.3.
34 Ibid., Book I.c.I.4.
35 Ibid., Book I.c.I.15.
36 Ibid., Book I.c.I.6.
37 Ibid.
38 Ibid., Book I.c.I.10.

Index

Note: *italic* page numbers denote references to figures.

8 House 103–104, *104*

Abbey of St. Denis 151–152, *153*
abductive reasoning 148
abstraction 35, 38, 39, 45–46, 88
Acropolis 86, *86*
Adams, Herbert *40*
aesthetics xix
A.I. (Spielberg) 129
Alberti, Leon Battista xv, xix, 19, 31, 62, 91, 131, 151, 154
allusion xxiii, 35
altruism 157
ambiguity 18, 60, 98, 100
analogies 3, 8, 23, 35, 88
Angelico, Fra 31
Angkor Wat 155–156
Aphrodite 81, 82, 90, 93, 103
Aquinas, Thomas 147
archetypes 6, 143, 144–147
Aristotle xix–xx, xxxi; craftsmen 33; *ethos* xviii, 85; fabrication 111; incorporeal souls 125; memory 41; metaphors 88; *pathos* 85, 89; *poiēsis* 116; rhetoric 82, 84
arrangement 101–102
artists 29, 30–31, 32, 37, 95, 119
arts 27–29, 155
Arts and Crafts movement 115
Ate 82
Athena 91, 130–131, 137
Augustine of Hippo 91
automata 4, 125, 126–129, 134, *135*, 141n80

Barasch, Moshe 119
Barcelona 63
Bateson, Gregory 16, 17
Batteux, Charles xix
Baudrillard, Jean 122
Bauhaus 115
beauty xix, 4, 89–94, 103, 109n52, 155

beliefs 10, 13, 22, 23, 156; beauty and truth 94; conviction of 107; persuasion 88; religious 11–12, 144–145
BIM *see Building Information Modeling*
Bjarke Ingles Group 103–104, *104*
Blur Building 59, *59*
body 34–35, *36*, 129, 156
body memory 41
Borobudur xx–xxi, *xxi*
Boston City Hall xxxi, 92, *93*
boundaries 16–17, 18–22, 57, 75, 149, 157
Breitenberger, Barbara 86
Brion Tomb *117*
Brown, Denise Scott xxxi, 57
Brown, Norman Oliver 69
Brown, Oliver xxxi
Brutalism 92
Buddhism xx–xxi
Building Information Modeling (BIM) 49, 62, 136, 152
Bulfinch, Thomas 55
Bundgaard, J.A. 150
Bundy, Murray Wright 30

Caicco, Gregory 85
Caixa Forum 70, *70*
Calatrava, Santiago 35
Cambodia 120, 155–156
Campbell, Joseph xvii, 145
Čapek, Karel 129
Cargo Cult 33
Carpenter Center for the Modern Arts xxxi, 92, *92*
Caryatids 86, *86*
Casey, Edward S. xxx, 37, 52n64
Cathedral of Light 97–98, *98*
cathedrals 8–9, 10, 35, *36*
Catholicism 8–10
ceremonies 12
certainty, workmanship of 115
Champigny sur Veude Chapelle *9*
change 56
chaos 9, 16, 19, 23

character xviii–xix, xxvi–xxviii, 27, 75–76; flaws 118–120; Hermes 74; judgment 150
charisma 4, 94, 97, 107, 152–154
Charlemagne 6
chiasmus xxviii, *xxix,* 1, 76
China 12, 104
Christianity 6, 8–10
Cicero, Marcus Tullius 101
cities 72
Citta Nuova xxxi, 72–73
Classical thought 30
codes of ethics xviii
Cole, Thomas 38–39, *39*
collective unconscious 6
Collignon, Giuseppe *64*
commodity (*utilitas*) 84, 85
communication 82, 87, 102–103
computers xxiii, 71, 103–104, 123, 133; *see also* digital media
concepts, architectural 31, 60, 101
Concert Hall, Los Angeles xxxi
Confurius, Garrit 80, 98
Conroy, Pat 61
Constructivism 88
controlledness 37
Convent Sainte-Marie de La Tourette 129, *130*
Cook, John W. 129
Cooly, Mason 32
cosmos 12, 21, 75, 124, 130, 156
Cox, Damian xxvii–xxviii
craftsmen 67–69, 113, 114–118; Aristotle 33; character traits 138; educated 131; Hephaestus xxxi, 124–125, 134; inspiration 130; Plato's critique of 119–120; role of architects as 70, 72, 74; technology 122; Vitruvius 156
creativity 27, 28, 33, 38, 143
Cresti da Passignano, Domenico 46
critical thinking 130–134, 138, 143, 147–148, 155, 157
culture 21, 58, 60, 63, 145, 156
customs 12, 13
cyberspace 123, 124

Daedalus xvii, xxix, 1–4, 11, 13, 22, 138; fabrication 125–126; fall of Icarus 15; flaws 130; Hephaestus compared with 118, 120, 125; order 7, 10, 19, 22, 23; play 16, 17, 18
daidala 3–4
dance 11
Dante Alighieri 31
deception 82, 95, 98, 99, 111

decision making 147, 148–150
Deconstructivism 34, 57
decoration 92
defining xxix, 1–23, 143; architect as definer 4–6; architect as measurer 7–10; boundaries and order 18–22; manner and mode 11–16; play 16–18; properties of definition 5
delight (*venustas*) 84, 89–90
delivery 101, 102
Delphic Oracle 97
demonstration 47, 60
Demosthenes 83, *83*
Derrida, Jacques 21
Descartes, René 91–92, 126, 147
design 1, 19, 31, 154–155
design thinking 147, 148
details 133
Deus Artifex 95
Diboutades 41, *42*, 43
digital media xxiii–xxiv, 49, 58–59, 100, 103, 123–124
Dionysus 28
the divine xxii, 5–6, 13, 32, 47, 126, 138
divine artists 31, 95
divine inspiration 29–32, 49
divining 47, *48*, 49
doing 71, 97
Douglas House 17
drawings 29, 48–49; dialogue 100; memory 42; persuasion 80, 86; play 18; scale 14; trust in 99–100; visualizing the future 45, 46

Eco, Umberto 87, 95–97
education 60, 62, 113, 120, 136, 155; broad-based 151; critical thinking 130–131; Hephaestus 134–135; knowledge of philosophy 157; love of learning xv; Roman architects 151
Egyptian architects 67, 95, 150–151
Egyptian hypostyle halls 32
Eiffel Tower 93
emotion xvi, 84, 85, 89, 91, 97
entasis 65, 77n39
envisioning 71–72, 74
Erechtheion 86, *86*
Erikson, Arthur 85
ethics xv, xviii, xxvii, 85, 104, 149–150, 157
ethos xviii, xxvii, 84, 85
Euripides 61

fabrication xxxi–xxxii, 71, 111–138, 144; architect as craftsman 114–118; architect as critical thinker 130–134;

161

architect as fabricator 120–125; architect as flawed 118–120; architect as inspired inspirer 125–130; decision making 149; definition of 111; digital 58–59, 124; Vitruvius 156

fantasy 30, 31, 39

Filarete 103

file-to-factory 124

firmness (*firmitas*) 84–85, 89

flaws 118–120

flexibility xv

form xix, 56, 88

Forster, Julia 37

Frampton, Kenneth 135

Frascari, Marco xvii, xxii, xxxi, 18, 125, 129, 133

Frazer, James George xxxii, 144–145

Frazer, John 123

French theorists xix

Frontisi-Ducrous, Françoise 3

Fuksas, Massimiliano and Doriana *137*

future planning 71–72, 74, 137

Gadamer, Hans-Georg xxi, 16, 21

Gaudí, Antonio 63

Gehry, Frank xxii, xxxi, 66–67, *66*, 71, 124

geometry 20

giftedness 154

Giuseppina Bianchi Danilo House 17

globalization xxv–xxvi, 57–58, 62, 105, 123, 149, 150

God 5–6, 31, 33, 95, 126

Gombrich, Ernst 100

the good 90–91

Gorgias 84, 97

Gothic architecture 151–152

Great Stupa shrine xx–xxi

Greek architects 22, 72, 120, 131, 144, 150–151, 155

Greek myths xvi–xvii, 22, 118, 125, 144; beauty and truth 90; charismatic personality of the gods 154; prophecy 97; Vitruvius 157; *see also* Daedalus; Hephaestus; Hermes; Muses; Peitho

Gropius, Walter 115

Guattari, Félix 123, 125

Guggenheim Museum 20, *20*, 66, *66*

habit 12, 13

Hadid, Zaha xxii–xxiii, 59, 98–99

Hagia Sophia 104, *105*

Hans, James S. xxix, 16, 17–18

harmony of parts 91

Harries, Karsten 82, 85

Heidegger, Martin xviii, xxvii, 54, 76n2, 122

Hephaestus *xvii,* xxxi, 111, *112*, 114, 120–122, 134–135, 138; altruism 157; as civilizing craftsman 124–125; creation of life by 126; flaws 117, 118–119, 120, 130; leadership status 136–137; wisdom 130–131

Heraclitus 84

hermeneutics xxvii, 54, 76n2

Hermes xvii, *xvii,* xxxi, 54–56, *55*, 74–76, 82, 114; altruism 157; hermeneutics xxvii; as inventor 71; as magician 67, 69, 70–71; medicine 156; as messenger 57, 59, 60; persuasion 86; resourcefulness 65; as thief 67; as traveler 61, 63

Herzog & De Meuron 70, *70*

Hesiod 28, 50n6, 50n8, 94, 111, 118

Hines, Gerald 152

Hobbes, Thomas 147

Hohauser, Stanford 14

Holl, Steven 13–14

Holocaust Museum xxx, 44, *44*

Homer xvii, 28, 50n8, 57, 85, 111, 114, 124, 138n2

honesty xv, 104, 157

Huizinga, Johan 16, 25n68

human body 34–35, *36*, 129, 156

Hume, David xxx, 38

huts 116

Icarus 15, *15*, 125–126

illusion xxiii, 4, 30, 97–99, 119, 125, 134

images 29, 37, 38, 47, 49; arrangement 102; memory 41; persuasion xxiv, 87, 101, 103; 'primordial' 145; rhetoric 82; seduction through 95; style 102; transitioning and transforming 56–57; trust in 99

imagination 27, 29–32, 37–39, 41, 46, 52n64, 87, 143

imaging xxix–xxx, 27–50, 143; architect as imaginer 37–39; architect as imitator 32–37; architect as prophesier 45–47; decision making 149; divine inspiration 29–32; memory 39–45; transitioning and transforming 56–57; Vitruvius 156

Imhotep 67, 95, *96*, 150

imitation xx, xxi, 32–37, 38, 69

indeterminacy 37, 39

Industrial Revolution 115, 117, 122

information gathering 148

Ingels, Bjarke 103–104, *104*

inspiration 28, 29–32, 45, 47, 49, 77n27, 115, 125–130

integrity xxvii–xxviii

intention xxvii, xxviii, 13, 45–46, 47, 56, 113

Index

interpretation xxvii, 54, 76n2, 150
intertextuality 54
invention: architect as inventor 71–74; intellectual act of 72; *invenzione* 31; in rhetoric 101; transitioning 56
Izenour, Steven 57

Jacquet-Droz, Pierre 141n80
Jakobson, Roman 87
Janus 75, *75*
Japan 120, *121*
Jencks, Charles 78n44
Jesus Christ 6
Jewish Museum Berlin 44, *44*
joints 116
Judaism 6
judgment xix, xxvi–xxvii, 22, 57, 76, 148–150
Jung, Carl xxxii, 6, 145
Justinian I 6

Kahn, Louis xxix, 19–20, 70, 129
Kallmann, Gerhard *93*
Kant, Immanuel xxvii, 13, 38, 98, 147
Kern, Hermann xxix, 11
Klotz, Heinrich 129
knowledge 33, 45, 119; craftsmanship 117; critical thinking 131; education 60; judgment based on 57; memory 41, 42; production and dissemination of 125
Kolarevic, Branko 136
Kostof, Spiro xxix, 19

La Caze, Marguerite xxvii–xxviii
labyrinth 1, *2*, 4, 22, 125; manner and mode 11, 13; meanders 18; measure 7; as metaphor of human existence 23; order 3, 10, 19, 20; play 17, 18
language 87, 97
Lascaux cave drawings 33–34
Le Corbusier xxix, xxxi, 19, 72, 92, *92*, 129–130, *130*, 156
Leach, Neil xix
leadership xv, 94, 136–137, 143, 149, 150–152
legal issues 157
Leonardo da Vinci 129
Lethaby, W.R. 129, 145
Levine, Michael P. xxvii–xxviii
Libeskind, Daniel xxx, 44, *44*
life, creation of 126
light 14, 129
Lincoln, Abraham 72
location 42, 97, 156
Locke, John 13, 147

logos 84, 85, 91
love 82, 90
Lyons, John D. 32
Lyotard, Jean-François 125

machines 122–123
magic 67–71, 97, 98
making 71, 100; *see also* fabrication
Malle, Bertram 45
mandalas 21, *21*
manner xix, xxix, 1, 11, 12–13, 16, 22
Martini, Francesco di Giorgio 35
mass customization 133
mathematics 91–92, 95, 155
Maulden, Robert 135
Mauss, Marcel 69
McEwen, Indra Kagis xvi
McKinnell, Michael *93*
McLuhan, Marshall 57, 58, 122
Meagher, Robert 122
meaning xxi, xxii, 23, 56, 130; architect as messenger 57–59; images 29; measurement of 10; rhetoric 87, 88
measure xxix, 1, 6, 22; architect as measurer 7–10; beauty connected to 91; units of 8, 34–35; Vitruvius 156
media 1, 29, 38, 48–49; persuasion 80, 88; seduction 94–95; trust in 99–101
medicine 156
Meier, Richard 17
memory 38, 39–45, 48, 98, 101, 102
mental impressions 39, 41, 42, 48
messenger, architect as 57–60, 74
metaphors 23, 35, 46; memory 43; persuasion 82, 86, 88
Michelangelo 31, 46, 129
Mies Van der Rohe, Ludwig xxxii, 49, 67
Milan 72
Miller, John W. 5
Milwaukee Art Museum 35
mimesis xxi, 32–33
Minotaur 1–4, *2*, 11, 13, 14, 17
Mnemosyne 40–41, *40*
mode xix, xxix, 1, 11, 13–16, 22
models 29, 48–49; dialogue 100; memory 42; persuasion 80, 86; play 18; scale 14; trust in 99–100; visualizing the future 45, 46
Modernism 72, 78n44, 92, 129, 149, 156
modernity 16
modesty 14–15
monomyths xvii, 145
Monument to the Third International 88, *90*
monuments 44
Moore, Richard 129

163

Index

morality xxvii; *see also* ethics
Morris, William 115
Morrissey, Lee xxxi, 82–83, 88
movies 129, 145–147
Mugerauer, Robert xxvii
Muses xxix–xxx, 27–28, *27*, 47–49, 143;
   divine inspiration 29–30, 32; education
   in arts and culture 155; imagination 31,
   37, 38; imitation 32; memory 39–41, 45
museums 44
Myanmar 155–156

National Parliament Building, Bangladesh
   20–21, *21*
nature 32, 33, 69–70, 125
Nazi Germany 97–98
Newson, Janice A. xxv–xxvi
Newton, Isaac 65–66
norms 10
Notre-Dame de Paris 10
Notre Dame du Haut 129

objects 33, 99–100, 134
ontology xxii
order 1, 18–22, 23; cathedrals 9; Daedalus
   xxix, 3, 7, 10, 19; Hephaestus 124,
   136–137
Otto, Walter F. 74
Ovid 32, 126

Pallasmaa, Juhani 13–14, 85
Pandora 66, 94, 111, 126, 131, *132*, 134
Pantheon xx, *xx*
paradigms 7, 8
parametric modeling 133, 135
Parthenon 91, *91*, 120, 155
pathos 84, 85, 89
The Peak 98–99
Peirce, Charles Sanders xxi, 148
Peitho xxxi, 80–82, *81*, 86, 103, 107; beauty
   and truth 90, 93; rhetoric 85; seduction
   81, 94, 99; trust 102
perception 37, 38, 52n64
Pérez-Gómez, Alberto xvii, xxviii, 3–4, 11,
   13, 85, 93–94
Pericles 74
persuasion xxiv, xxxi, 60, 80–107, 144;
   architect as developer of trust 99–102;
   architect as persuader 86–88; architect
   as rhetorician 82–85; architect as
   seducer 94–99; architect as seeker of
   beauty and truth 89–94; decision
   making 149; Hermes 57; Vitruvius 155,
   156
phantasia 30

phenomenology 60
philosophy 157
Piano, Renzo 71, 78n70
Piranesi, Giovanni Battista 88, *89*
place 85
Plato xix–xx, xxxi, 3, 139n38; on architects
   61–62; on craftsmen 119–120; critical
   thinking 147; fabrication 111; imitation
   69; inspiration 77n27; memory 41;
   mimesis 33; Muses 28; poetical
   enthusiasm 31; *technê* 122
play xxii–xxiii, 16–18, 21, 25n68, 56, 110n80
Pliny 3, 32, 41
Plotinus 90
poièsis xxi, 116, 125
post-structuralism 57
postmodernism xxiii
praxis 111
precedents 65, 66, 67, 74, 148, 155
precision 110n79
problem identification 148
Prometheus *xvii,* 1, 64, *64*, 66, 120, 125,
   131
propaganda 80, 82, 97, 105, *106*
prophecy 45–47, 97
proportion 19, 26n74, 35, 91, 155, 156
Pruitt-Igoe housing project 65, *65*, 78n44
pure possibility 37–38, 39
Pye, David 115
pyramids 7, *8*

Raphael *84*
Rappaport, Roy 11–12
reasoning 84–85, 157
reference standards 7–8, 24n31, 88
regionalism 11
Regnault, Jean-Baptiste *42*
religious beliefs 11–12, 144–145
Renaissance xvii–xviii, 30–31, 72, 91, 95,
   156
repetition 17
representation xix–xxiii, 18
resemblance 43–44
resourcefulness xv, 65
rhetoric 82–85, 86–87, 88, 100; Cicero 101;
   importance of 107; magic and illusion
   97, 98
Risatti, Howard 115–116
risk, workmanship of 115–116
ritual xxix, 1, 11–12, 13, 33, 69
Rockwell, Anne 151–152
Romans xvii–xviii, 34–35, 117, 150, 151,
   154–155, 157
Romantic period 129
Rotundi, Michael xxiii

164

Rubens, Peter Paul *112*
rules 16, 17, 19, 57, 75–76, 125
Ruskin, John xxxi, 92, 115, 138n17
Rykwert, Joseph xix, xxxi, 116

Santayana, George xix, 90
Sant'Elia, Antonio xxxi, 72–74, *73*
Sauvage, Henri 73–74
scale 7, 14, 24n31, 35, 156
Scarpa, Carlo xxxii, 29, 116–117, *117*
Schumacher, Patrick 135–136
Scolari, Massimo 44–45
seduction 4, 81–82, 93, 94–99, 103,
    104–105, 107
self-containedness 37
self-evidence 37
self-reflexivity 66, 102
semiotics xxi, 59
Semper, Gottfried 116
Seneca, Lucius Annaeus 32
Sennett, Richard xxxi, 117, 125
Shelley, Mary 126–129, *128*
Shenzhen Bao'an International Airport 1*37*
Shwedagon Pagoda 155–156
signs xxi, 45, 47, 82, 87
simulation 71
Sistine Chapel 6
sketches 14, 100, 110n81
skills 27, 32, 48, 67, 138; craftsmanship 114,
    115; Hephaestus 134; persuasive 80,
    107; seductive 95, 97
Smith, Albert 122
Smith, Amy C. 81
Socrates 90, 109n52, 147
software 49, 58, 71, 136
Solomon 5–6
solutions, finding 148
Sophists 84
soul 33, 130
spatial memory 42, 44
special effects 119
specialization xxvi, 71, 149, 150, 152
Speer, Albert 97–98, *98*
Spielberg, Steven 129
Spinoza, Baruch 13
spirituality 10, 129, 130
spontaneity 37
'starchitects' 105
Stein, Murray 74–75
Stoics 30, 84
strategic thinking xv
style xix, 11, 12, 32; personal 67; rhetoric
    101, 102
Suger, Abbot 69, 151–152
Summers, David 30, 31

Sumner, William Graham 147
sustainable materials 104
symmetry xix, 26n74, 156

Tafuri, Manfredo 88
talent 27, 31, 32, 48, 95, 97, 152–154
taste xix
Tatlin, Vladimir 88, *90*
Tavernor, Robert xix
technē 4, 122, 125
technology xxiii–xxiv, 62, 64, 71, 117,
    120–124; critical thinking 133–134;
    fabrication 111, 135–136, 137;
    Hephaestus 120, 125, 134–135; misuse
    of 131; persuasion 103; technicians and
    technologists 113, 134; theory and
    practice 113; *see also* digital media
tectonics 135–136
The Temple of Jerusalem 5–6, *6*
temples 6, 65, 91, 120, 155–156
Terzidis, Kostas 124
Thales 7, *8*
theory xvi, 136, 137–138; Vitruvius 56, 62,
    113, 117, 118, 131, 156
Therme Vals xxxi, 60
thieves 64–67, 74, 155
Tianducheng 104
tools 7, 33, 155
Tower of Babel *xxx*
traits xv, xxxi, 138, 143, 155–158
transforming xxx–xxxi, 56–57, 71, 72, 75
transitioning xxx–xxxi, 56–57, 61, 75
translating xxx–xxxi, 56, 57, 60, 63, 75
traveler, architect as 60, 61–64, 74, 155
trust 94, 99–102, 103, 104, 107
truth 33, 115, 125, 138n6; beauty and
    89–94, 109n52; seduction and 103,
    104–105; Vitruvius 155
Turner, Victor 12

units of measure 8, 34–35
utilitas 84, 85

van Babure, Dirck *xvii*
Vasari, Giorgio 30–31
Vaucanson, Jacques 141n80
Venturi, Robert xxxi, 57
venustas 84, 89–90
verbal skills 80
vernacular architecture 13, 20–21, 120
Vesely, Dalibor xix, xxi, xxii
Vico, Giambattista 111–113
Viollet-Le-Duc, Antoine xix
virtue xix
visionary thinking xv

visualization 39, 48–49
Vitruvius xvii–xviii, xxxii, 154–157; architect as prophesier 46–47; balance of theory and practice 56, 62, 117, 118, 136; Caryatids 86; commodity 85; education 62, 113, 131, 150, 151, 155; *firmitas, utilitas* and *venustas* 84–85, 89; proportion 19, 26n74, 35; rhetoric 82, 84; Roman architects 151; symmetry xix
Voltaire 32

Wagner, Otto 73
Walt Disney Concert Hall 66
Warner, Olin *40*

Wardy, Robert 97
Washington Monument *43*
Weinsheimer, Joel 17
Westfall, Carroll William xix
Willis, Dan 133
wisdom 130–131
Wittkower, Rudolf and Margot 31
Wollheim, Richard 45–46
Woodward, Todd 133
'workmanship of risk' 115–116
Wright, Frank Lloyd 20, *20*

Yates, Frances 42

Zumthor, Peter xxxi, 60